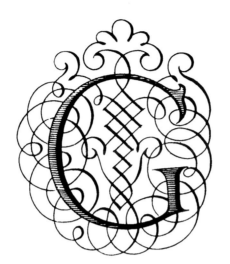

The Gilbert Collection

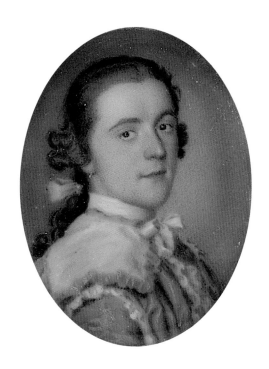

Portrait Miniatures
in Enamel

SARAH COFFIN and BODO HOFSTETTER

PHILIP WILSON PUBLISHERS

IN ASSOCIATION WITH THE GILBERT COLLECTION

First published in 2000 by
Philip Wilson Publishers Limited
143-149 Great Portland Street
London W1N 5FB

Distributed in the USA and Canada
Antique Collectors' Club Limited
Market Street Industrial Park
Wappingers' Falls
NY 12590

ISBN 0 85667 513 X

This publication has been made possible by a
grant from the Heritage Lottery Fund.

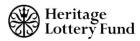

Designed by Peter Campbell
Edited by David Girling

Printed and bound in Italy
by Società Editoriale Lloyd, Srl, Trieste

Contents

Foreword

Portrait miniatures in enamel comprise the smallest part of the Gilbert Collection. Like the other main components of the collection, however, this area has grown to the point of presenting a rounded and comprehensive overview of its subject. Today the collection includes over a hundred works in this specialised branch of miniature painting, from its appearance in the first half of the seventeenth century to its final flowering in the nineteenth. The output of nearly all the leading artists in the medium are represented, as are most centres of production throughout Europe.

Arthur Gilbert's collection of enamelled miniatures grew from chance beginnings. Just as his interest in gold boxes was originally sparked by one or two examples which he bought because they contained micromosaics, so his first enamelled miniatures were integral parts of snuffboxes. From these he came to appreciate the special qualities of enamels and started to collect them in their own right. The features that appealed most directly to Gilbert were their colour-fastness and the impressive technical demands of the process. The former has an obvious attraction to a collector living in the sun-drenched climate of southern California, while the latter reflects the strand that runs most consistently through all the disparate elements of the Gilbert Collection, namely a passion for virtuoso and painstaking craftsmanship.

British public collections are well-endowed with portrait miniatures but the distinction of the Gilbert Collection is that it is almost exclusively composed of portraits in enamel rather than watercolour. As such it provides a rare opportunity to study the development of the medium. It is symptomatic of the rarity of such a focus that this is the first major modern publication to concentrate on enamelled miniatures and the essays that precede the catalogue section set out the present state of knowledge on the subject. Bodo Hofstetter's essay maps the spread of the technique through the movement of artists from court to court, while Sarah Coffin's examines the portrait miniature's development in England and the gradual advance of its academic respectability as evidenced by its increasing prominence in the annual exhibitions of the Royal Academy which, in the late eighteenth century, were held in Somerset House.

Quite apart from their intrinsic interest, the portrait miniatures have a special place in the Gilbert Collection as a whole in that they provide a visual reference to the world of which so much else in the collection was a product. Indeed, many of the sitters owned or were associated with other objects in the collection. Sir Robert Walpole's patronage was the cause of some of the most distinguished English silver in the collection; one of the most sumptuous gold boxes was the mark of Catherine the Great's gratitude to her English doctor, Thomas Dimsdale, and his son; and the spiritual qualities of Pope Pius VII, donor of Napoleon's great clock with mosaics by Raffaelli, shine out from his portrait by Bianca Boni.

I would like to extend my thanks to the authors, Sarah Coffin and Bodo Hofstetter, for their constant enthusiasm for this project and to Katie Coombes of the Victoria and Albert Museum for her initial guidance and advice. Special thanks too are due to Rachel Layton who, as Assistant Curator at the Gilbert Collection, worked closely with the authors, throwing light on a number of issues and co-ordinating all aspects of the project.

Timothy Schroder
Keeper of the Collection

Acknowledgements

We are grateful for the help of many people during the course of our research. Those listed below were especially generous with their time and knowledge and we thank them for their generosity.

Sarah Coffin and Bodo Hofstetter

Dr Derek Adam, Nottinghamshire
Mr Alan Derbyshire, London
Mr Mariano Aldao, Buenos Aires
Dr Hans Boeckh, Geneva
Mr David Bowney, London
Dr Görel Cavalli-Bjorkman, Stockholm
Miss Katherine Coombs, London
Dr Stephen Duffy, London
Miss Alexandra Fennell, London
Dr Jean Gérardin, Paris
Mr Alexis Kugel, Paris
Mr Nicolas Kugel, Paris
Mrs Halgard Kuhn, Hanover
Miss Céline Le Prieur, Paris
David Lavender, London
Dr Stephen Lloyd, Edinburgh
Martin Norton, S.J. Phillips, London
Ms Hannelore Nützmann, Berlin
Dr Magnus Olausson, Stockholm
Miss Caroline Page, London
Mr Pierre Papeloux, Paris
Mr Alejandro Pongo Morán, London
Ms Anne Puetz, London
Dr Aileen Ribeiro, London
Ms Rosalind Savill, London
Drs Karen Schaffers-Bodenhausen, The Hague
Miss Elle Shushan, New York
Miss Fabienne-Xavière Sturm, Geneva
Col Peter Wattoned, Kent
Dr Peter Wegmann, Winterthur
Mr Haydn Williams, London

Enamelling Techniques

SARAH COFFIN AND BODO HOFSTETTER

SINCE ANTIQUITY, numerous enamelling techniques have been developed, including *champlevé, cloisonné, plique-a-jour, flinqué, basse-taille* (including *taille d'épargne*) and *Limoges*. These techniques, however, are not relevant to the enamel portraits described in this work and hence will not be discussed.

What is enamel? Simply put, it is a type of glass coloured by metal oxides and fused to a metal or porcelain base by firing. Virtually all the miniatures discussed in this book are on a metal base. Enamel on metal is fired at a higher temperature than porcelain, thus producing a harder surface which is more resistant to abrasion.

The earliest portrait enamellers came from a goldsmithing and watchmaking tradition, and had found the convex surface of the watchcase to be a receptive ground for enamel. However, when trying to imitate full-scale paintings, artists such as Petitot initially attempted to work on as flat a support as possible. These supports included gold, copper, silver and iron. At first, deriving from the watchcase tradition, gold was more frequently used. However, there was no visible advantage in using it as it was completely obscured by the painting. Increasingly, copper became the commonest support. It was not only less expensive, but, in addition, could survive firing of temperatures of up to 1900 F ° (1037° C) as opposed to 18k gold at 1700° F (927° C).

The greater flexibility of gold creates an additional conservation hazard: being softer, it can separate from the enamel paint, which causes cracks in the enamel. On the other hand, unlike gold, copper oxidises, rendering it vulnerable to *verdigris* caused by humidity. The *verdigris* can expand and lift the enamel from its support and causes cracks, if left unchecked.

To prepare the support for enamelling, the metal is first cut into a thin plaque, often less than 1 mm thick, and then hammered to create the slightly curved surface which helps to keep the plaques from warping during the firing process. The larger the plaque, the greater the potential for warping, and even cracking, at high temperatures. The technical difficulties associated with greater size made it a challenge which was taken up by some artists, from Jean Petitot to Charles Boit and Henry Bone, with varying degrees of success. Boit's largest successful miniature, made in 1703, was 36 × 46 cm (14 × 18 in). He was unable to execute one of 46 × 72 cm (18 × 28 in). About 100 years later, Bone's largest enamel was a copy of Titian's *Bacchus and Ariadne*, measuring 40.5 × 46 cm (16 × 18 in).

In addition to the preparation of the support, the paints have to be made. To create enamel paints, small lumps of coloured metal oxide are put into a mortar with water and then finely ground with a pestle. The result has the consistency of talcum powder. Oil – either sandalwood or lavender – is added to transform the powder into paint.

Before colours can be used, layers of white base enamel must be applied and fired to both front and back. Even if nothing is to be painted on the often concave reverse, it needs this enamel coating to avoid distortion of the metal. Hence it is called the counter enamel. The portrait is usually painted on the convex side. If there is no other painting on the counter enamel, it may be used for inscriptions, such as the signature, date and the name of the subject (see p. 10).

After the white has been fired, the artist can begin painting with colour. Each colour has a different melting point and must be applied individually with a brush, almost in a painting-by-numbers fashion, with one colour at a time. The artist starts with the colour that needs the highest temperature in order to fuse onto the preceding layer. Subsequent applications of colour require separate firings with descending temperatures. Before the invention of electrically heated kilns, the firings took place in an oven, generally fuelled by charcoal or wood to a temperature of about 800°C (1,472°F), with each firing lasting from between two and fifteen minutes, the longest firing being first.

This creates permanent colours and requires the artists to have mastered the chemical properties of the different colours, as there is no way of correcting a mistake. The Swiss enameller Salomon Counis observed: 'in painting enamel everything must be calculated and foreseen, one is never helped out by those happy chances, by those accidents of the brush, which are not so rare in oil painting [...] The hand often engages the head, in enamel painting, on the contrary, it is always the head which must drive the hand'.[1]

With every firing, the risk of damaging or destroying the piece increases. The most common problem is air bubbles, which create small holes in the surface,

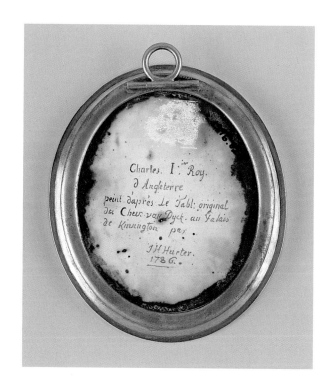

Inscription on counter enamel of Charles I, cat. no. 31 (see p. 79).

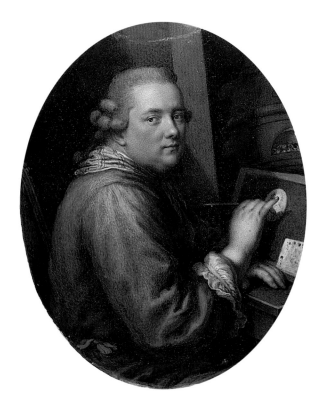

Giuseppe MacPherson (1726–80), self-portrait with enamelling kiln, enamel, eighteenth century; Hamburg, Kunsthalle, inv. 197.

or falling ash which can pit the surface. Additionally, a miscalculation or difficulty in maintaining a constant kiln temperature can cause certain colours to burn, creating black marks or loss of colour.

With time, these pitfalls were better understood, and precautions could be taken to control the causes of technical mishaps. Although colours were constantly being improved and new ones introduced, little else changed in the techniques of enamel painting between the seventeenth century and around 1800.

At about the latter date, and with no apparent connection, enamellers in Geneva, and Henry Bone in England developed techniques for making a final transparent *glaze-fondant* to finish their enamels. This both heightened the surface gloss and evened it up, helping to hide irregularities. Bone also developed for his plaques the technique of putting a layer of clear flux (a coat of enamel) over the white *fondant* before applying the colour to avoid hairline cracks. In addition, he mixed pulverised flux with the colours to equalise them and to help fusion to the grounding.

This technique had undoubtedly been inspired by Bone's experience as a porcelain painter. With the

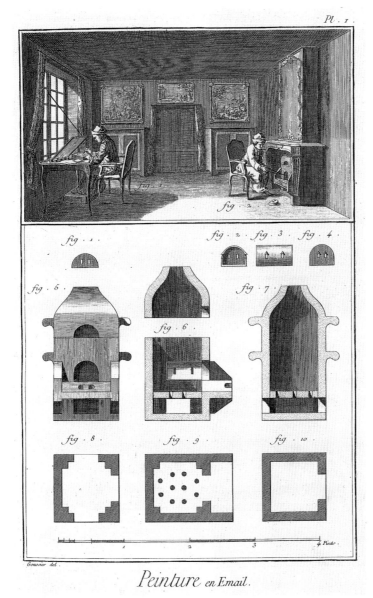

Peinture en Email.

Workshop and kiln of an enameller, from Diderot/d'Alembert, Encyclopédie, Paris 1751–65.

increased popularity of hard-paste porcelain, more painters were working on porcelain, and it was added to the list of the supports used for enamel portrait miniatures. Various enamel artists were drawn to working in this medium, including Louis Bertin Parant, Jean-François Soiron, Abraham Constantin and John Simpson.

The individual techniques of enamel painting that the different artists adopted are illustrated in the various catalogue entries.

¹ Translation of Sturm 1975, p.3.

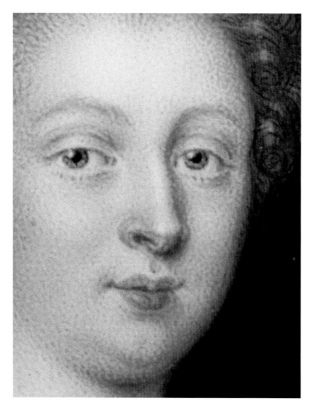

Lady with a Blue Cloak (cat. no. 27) by Huaut.

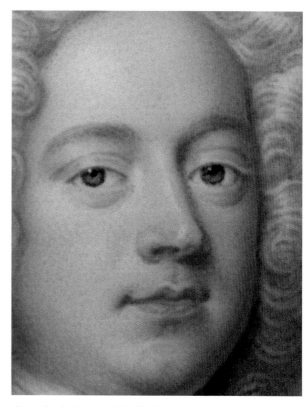

Baron Brooke (cat. no. 62) by Zincke.

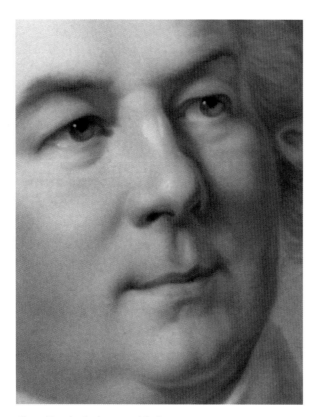

Count Zavadovsky (cat. no. 50) by Soret.

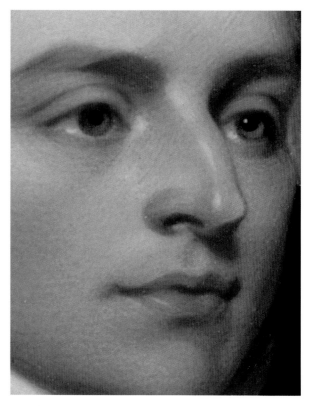

Capt Whitby (cat. no. 7) by Bone.

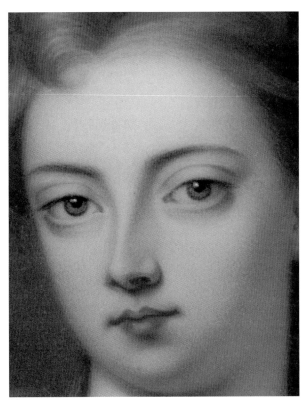

Lady Anne Churchill (cat. no. 4) by Boit.

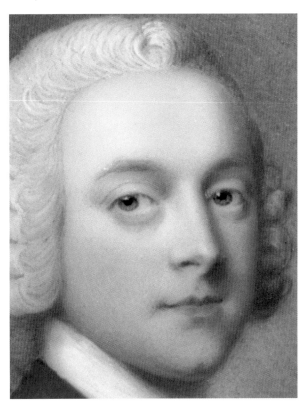

Mr Tilson (cat. no. 53) by Spencer.

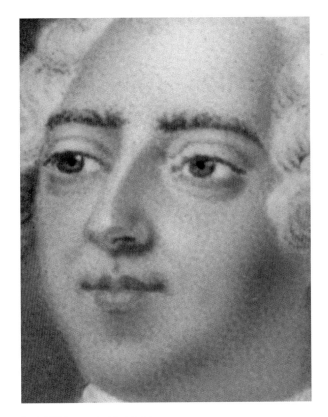

Louis XV (cat. no. 40) by Mathieu.

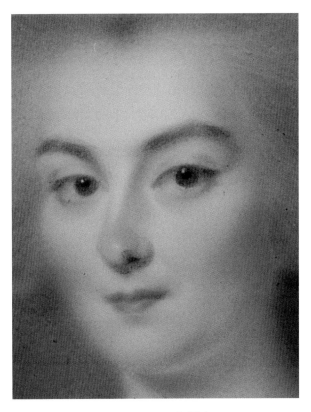

Young Lady in a Blue Dress (cat. no. 61) by Weyler.

Continental Enamelled Portrait Miniatures

BODO HOFSTETTER

In art history, research in the field of enamel painting has been neglected. Of the many good reasons for this, the most important may be the inherent difficulty of classifying enamel painting. Should it fall under the category of applied arts, jewellery or painting? Whereas the first enamellers came from a background associated with the goldsmith, jeweller or watchmaker, many renowned enamellers of the eighteenth and nineteenth centuries were initially pastellists or oil painters. Many enamels are mounted on gold boxes – how then could a museum curator classify those as paintings? From the eighteenth century onwards, enamellers often worked in porcelain factories, so the ceramics context supplies a further aspect – although not one that really helps the researcher – because of the anonymity of the porcelain painter within the factory current at the time.

The general ignorance about enamel painting results mainly from a lack of sources. Apart from those relating to enamellers who worked for the court, no documents appear to have survived. The only 'sources' available are the enamel portraits themselves. These are frequently mounted on gold boxes or in lockets so that in many cases it is risky or impossible to check the signatures which are often enamelled on the reverses, called counter enamels.

Whereas the history of the enamel miniature in England seems to have few gaps in which there are only mysterious and undocumented artists, the situation on the Continent is different. It is a strange phenomenon that most enamellers seemed to prefer a nomadic life, looking for work in many geographically far apart places. This makes research in the archives almost impossible, as documents easily available for 'sedentary' artists, such as certificates for births, baptisms, marriages, contracts and deaths, may be scattered among many different archives. So it is not surprising that there are no primary sources on quite a number of enamel painters, even at such a late date as the nineteenth century. Equally, no sources are available about the commissioning and purchase of enamel on the Continent or the reactions of those involved. Like its watercolour cousin, the enamel miniature appears to have been an everyday object for those who could afford it, not worth the slightest written comment.

Not surprisingly, the present essay does not in any way claim to be complete. In attempting to present the most significant artists who have left a trace in the field of enamel painting, it may appear to be an endless sequence of biographies but, at the present stage of research, this is the only way to proceed. It is to be hoped that the documented elements compiled in this essay may encourage a greater interest in the challenge of further research.

THE ORIGINS OF ENAMELLING

The technique of enamelling has been known from the earliest times. Its name is supposed to have derived from the Hebrew word *Haschmal* used by the prophet Ezekiel. Enamelling was used in the decoration of jewels by the Egyptians, the Greeks, the Romans, the Byzantines and the artists of the Middle Ages. The family workshops of enamellers in Limoges in the fifteenth and sixteenth centuries produced not only beautiful and durable decoration for everyday objects, such as dishes and boxes, but also small portraits painted in a linear *grisaille* technique by alternating opaque and translucent enamel layers. The Pénicaud and Limousin families in particular were known for these rather naïve-looking enamels which today are strictly separated from the enamel miniatures dealt with in this publication.

The transition from using enamel in a purely decorative way to the production of independent miniature likenesses must have been completed as late as the first third of the seventeenth century. It is only at this point that the enamel miniature became an alternative to the portrait miniature painted with watercolour and body colour on vellum or parchment, a technique which became fashionable at royal courts from the late 1520s. The tradition of the watercolour miniature came from the book miniatures painted by the limners of the Bruges-Ghent school, whereas the enamel miniature originated from the studios of goldsmiths and watchmakers from Blois, Châteaudun and Paris.

It is not surprising therefore that the first signed and dated independent enamel portrait is by the hand of the son of an artist, Jean Toutin, famous for his enamelled watchcases and lockets. Henry Toutin (1614–83), the author of the world's first recorded enamel miniature,[1] proudly signed the work on the reverse, *Henry Toutin Orphevre / aparis a fait ce cy lan / 1636* (see fig. 1). The colours of this portrait, unlike those of the enamel portraits produced by the Pénicaud and Limousin families, have not been applied in layers. The brushstrokes form a visible

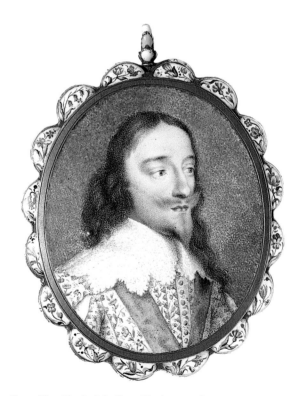

Fig. 1. King Charles I, by Henry Toutin, enamel on copper, Mauritshuis, The Hague.

stipple (*pointillé*) which imitates the watercolour/ body colour technique used by the limners of their time. Toutin used the same technique for the few watchcases and lockets known to have been decorated by him.[2]

Although it is most likely to have been painted in Paris, the first enamel portrait depicts Charles I of England. It is the only enamel portrait by Toutin hitherto recorded, but it can be assumed that Toutin painted other portraits which are either unsigned and therefore unidentified or lost. From this starting point, there follows chronologically a series of enamels painted by Jean Petitot (1607–91), the most celebrated enameller of all time.

FRANCE

Jean Petitot and the Heyday of Enamel Painting: from Geneva via London to Paris

For centuries Jean Petitot's name has almost been synonymous with enamel painting. The son of a Huguenot refugee, he was born in Geneva and is thus the founding father of the long tradition of Geneva enamellers. He completed his apprenticeship as a goldsmith in 1626, but where and how he learnt the enamelling technique is uncertain. It has been suggested that he met the Toutins in Paris in about 1633, but it is impossible to substantiate this hypothesis.[3] The fact is that in 1638, only two years after Toutin's portrait of King Charles I, Petitot signed and dated his first three recorded enamel miniatures: the portraits of Charles I of England, his wife, Queen Henrietta Maria, and their eldest son, the future Charles II.[4] These three oval enamels and the dozen others he signed and dated in England until 1643 are all considered masterworks of enamel painting. They mainly depict Charles I, his family and his courtiers and are all copies after large-scale oil portraits, mostly by the King's court painters Anthony Van Dyck and Gerard van Honthorst.

However, the exact years of his arrival in England and his return to the Continent are unknown. It is known that Petitot was in France in 1651, as he was married there that year. He may have been introduced at the court of Louis XIV by the King's aunt, Queen Henrietta-Maria of England, who had returned to her native country after the execution of

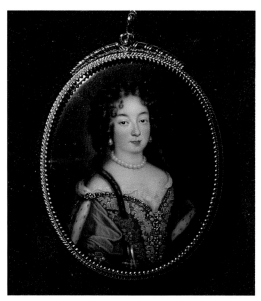

Fig. 2. The Dauphine Maria Anna, by Jean Petitot, enamel, Buenos Aires, Museo Nacional de Arte Decorativo.

her husband in 1649. Despite his Calvinist religion, Petitot was appointed Court Painter in Enamel to the Sun King. With the Revocation of the Edict of Nantes thirty years later, in 1685, the persecution of the Protestants started again and Petitot was thrown into prison in 1686 when he refused to renounce his faith. Forced by illness to give in, he signed his abjuration and returned to Geneva, where he died in 1691.

During his time in London, Petitot appears to have worked on his own, but his works were so much in demand at the court of Louis XIV that he had to find associates and apprentices. The few enamels executed in England between 1638 and 1643 are all of exquisite quality, painted with a very fine stipple resulting in expressive and strong portraits. Also their size, mostly over 5 cm (2 in) high, seems important compared with that of the French works, which are, with some rare exceptions (see fig. 2), mostly the size of a thumbnail. The rather generalised representation of the sitters, mainly copied after Beaubrun, Gobert or Mignard, makes their identification today almost impossible.

Because of the mass-production required by the Sun King and his court, it is sometimes difficult to distinguish the works of the master from those created by the hands of his assistants. Nevertheless, two of these helping hands are almost equal in skill to Petitot's. Jacques Bordier (1616–84) was born in Geneva and, like Petitot, trained as a goldsmith. He is said to have met his fellow countryman in London and married Petitot's sister in 1651. It is not clear to what extent he was working for Petitot, but the superb quality of his signed works makes it most unlikely that he was taken on to execute inferior tasks in Petitot's studio. On the other hand, only three enamel portraits bear his famous monogram 'JB', including his masterwork, the celebrated portrait of the printer Vitré (see cat no. 18). Bordier's activities as a diplomat may have prevented him from developing his artistic activities further.

Of Petitot's fourteen surviving children, only one took up his father's artistic career. Jean II Petitot (1653–1702) was apprenticed to a miniaturist, one of the famous Cooper brothers, in 1677. He worked for Charles II from 1677 to 1682. In the following year, he married his cousin Madeleine Bordier. On Jacques Bordier's death in 1684, he succeeded his uncle as a Genevan diplomat at the French court. His enamel miniatures are very rare and it is often difficult to distinguish between the work of the father and that of the son. Other enamellers active in seventeenth-century France include the Du Guernier brothers, Louis (1614–59) and Pierre (c. 1624–74). Only two enamel portraits signed 'Du Guernier', without initial, are recorded, one in the Royal Collection and the other in the Collections of the House of Orange-Nassau. Of even greater rarity are the enamels by Jean II Toutin (1619–after 1660), Henry Toutin's younger brother, Robert Vauquer (1625–70), Louis de Chatillon and Jacques-Philippe Ferrand.

Enamellers in France under the Regency and Louis XV

During the first three quarters of the eighteenth century, the art of the enamel miniature was practised by a restricted number of artists whose clientele was essentially the royal family and their court. The enamellers gained their living, as did their fellow artists painting in watercolours, by a kind of mass-production of portraits depicting Louis XV, copied after the official large-scale oil paintings. These small miniatures were mounted in jewels and precious snuffboxes to be distributed as political presents, a custom which had already started under Louis XIV. The French rulers must have been conscious of the advantages of enamels over the fragile watercolour miniatures, as they sponsored the enamellers in a quite exceptional way. They facilitated their admission to the Académie Royale de Peinture (which was reserved for Catholic subjects) and provided them with highly sought-after lodgings with studios in the Louvre.

When the Swede Charles Boit (1662–1727),[5] former court enameller to William III and Queen Anne and a great traveller, arrived in Paris in 1717, he was admitted to the Académie Royale de Peinture despite being a Protestant. His *pièce de réception*, the *Charité*, is now in the Louvre. The Regent, the Duke of Orléans, showered him with commissions; Boit's French sitters include a posthumous Louis XIV, numerous versions of Louis XV as a young boy, Mademoiselle de Clermont, and the Regent himself. After a two-year sojourn in Dresden, he returned to Paris in 1723, where he died in 1727. The famous miniaturist Jean-Baptiste Massé (1686–1767) is also said to have painted enamels but not a single example seems to have survived. He was one of Jean-Etienne Liotard's masters in Paris from 1723 to 1726 but it is impossible to discern if Massé influenced Liotard as an enameller.

A greater traveller even than Boit, Liotard passed through France several times and executed enamels in Lyons and Paris. His huge rectangular enamelled iron plaque depicting Empress Maria Theresa, now in the Rijksmuseum, Amsterdam, is signed and dated *à Lyon 1747*, and a superb oval enamel of the same sitter is signed and dated *Juin 1748 a Paris*.[6] During his second stay in Paris, 1748 to 1753, he painted several other ravishing enamels, such as the so-called *Marquis de Marigny*, dated 1749,[7] and *La Liseuse* (his niece, Mademoiselle Lavergne from Lyons), dated 1752.[8] As Liotard was not proposed for admission to the Académie Royale, he was elected to the Académie de Saint-Luc des maîtres peintres, where he exhibited in 1751, 1752 and 1753. It was only in 1752 that his exhibits included an enamel, one of his self-portraits.

Whereas enamels represented a minute part of Liotard's *œuvre*, three other contemporaries active in Paris in the mid-eighteenth century specialised entirely in enamels: Louis-François Aubert, Jean André Rouquet and Jean-Adam Mathieu. Louis-François Aubert (d. 1755) is now less known for his beautiful enamel portraits than for his *émaux en relief* which he fired, following the old goldsmith-enameller's tradition, on gold snuffboxes and gold watch-cases. He was particularly famous for his flower decorations. He was authorised to bear the title of *peintre en émail du roy* (king's enamel painter). The three enamel portraits recorded as by his hand all depict Louis XV and date between 1752 and 1753.[9] They are finely stippled but stiff and official compared with the magnificent enamels painted by Liotard at the same time.

Although Jean André Rouquet (1701–58) was born in Geneva, most of his many enamel portraits are strongly influenced by Christian Friedrich Zincke who dominated the field of enamel portrait painting in England for almost half a century. Because of their close resemblance, Rouquet's works are often wrongly attributed to Zincke, although they are finer and less stereotypical than Zincke's works. Having spent thirty years in England (see cat. no.98), Rouquet left for Paris in 1753 and was subsequently admitted to the Académie Royale in 1754, despite being a Protestant, which necessitated the *ordre exprès du Roi*.

From 1753 to 1757, Rouquet exhibited at the Paris Salon, showing enamels depicting celebrities of his day such as Louis de Sylvestre, Chochin and the Marquis de Marigny, brother of his patron the Marquise de Pompadour. The portraits of Marigny and of Louis XV after Liotard's pastel, now both in the Louvre, are among the masterworks of French enamel miniature painting. Rouquet's enamels from his unfortunately short French period are characterised by an incredibly fine, pastel-like brushstroke, tasteful colours and a perfect mastery of the firing technique. Some of them are so close to Liotard's ingenious works that they have been erroneously attributed to Liotard.[10] Rouquet's chameleon-like talent enabled him to paint in London '*à la Zincke*' and later in Paris '*à la Liotard*'. Nevertheless, his professional success was overshadowed by the death of his wife in 1753 and his own temporary hemiplegia. After the death of his beloved servant who had worked for him for eighteen years, he lost his mind. When his contemporaries noticed signs of dementia in his behaviour, such as throwing bottles out of his window and walking half-naked in the streets, he had to be confined to Charenton Hospital in August 1758. He died there in December of the same year.

On his admission to the Académie Royale in 1754, Rouquet was granted a lodging in the Louvre, which had become available on the death of another enameller of renown, Jean-Adam Mathieu. This flat in the Louvre, formerly occupied by the enameller Louis de Chatillon, had been coveted by numerous artists of the Académie Royale including Massé, but the Swedish Ambassador succeeded in securing it for his protégé, Jean-Adam Mathieu, born in Stralsund (Pomerania) in about 1698. Mathieu was a goldsmith, porcelain painter and enameller. During the second quarter of the eighteenth century, he was undoubtedly the most fashionable enameller in France. Many oval enamel miniatures by his hand depicting Louis XV are known; the list of his other sitters is just as impressive and includes Queen Maria Leszczynska and her father Stanislas, King of Poland, the Duke and Duchess of Orléans, the Prince de Condé and the Marquise de Pompadour. Two months before his death, on 18 April 1753, he was appointed *Peintre Orfèvre du Roi en Email*. All those honours appear exaggerated considering the poor artistic quality of his enamels. Like all his contemporaries, he used a visible stipple, just as Liotard had done. Nevertheless, Mathieu's enamels appear wooden, affected and extremely stylised. But the stiff, official aspect of his enamels, reminiscent of the state portraits under the reign of the Sun King, may have met the expectations of his princely clients.

The Louis XVI Period: a Revolutionary Wind

During the Louis XIV and Louis XV periods, the art of painting portrait miniatures in enamel had been confined to a limited number of artists working for the court and the high aristocracy. From the 1770s onwards, a popularisation of both the watercolour and the enamel miniature can be seen. In response to an increasing demand for small likenesses coming from a financially strong and socially confident bourgeoisie, many miniature painters and enamellers arrived whose work was not always of such a high artistic standard as that of the older generation. Other enamellers were forced into mass-production in order to satisfy the demands of their clients. A prime example of this decline in standards is the work of Nicolas-André Courtois (1734–97). He was admitted to the Académie Royale as an *agréé* in 1770 and exhibited in the Paris Salon from 1771 to 1777.

Although Courtois was peintre du roi, Clouzot[11] said of him that '*il travaille pour des gens de toute condition. Impossible de mettre des noms sur les portraits d'hommes, d'enfants ou de femmes . . .*'

His work is characterised by a poor technical quality and a total lack of variety in the representation of his models. This may have resulted from the fact that he must have been one of the first enamellers who, rather than copy from others, painted *ad vivum* as far as it was feasible considering the complex enamelling technique. His boring, small bust-length portraits of French bourgeois in black coats characterise the lower end of the French enamel market of the Louis XVI period, along with the works of other artists such as Nicolas-Claude Vassal, Carpentier of Rouen and also Pierre Pasquier.

The reputation of Pierre Pasquier (1734–1806) is not borne out by the disappointing standard of the majority of his work. In 1769, he was admitted fully to the Académie Royale de Peinture. Five years later, he was granted one of the highly coveted lodgings in the Louvre. From 1769 to 1783 he exhibited in the Paris Salon, and the names of his sitters include Marie-Antoinette as Dauphine, Louis XV and Christian VII, King of Denmark, the Comtesse d'Artois and Princesse Sophie of France. During the French Revolution, he was imprisoned, but freed after the fall of Robespierre. His most successful period appears to have been the years 1770–80. After that date, a new and revolutionary technique and style had been established in France and gained the favour of the public.

The Triumph of Hall, Weyler and their Competitors from Geneva

Enamel painting in France under the last years of the ancien régime, as represented by French enamellers such as Courtois and Pasquier, creates rather a poor impression.

The arrival in Paris of the Swedish oil painter, miniaturist and enameller Pierre-Adolphe Hall (1739–93) introduced an entirely new technique which opened the way to a completely different artistic conception of painting both enamel portraits and watercolour miniatures. The technique of stipple, or *pointillé*, had been used on the Continent from the seventeenth century. The modelling of a face by creating shadows, the indication of the darker and lighter parts of a dress were achieved by painting small dots or hatches shaped as short commas spaced closely together or further apart, so that the dark areas would have a high concentration of dots and the light areas many less. The finer and less visible these dots were, the smoother the general aspect of the miniature was.

Petitot's best works are so finely stippled that strong magnification has to be used to see the work of the brush. Liotard, on the other hand, used quite a thick and visible dotting which gives a strong impression when seen from afar but is best not scrutinised under magnification. It was a technique similar to that used by Signac and Seurat in their work in the late nineteenth century. Hall's innovation consisted of complementing the stipple with the use of broad brushstrokes as used by Frans Hals. He thus imitated the technique of oil painting and created miniatures, which were as natural and lively as large-scale paintings. The growth in popularity of a polished ivory slip as a ground facilitated the 'ingenious' brushstroke as the glossy surface – in contrast to the quite rough surface of vellum or parchment – did not provide any resistance to the gliding of the brush. This technique was immediately adopted by many watercolour miniaturists and enamellers. Enamel miniatures signed by Hall are very rare, although he is said to have preferred his portraits in this technique to his watercolour and gouache miniatures.

The real exponent of this new style is Jean-Baptiste Weyler (1747–91) from Strasbourg. Schidlof[12] considered him as undoubtedly the best French enameller of his time, although he was also an accomplished watercolour miniaturist and pastel painter. The large enamel miniature depicting the Comte d'Angiviller (see cat. no. 59) is both characteristic of the new style of enamelling in France and Weyler's œuvre. It is such an extreme example of the free technique that it almost gives the impression it is unfinished. Weyler concentrated mainly on copying both contemporary and old master subjects and executed very few 'real' portraits (see cat. no. 61).

Hall and Weyler had to face real competition in the field of the enamel portrait miniature. By 1770, several highly talented enamel painters from Geneva had settled in Paris. Charles-Louis Loehr, Pierre-François Marcinhes, Jean-François Favre and Jaques Thouron merged the new, 'free' brushstroke with the

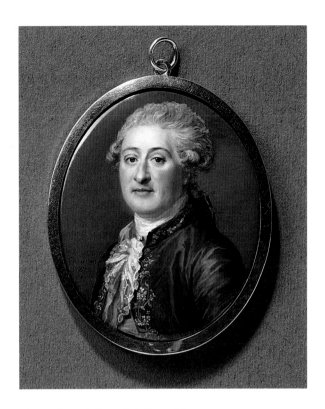

Fig . 3. Baron de Breteuil, by Jaques Thouron, 1787, enamel on copper, private collection.

traditional meticulous, incredibly fine 'Geneva' stipple and created enamels full of life, which imitated the technique of the large-scale oil painters. Whereas works by Loehr and Marcinhes are excessively rare, both Favre and Thouron were quite prolific enamellers.

Jaques Thouron (1749–89) was apprenticed to the Geneva enameller Pierre François Marcinhes (1739–78) in 1764 for four years. From 1770 onwards, he is recorded in Paris where he entered the workshop of the Geneva enameller Charles-Louis Loehr (1747–78). It is in Loehr's studio that he probably met another compatriot, Jean-François Favre (1751–1807). They soon set up a business on their own, producing enamel plaques depicting mythological and historical scenes for mounting on snuffboxes and other objects of vertu. From the late 1770s onwards, both associates appear to have progressed to painting enamel portraits, and at least from 1778/79 onwards, signed and dated masterworks of enamel painting by their hand are known. Thouron counted among his clients both the wealthy Geneva bourgeoisie, such as the Neckers, Tronchins,

Pictets and Turretinis, and the French high aristocracy, including the Orléans, Luynes and Gramont families. His portraits are almost exclusively copies after oil paintings, mainly by Elizabeth-Louise Vigée-Lebrun, Henri-Pierre Danloux and Jean-Baptiste Greuze. He was appointed *'Peintre de Monsieur'*, painter to the Comte de Provence, later Louis XVIII but also supplied enamels for the Comte d'Artois, later Charles X. Jaques Thouron died at the age of forty, only four months before the outbreak of the French Revolution. His masterfully executed enamels are considered the best of the Louis XVI period (see fig. 3) and his works have been compared to those of Petitot and Liotard.

The career of his contemporary Jean-François Favre was overshadowed by Thouron's reputation. Favre is said to have been forced to return to Geneva for health reasons, and his enamels are rarer than those of the artist who was briefly his associate. Unlike Thouron, Favre also executed watercolour miniatures and drawings. Nevertheless, his masterworks are his enamel miniatures and the portrait of Mounier (see cat. no. 21) is a typical example of his work, giving a 'down-to-earth' impression in contrast to Thouron's spiritual, 'flashy' portraits.

Enamel in France during the nineteenth century

The success of Thouron, Favre and several of the other Geneva enamellers in Paris encouraged many foreign enamellers to try their luck there too. The younger ones were keen to take lessons with the celebrated large-scale oil painters *à la mode* such as Gérard, David, Gros or Girodet, and the older ones tried to find new clients at the recently founded imperial court. With the dissolution of the French Royal Academy in 1792, the Paris Salon was now open to all artists and did not limit access solely to the members of the Royal Academy. For up-and-coming artists, this was the best way to court the public. Among the many immigrants was a unique artist, German-born Carl Christian Kanz (1758–c. 1818). He came from Plauen and had established himself in Paris in the 1780s. He exhibited at the Paris Salon in 1808 and specialised successfully in *'têtes d'expression'*, which were erotic fantasies in enamel (see cat. nos. 32 and 33). Most of the other foreign artists who tried to conquer the Paris 'market' were from Geneva, such as Jean-Jacques Soutter (1765–1840), Salomon

Guillaume Counis (1785–1859), Abraham Constantin (1785–1855) and his pupil Pierre-Henri Sturm (1785–1869), and the best known of them, the highly talented Jean-François Soiron (1756–1812). Most of their technically highly accomplished enamels were copies after large-scale oil paintings, and their favourite model was, obviously, the Emperor Napoleon.

But none of the enamellers could gain an audience with the Emperor in person; oil paintings by Gérard or miniatures by Isabey had to be used as models. Napoleon does not appear to have understood the advantages of enamel miniatures over ivory miniatures. Jean-Baptiste Isabey (1767–1855) was inundated with commissions for watercolour miniatures which were mounted on gold presentation snuffboxes, so much so that he had a whole studio 'producing' the imperial portraits, each of which he finally had to sign. The existence of some rare enamels signed *Isabey* proves that Isabey mastered this technique but did not really benefit from his enamelling skills. Correspondence between the imperial administration and enamellers such as Louise Kugler (fl. 1802–12), the pupil and widow of Jean-Baptiste Weyler, prove that there was no special interest in enamels at the imperial French court. Even the famous French miniature painter Jean-Baptiste Jacques Augustin (1759–1832), who occasionally painted enamel miniatures of incredibly fine quality, did not succeed in breaking the Imperial preference for Isabey's ivory miniatures. After Napoleon's fall in 1815, the enamellers tried their luck with Louis XVIII and his brother and successor Charles X, and later with Louis-Philippe. Only Jean-Baptiste Duchesne de Gisors (1770–1856) succeeded as a court painter, executing many enamels of the Duc de Berry and his family, Charles X and, under Louis-Philippe, the Orléans family. In 1840, Louis-Philippe specially commissioned him to 'continue' the series of Petitot enamels owned by the Louvre.

Although Abraham Constantin was awarded a gold medal for his exhibits in the Paris Salon of 1819 and received the Legion of Honour in 1828, he slowly abandoned the enamelling technique for the porcelain miniature. He joined the Royal Porcelain factory at Sèvres in 1826 and had enormous international success with his huge porcelain plaques depicting copies after old master and contemporary paintings. Constantin had realised that, after 300 years of existence, the enamel miniature portrait had gone out of fashion, at least as a way to represent images of loved ones. Another miniaturist better known for her porcelain plaques than for her enamel miniatures is Fanny Charrin (d. 1854) who extensively copied enamels and porcelain miniatures in the style of Petitot. By the mid-nineteenth century, the enamel miniature had become more and more a curiosity and a collector's item. Enamel miniatures by Petitot had always been considered at the height of enamelling art and were copied (and signed) by enamellers such as Pierre Pasquier and Fanny Charrin. From the mid-eighteenth century Petitot enamels had been popular with collectors and by the nineteenth century, clever enamellers knew how to satisfy the increasing demand for them. Even today, many well-painted mid-nineteenth century 'Petitots' can cause embarrassment to collectors and even to museum curators. The Petitot revival constituted a rather deplorable end to the art of the enamel miniature in France.

SWITZERLAND

Strangely enough, the Swiss enamel miniature continued well into the nineteenth century; and in the second half of the nineteenth century a great number of highly talented Geneva artists were working, such as Charles-Louis Glardon (1825–87) and his older brother Jacques Aimé Glardon (1815–62), Philippe Prochet (1825–1890), Jules Hébert (1812–97) and his daughter Juliette Charlotte Hébert (1837–97), and Rodolphe Piguet (1840–1915). These artists also worked extensively in the Geneva *Fabrique*, which is the typical Geneva industry producing watches, watchcases, snuffboxes and gold jewellery, all decorated with enamel. From the late seventeenth century, the Geneva *Fabrique* had provided work for many enamellers. The rise of the watchmaking industry resulted in an ever-increasing demand for craftsmen of high technical standards. Thus, the enamellers' workshops in Geneva assured the tradition of the enamelling skills, although it is true that the mass-production within the workshops of the *Fabrique* sometime resulted in a kind of slavery. The enamelling workshops were often a family business, and the dynasties of the Huauts, the Mussards,

the Andrés and the Gardelles supplied enamels both for watchcases, gold box tops and also enamel portraits. The most talented enamellers tried to escape from the depressing fate of spending their life decorating watchcases by leaving Geneva. Towards the end of the eighteenth century, an economic and political crisis caused a further exodus of Geneva enamellers, which explains the presence of Geneva enamellers in almost all European countries. Among those who stayed in Geneva, Elizabeth Terroux (1759–1822) is probably the best known but not the only one. This guaranteed the survival of the Geneva tradition of enamel painting.

SCANDINAVIA

One of the first countries to receive a Geneva enameller was Denmark. Paul Prieur (c. 1620–c. 1683) (see p. 94). The son of a Geneva goldsmith, he was active in Copenhagen from 1655 onwards at the latest. He worked extensively for the court of kings Frederick III and Christian V. Prieur was succeeded by Strasburg-born Josias Barbette (1657–1732), again the son of a goldsmith. Christian V and Frederick IV were generous sponsors of this highly talented artist (see cat. no. 1). In the year of Barbette's death, Heinrich Jacob Pohle (fl. 1729–47) was appointed court miniaturist. He executed both watercolour and enamel miniatures. During the second third of the eighteenth century, lesser-known artists such as Hans Jacob Schrader, Jorgen Gylding and particularly Joseph Brecheisen continued the tradition of the enamel miniature in Denmark. Brecheisen (c. 1720–after 1766), whom Colding[13] considered to be the most important enameller active in Denmark after Prieur and Barbette, is recorded in Denmark from 1758. He worked for the court of Frederick V, producing both miniatures in watercolour, enamel miniatures and enamelled boxes. Towards the end of the eighteenth century, as watercolour on ivory miniatures became more and more popular, enamel miniatures went out of fashion. Lesser-known artists such as Christopher Ruch, C.F. Schrader and Georg Seiptius are the last representatives of this art in Denmark. A similar phenomenon can be seen in Sweden. Jean Toutin II (1619–after 1660) came to Sweden in about 1645 and became enamel painter to Queen Christina, although not a single piece by his hand can be ascribed to him with certainty. In 1646, Queen Christina's agent in Paris engaged the French enameller Pierre Signac (1623–84). Signac, a pupil from the Toutin workshop, was appointed court painter to Queen Christina on 1 January 1647. He painted many portraits in watercolour and enamel of the Queen and of her followers Charles X Gustav and Charles XI.

Signac's pupil Charles Boit (see pp. 50–52) made a brilliant career outside Sweden, as did another Swede, Martin van Meytens (see cat. no. 41). The tradition of enamelling was continued by lesser known and talented artists such as Eric Utterhielm (1662–1717), Andreas von Behn (1650–1715) and Elias Brenner (1647–1717), Signac's successor as court miniaturist. After its short heyday in the second half of the seventeenth century, the enamel miniature quickly lost its popularity. The last miniaturist bearing the title of Swedish court enameller was Johan Georg Henrichsen (1707–73) who painted many portraits of the ill-fated Gustav III.

GERMANY AND AUSTRIA

The art of enamelling was particularly widespread in seventeenth- and early eighteenth-century Germany. Three courts sponsored this form of art in a quite exceptional way: the Court of the Electors of Brandenburg, later Kings of Prussia, in Berlin and Potsdam, the Court of the Electors of Saxony, sometime Kings of Poland, in Dresden, and the Court of the Electors Palatine in Düsseldorf.

Brandenburg-Prussia

Many enamel miniatures depicting Elector Frederick William of Brandenburg (1620–88), called 'The Great Elector', have survived. Unfortunately, most of them are unsigned and it is very difficult to ascribe those pieces to the enamellers whose names are recorded in Berlin from c. 1685 onwards. Lorenz Eppenhoff came from the Netherlands to Berlin in 1685. Not a single piece has been attributed to him with certainty, although it is recorded that in 1689 he received an annual salary of 300 *Reichsthaler* for supplying at least six enamels per year. He got 30 *Reichsthaler* for any supplementary enamel.[14] Pierre II Huaut (1647–98), son of the Genevan enameller Pierre I Huaut arrived in Berlin in spring 1685 and

immediately began working for the Great Elector. He returned to his home town one year later, and a beautiful example of his work from this short Geneva period is in the Gilbert Collection (see cat. no. 27). On his return, he recommended his two younger brothers Jean-Pierre (1655–1723) and Ami (1657–1724) to replace him. Thus, on 7 June 1686, the Electoral Prince of Brandenburg had to write to the Geneva city council to apply for an authorisation for the brothers to leave.[15] His request was granted and the two brothers became court painters until 1700, when they returned to Geneva. Their elder brother had rejoined them in Berlin in 1689 and was appointed painter to the new Elector, the Great Elector's son Frederick III, on 19 September 1691. Pierre II Huaut died in Berlin seven years later.

In the meantime, a native Berliner, Samuel Blesendorff (1663–1706) had arrived at court. After purportedly working at The Hague in 1679, he painted his first enamel of the Great Elector in 1686. He later portrayed his son Elector Frederick III, who styled himself the first King in Prussia as Frederick I in 1701, many times. Whereas the enamel miniature was highly appreciated during the reigns of the Great Elector and Frederick I in Prussia, the Soldier King, Frederick William I, did not show any interest in the arts. Nevertheless, the Swedish-born painter and enameller Johann Harper (Stockholm 1688–1746 Potsdam), a pupil of Martin van Meytens, arrived in Berlin in 1712. He was styled *Hof-Kabinettmaler* in 1716. Judging from the only recorded enamel portrait by his hand,[16] he was an enameller of exceptional talent.

Like his father, Frederick the Great did not show a great interest in miniature painting. Most of his official miniatures are painted in body colour and watercolour by Anton Friedrich König.

Berlin-born enameller Carl-Friedrich Thienpont (1730–96), a pupil of Antoine Pesne, painted enamels from 1751 onwards and studied with Ismael Mengs in Dresden in 1753. He painted his beautiful enamel self-portrait in Berlin in August 1761, worked in Stettin in 1762 and then moved to Warsaw, where he died in 1796. Among the best-known artists during the reign of Frederick the Great was Daniel Chodowiecki (1726–1801). Apart from executing ivory miniatures, drawings and engravings, he painted enamel miniatures, mostly for enamelled snuffboxes. He was probably the last enameller working in Prussia.

Dresden

The splendour of the court of Augustus the Strong (1670–1733), Elector of Saxony as Frederick Augustus I and King of Poland as Augustus II, necessitated the presence of many enamellers. The art of the goldsmith and of the enameller were so closely related in Dresden that they were often shared as a family business. The prime example is the case of the celebrated court goldsmith and jeweller Johann Melchior Dinglinger (1664–1731) who worked with his younger brother Frederick George Dinglinger (1666–1720). The gold jewellery executed by Johann Melchior was usually enamelled by his brother, who also executed beautiful enamel portraits of Augustus the Strong. Overshadowed by the fame of the Dinglingers was Johann Melchior Dinglinger's son-in-law, court enameller Isaac Benjamin Vallier (fl. 1716–31). His signature is to be found on an enamelled gold sweetmeat box in the Green Vaults and on two rare enamel-on-gold miniatures, including a portrait of Augustus the Strong of 1721, in the Kunst und Gewerbe Museum, Hamburg. Nevertheless, the most beautiful enamel portraits depicting Augustus the Strong were executed by the great traveller Charles Boit, who stayed in Dresden in 1719/20.

Ismael Mengs (1688–1764) was a pupil of Johann Harper. Although he was court enameller in Dresden, very few works can be attributed to him apart from two large enamel plaques depicting religious subjects in the Green Vaults, Dresden. Under the reign of Augustus the Strong's only legitimate son Frederick Augustus II, King of Poland as Augustus III, the interest in the enamel miniature was boosted by the increasing fashion for Meissen porcelain. Johann Martin Heinrici (1713–86), best known for his decoration of Meissen porcelain, executed both beautiful miniatures on porcelain boxes and enamel portraits of the Elector and his family. From the 1740s onwards, the use of the firing technique became increasingly confined to the decoration of porcelain snuffboxes, with the portraits being directly painted on the inside of the porcelain box lid (see cat. no. 90). Enamellers as such ceased to work in Saxony after this period.

The Palatinate

Nowadays Düsseldorf is not particularly known as an artistic centre, but at the beginning of the seventeenth century it almost rivalled both Dresden and Berlin. During the reigns of Electors Palatine Jan Wellem (1658–1716) and Charles III Philip (1661–1742), Düsseldorf became one of the centres of enamel painting in Germany. At least four enamellers of repute were able simultaneously to benefit from the generous patronage of the art-loving Palatines: J.M. Khaetscher, Charles Boit, Peter Boy and Johann Frederick Ardin.

Khaetscher, whose first names and dates are unknown, is the most mysterious artist of this group. His signature is to be found on a series of enamels depicting members of the family of Palatinate-Neuburg.[17] An Electoral portrait by him is in the Gilbert Collection (see cat. no. 34). From an artistic point of view, he did not reach the level of his fellow enamellers at court.

Charles Boit, whose name appears frequently throughout the present publication, included Düsseldorf in his visits. He must have arrived there from the Netherlands after a short visit to the court of Clement Augustus, Prince Elector of Cologne. A witness to this visit is a beautiful enamel miniature of Clement Augustus, signed *C. Boit pinx. a Bonn 1700*.[18] Boit's stunning enamels of Palatine Elector Jan Wellem and his wife, both signed with his monogram and dated 1700, are in the Bayerisches Nationalmuseum, Munich, now the home of the fantastic miniatures collection of the House of Palatinate-Neuburg.[19] Boit's monogram had for many years been mistaken for that of Peter Boy.

The celebrated enameller and goldsmith Peter Boy (c. 1650–1727), who had formerly worked for the Prince-Elector of Trier, is recorded in Düsseldorf from 1696 onwards. He painted splendid enamel portraits of Elector Jan Wellem and his wife Maria Anna Luisa de Medici, but his absolute masterwork, and certainly one of the most impressive enamel miniatures ever painted, is the *Entombment of Christ* after Adriaen van der Werff, signed and dated 1716. This huge enamel plaque arrived, after the extinction of the Palatine-Neuburg line, via Karlsruhe and Mannheim in Munich.[20] A pupil of Boy was Johann Friedrich Ardin, none of whose personal details are known. Nevertheless, his *œuvre* is vast. Most of the enamel miniatures depicting Elector Jan Wellem and his brother and follower Charles III Philip are by his hand. The Bayerisches Nationalmuseum in Munich has at least twenty-four enamels by his hand, depicting almost the entire family of the last Palatine-Neuburgs. With the transfer of the Palatine residence under Charles III Philip, Düsseldorf lost its role as one of the leading centres for enamel painting.

Enamel portrait miniatures in Germany were, however, not restricted to Berlin, Dresden and Düsseldorf. In Augsburg and Nuremberg, centres of the art of the silversmith, enamellers did not only decorate pieces of gold, silver or silver-gilt, but also painted portrait miniatures in this technique. Artists such as Georg Strauch (1613–75), from Nuremberg and Johann Conrad Schnell I and II produced enamel portraits of great quality.[21]

From the 1740s onwards, the linking of goldsmith with enameller had an alternative in the porcelain painter and enameller combination. Johann-Andreas Bechdolff (1734–1807), who was enameller at the porcelain factory of Ellwangen ('*Schmöltzmaler bei der feinen Porzellain fabrique*'), is totally unknown to today's public. The only enamel miniature known to be by his hand[22] is certainly a beautiful portrait of high artistic standard.

Vienna

The capital of the Holy Roman Empire showed, surprisingly, no major interest in the enamel miniature. The Swedish traveller Charles Boit's huge family portrait of Emperor Leopold and his family,[23] one of the largest enamels ever painted, 38×46 cm ($14^{15}/_{16} \times 18^1/_8$ in), is signed and dated *Carolus Boit ad vivum pinx. anno 1703*. It is probably the first enamel miniature painted in Austria and did not encourage any Austrian artists to continue this technique in their country. On the contrary, Joseph Brecheisen, born in Vienna and trained at the Vienna Academy from 1728 to 1730, left Vienna for Berlin (in about 1748), eventually making a career at the court of Copenhagen.

Another Swede, Boit's pupil Martin van Meytens (1695–1770) (see cat. no. 41), arrived in Vienna in 1721 after having spent the preceding year in Dresden. During his two years' stay in Vienna, he is said to have painted enamel portraits of the imperial family. After lengthy travels in Italy, he returned to Vienna around 1729 and became an imperial cabinet painter. Meytens, who is better known for his large-scale oil portraits, later became the favourite painter of Empress Maria Theresa and was appointed Director of the Imperial Academy in 1759. A series of beautiful enamels in the Imperial Austrian Miniatures Collection has been wrongly associated with Liotard's name but is in fact by Meytens.[24] The attribution to Liotard was tempting, but, during his visits to Vienna, Jean-Etienne Liotard does not appear to have painted enamel miniatures. Indeed, his enamel portraits of Empress Maria Theresa were painted in Lyons and in Paris.

One of Liotard's contemporaries, the Bohemian artist Wenceslas Chudy (c. 1730–after 1790), painted both on porcelain and enamel. He worked in Vienna and his artistic output, of mediocre quality, included allegories and portraits. At the end of the eighteenth century, only two enamellers were active in Vienna: Carl Dachtler and Jacob Conrad Bodemer. Short-lived Dachtler (1770–1803) was trained in Vienna and Paris, possibly by Jean-Baptiste Weyler. The quality of his work is excellent, but his enamels are extremely rare. Of equally high quality are the enamels by German-born Jacob Conrad Bodemer (1777–1824). He learnt enamelling technique in Geneva and arrived in Vienna in 1799. His masters at the Vienna Academy include Füger and Lampi. Nevertheless, his work has nothing 'Fügerish' about it, for he painted using the fine, tidy technique of the Geneva enamellers. Bodemer, who exhibited his works in Vienna from 1801 to 1813, had a high-ranking clientele including the imperial family and Viennese aristocracy. His success did not encourage any Austrian imitators and he may be considered as the last Viennese enameller.

RUSSIA

From the very beginning of the art of the portrait miniature onwards, the enamel miniature played a key role in Russia, and for about hundred years it was certainly the most appreciated form of miniature painting in Russia. The absence of the art of limning, which could have generated the technique of water-colour miniature painting, and the lack of small-scale oil portraits as an alternative approach left the field of miniature painting open to the art of enamelling.

During his extensive travels through Europe, the discoveries of the young Tsar Peter the Great (1672–1723) included enamel portrait miniatures. Although the technique of enamelling was far from unknown in Russia, its use for real-life likenesses was new to Peter the Great. His first contacts with an enameller took place in England during his first visit to London where he met Charles Boit in 1697/98. Cavalli-Björkman (1981, p. 41) and Odom (1996, p. 82) state that Boit painted the Tsar as early as 1698, after a painting by Kneller. Nevertheless it was not until 1717, when he was in Paris, that Boit executed any major work for the Tsar. Peter the Great is said to have commissioned forty of his portraits from Boit, who also had to copy Nattier's portrait of Peter's wife Catherine, painted at The Hague in 1717 (see Reynolds, 1999, p. 275, no. 402). These enamels were presented by the Tsar to servants of the state as rewards and worn like orders. It is not known if the Tsar tried to attract Boit to come with him to Russia, but the Tsar's offer to Boit's pupil Martin van Meytens was turned down.

Obviously, as no Western enameller was prepared to work in the newly founded St Petersburg capital, local artists had to be trained. The first dated Russian enamel portrait miniature is signed and dated on the counter enamel *St Petersburg 1712*, and the artist's name is Grigory Semenovich Musikiysky (1670/71–c. 1739).[25] It depicts Peter the Great in profile and is nowadays held in the Hermitage. Numerous other enamels by this artist dated between 1712 and 1727 are kept in the same museum and also in the Russian Museum, St Petersburg. They all represent the Tsar and members of his family. Musikiysky was not afraid of complicated group portraits, but the result is so hilarious, with bodies totally out of proportion, that the Tsar's wish to hire a Western enameller is perfectly understandable. The works of Andrei Ovsov (1678/79–c. 1740) are of distinctly better artistic quality and show that he must have seen Charles Boit's works. Again, they mainly depict Tsar Peter and his family and are dated between 1725 and 1727. During the reign of Peter's daughter, Empress Elizabeth Petrovna (see cat. no. 96) ivory miniatures were introduced into Russia. The enamel miniature nevertheless remained extremely popular at court and many enamel portraits of the Tsarina, mostly after Louis Caravaque,

are recorded, although the names of the artists are unknown. The heyday of the Russian enamel portrait miniature coincides with the reign of Empress Catherine the Great (1729–96). During the first years of her reign, Andrei Ivanovich Cherny (or Chorny or Chernov), a porcelain painter from the newly founded imperial porcelain factory, executed finely stippled but rather stiff enamel miniatures of the Tsarina and members of her court, such as her lover Count G.G. Orlov.[26] During the last quarter of the eighteenth century, the ivory miniature became increasingly popular in Russia and Petr Gerasimovich Zharkov (1742–1802), a member of the St Petersburg Academy of Arts painted in both media. From 1783, he held a class in miniature painting at the Academy, and, in 1791, a class specifically for painting in enamel was added to his responsibilities.[27] Although his enamels are finely painted, they are still considerably inferior to the enamel portraits by his contemporaries in Western Europe. It is not surprising, therefore, that Empress Catherine the Great, used to the highest artistic standards, longed for enamels from the West. When in 1787 her Parisian agent, Baron Frédéric Melchior de Grimm, negotiated the sale of a collection of fifteen enamel miniatures by Johann Heinrich Hurter, she was happy to pay the considerable price of 661 *louis d'or*. Her great expectations were disappointed when the pieces finally arrived in St Petersburg, and she severely blamed Grimm for the acquisition of this collection of low-quality enamels, which were all copies after oil paintings.

At about the same time, Geneva enameller Nicolas Soret (1759–1830) arrived in St Petersburg and was introduced at court by Prince Potemkin (see pp. 101–02). Soret's outstanding talent was recognised by the Tsarina and he had soon painted many enamels of Tsarevich Paul, his wife Maria Feodorovna and their sons.[28] Soret held the title of *peintre ordinaire* of the Empress. As well as the artistic qualities he possessed, he also knew how to flatter the ego of the sixty-year-old Tsarina. He explained the success of his portraits thus: 'With a little bit of resemblance, I had the art to make her younger and furthermore very beautiful; my paintings had, by the way, nothing special.'[29] Catherine's death in 1796 changed his outlook. Although he was on good terms with Maria Feodorovna, he suffered from panic attacks in the presence of Tsar Paul who, as he wrote in his *Souvenirs*, 'sent people so easily to the borders or to Siberia.'[30] In the circumstances, Soret preferred to return to Geneva. The two last Russian enamellers of international reputation were Dimitri Evreinov and Pietro di Rossi.

Evreinov, who learned painting with Jacques Saint-Ours and enamelling with Jean-François Soiron in Geneva, was admitted to the St Petersburg Academy of Arts in 1775 and became Councillor in 1799. He painted enamel portraits of Tsar Paul I and of Tsarina Elisabeth Alexeievna and died in 1813. Pietro di Rossi (1761/65–1831) attended the class on enamel miniatures taught by Petr Zharkov at the Academy of Arts and was made a member of the Academy in 1813. Both his smoothly painted miniatures on ivory and his rare enamels are of excellent quality. He can be considered as the last enameller of renown in Russia.

SOUTHERN EUROPE

In general, portrait miniature painting was not fashionable in Southern Europe. This applies, to an even stronger degree to enamel painting. Northern Europe's enthusiasm for enamels is diametrically opposed to the attitude of Southern Europe.

The few Italian-born watercolour miniaturists of talent, such as Rosalba Carriera and Ferdinando Quaglia, found their clientele outside their country. For an enameller, the warm temperatures and sunlight of the South which are so destructive to the fragile ivory miniatures would have provided the ideal environment. However, this situation was not taken advantage of.

Italy

Only two Italian towns would appear to hold any interest for the student of the history of the enamel miniature: Florence and Milan. The only miniaturist to master the enamel technique in seventeenth-century Italy was Giovanna Fratellini, *née* Marmocchini (1666–1731). Court painter to Grand Duke Cosimo III de' Medici, she painted pastels, oil paintings, miniatures and also enamels. Only one enamel miniature signed by her hand, the portrait of Ferdinando di Cosimo III de' Medici[31] is recorded. During the third quarter of the eighteenth century,

James MacPherson worked as a miniaturist and enameller in Florence. Fifty years later, Napoleon Bonaparte's sister, Elisa, Grand Duchess of Tuscany, wanted to hire a Swiss enameller as her court enamel painter. Since Geneva-born Abraham Constantin politely turned down her offer, she found Salomon-Guillaume Counis (1785–1859) who accepted her offer with enthusiasm and left for Florence in 1810. Until the fall of the Empire, Counis painted beautiful enamels, depicting the Grand Duchess and her family, executed in the fine, glossy technique of the Geneva tradition. He went back to Geneva in 1815, but fifteen years later Counis returned to Florence, only to die without having painted any further major enamels. His direct contemporary and competitor Abraham Constantin (1785–1855) spent several years in Florence, working not on enamelling portraits but on copying old master paintings on huge porcelain plaques, which was a great commercial success.

Two very different reasons made Milan important in the history of enamel painting. Brescia-born miniaturist Giambattista Gigola (1769–1841) was the only Italian miniaturist to master the enamel technique. Both his watercolour and his enamel miniatures are painted in a naive, provincial manner, but the local aristocracy, notably the Trivulzio family, must have appreciated his works. Among Gigola's clients was the man who probably commissioned the most important number of enamels ever painted. The Milanese Count Giovanni Battista Sommariva (1760–1826) was an incredibly rich and passionate collector of paintings and sculptures. Eager that his beloved paintings should be immortalised in the enamel technique, he hired several enamellers to copy his huge collection in enamel, including the Italian Gigola, the French Adèle Chavassieu d'Audebert and the Swiss Henri L'évêque. The extent of this enterprise is revealed by the eight pages by Henri Clouzot (1924, pp. 219–26) listing Chavassieu d'Audebert's enamels executed for the Count. Henri L'évêque's 'Sommariva' enamels fits on one page in Clouzot, but the list is still impressive.

The further south we move, the less the enamel miniature seems to be appreciated. One may wonder why there are no Neapolitan enamel miniatures. The kingdom of Ferdinand IV and his wife Maria Carolina would *à priori* have supplied the perfect basis for this art. The presence of a porcelain factory would have facilitated the training of enamel painters. Furthermore, Naples was, at the end of the eighteenth century, together with St Petersburg, the only city in the word where miniature painting was taught at the Academy. The royal family was an important client for the local miniaturists, as their princely relatives in Madrid, Vienna, Parma, Milan and Paris demanded images of the steadily growing royal family. Also, the hot climate and strong sunlight would have justified the choice of a more resistant support than ivory or parchment. The explanation may be that the enamel technique was too slow for the impatient royal clients? It is certain that the quality of the innumerable Neapolitan royal miniatures is extremely low and could only be the result of a mass-production.

The Iberian Peninsula

If the interest in enamel miniatures in Italy was limited, in Spain and Portugal it was almost non-existent. Queen Maria-Luisa of Spain, who loved her graceless features to be immortalised by her court painter Goya, must nevertheless have commissioned some enamel miniatures. During the first years of the nineteenth century, two enamellers of foreign origin worked at the Spanish Court. Franz Nickel (1783–1845) from Hanau painted miniatures in both enamel and watercolour. He was, for a time, assistant at the Academy of San Fernando. A small oval enamel by his hand after a miniature by Joseph Bouton representing the Queen (dated 1805) and a circular enamel of 1806 depicting her lover Don Manuel Godoy have survived.[32] Henri L'évêque (1769–1832) – from Geneva – was, after Liotard, probably the most adventurous peripatetic enameller. He worked in France and England but also stayed during the first few years of the nineteenth century in Spain and Portugal. His enamel portrait of Jean Chaponniere-Verdier[33] is signed and dated 1802 and bears an address 'Aranjues', the only trace of his activities in Spain, and more precisely, at court. His great invention was a 'portable' kiln which allowed him to execute enamels on the road. Works from his visit to Portugal are less rare than his 'Spanish' enamels and three large circular enamels are recorded depicting high-ranking Portuguese army officers.[34]

The last enameller active in Spain was Vicente Baus, an artist whose name is not recorded in any dictionary, although his signature appears on two large circular enamels. The earlier one depicts Ferdinand VII of Spain in an allegory on the first Spanish Constitution of 1812 (see fig. 4), and the other one, in a Paris private collection, glorifies the King's third marriage to his niece Princess Maria Isabella of Portugal in 1816. Both pieces are well painted and in no way inferior to most enamels of their period. It is only too typical of the current state of research that a competent enamel painter who obviously worked for the king of Spain is not even documented. May the publication of the miniatures in the Gilbert Collection constitute a small step forward in the connoisseurship of the enamel miniature in Europe!

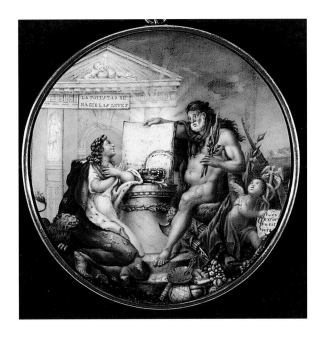

Fig. 4. King Ferdinand VII of Spain, by Vicente Baus, 1812, enamel on copper, private collection.

NOTES

1 Schaffers-Bodenhausen/Tiethoff-Spliethoff, 1993, pp. 19–20, fig. 12.
2 Schneeberger, 1958, pp. 90–3.
3 ibid., p. 118.
4 ibid., pp. 121–2, and Schaffers-Bodenhausen/Tiethoff-Spliethoff, 1993, p. 199.
5 See also pp. 31–32, 50–52.
6 German private collection, formerly sale Koller, Zurich (12–18 November 1987, lot 1792).
7 Schneeberger, 1958, p. 151, figs. 53, 54.
8 Keil, 1999, p. 229, no. 513.
9 Schidlof, 1964, III, pl. 21, no. 41; German private collection, formerly sale Koller, Zurich (12–18 November 1987, lot 1752); French private collection, formerly sale Christie's, Geneva (16 May 1995, lot 198).
10 For example exhibition catalogue Geneva/Paris, 1992, pp. 160–1, no. 86.
11 Clouzot, 1925, p. 149.
12 Schidlof, 1964, II, p. 898.
13 Coldin, 1991, I, p. 82.
14 Exhibition catalogue Berlin, 1991, p. 30.
15 Clouzot, 1925, pp. 212–13.
16 German Private Collection, formerly Christie's, Geneva (14 May 1991, lot 135), depicting the Soldier King, signed and dated Berl. / 1733.
17 Buchheit, 1911, pp. 73–4.
18 Formerly in the List Collection, Magdeburg, sold Lange, Berlin (28–30 March 1939, lot 504).
19 Buchheit, 1911, p. 64, pl. XVII.
20 Clasen, 1993, p. 137, fig. 207.
21 Boeckh, 1996, pp. 90–1.
22 British Museum, London, inv. AF 3026.
23 Cavalli-Björkman, 1981, pp. 43–5, pl. 16.
24 Keil, 1999, pp. 231–2.
25 This artist was transferred from the Moscow Kremlin Armoury enamelling workshop to St Petersburg, probably in 1711.
26 Komelova/Printseva, 1986, pl. 20, 21, pp. 48–9, 304–5, one signed and dated 1765.
27 Odom, 1996, p. 92.
28 Blondel, 1907, pp. 25, opp. p. 28, p. 29 and Hofstetter, 1999, pp. 70–1.
29 Naville, 1974, p. 358.
30 Naville, 1974, p. 359.
31 Langedijk, 1981, p. 833, no. 35.
32 Tomás, 1953, pl. IX.
33 Geneva, Musée de l'Horlogerie, inv. E. 273.
34 One is in a private collection in Paris, and the other two are illustrated in Hofstetter, 1999, p. 73, nos. 98 and 99.

Enamelled Portrait Miniatures in England

SARAH COFFIN

ENAMELLING IN ENGLAND

Enamel miniature painting has generally been seen as a foreign aberration in the history of the indigenous English limning tradition. In reality, when this imported technique became allied to the demands of local patronage, it evolved from a novelty into the principal form of miniature painting in England during the first half of the eighteenth century.

The Gilbert Collection, which contains both Continental and English enamel miniatures, provides the evidence for these works to be seen in the broader context of English art. The early practitioners of enamelling in England were born and often trained on the Continent, as were many other of England's artists and artisans. Some were Huguenot refugees from religious persecution in France, many of whom came with the prospect of patronage from the monarchy, particularly from William and Mary. Since Henry VIII's break with Rome and the creation of the Church of England, the subsequent tension over religious affiliations had made religious subjects politically too sensitive to be depicted. Portraiture became the dominant pictorial art form in Britain.

Many of the silversmiths and goldsmiths born on the Continent and who emigrated to England in the late seventeenth and early eighteenth centuries are now regarded as English, so it would be inconsistent to characterise the enamellers who worked in England as 'foreign', as had been done in the past. Like the silversmiths and cabinet makers who brought new styles and techniques with them,

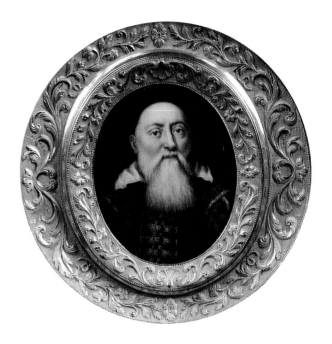

Fig 5. *Theodore Turquet de Mayerne, possibly by Jean Petitot. Collection of John S. Walker, photograph courtesy of Elle Shushan.*

enamellers responded to the wishes of their British patrons to produce works which could not have been produced anywhere else, in the process altering permanently British styles.

While the enamelling of portraits arose out of the goldsmithing and watchmaking tradition, it should be noted that some of England's earliest miniaturists in the limning tradition, most notably Nicholas Hilliard (1547–1619) also trained as or were related to goldsmiths. It is from the Swiss watchmaking and goldsmithing tradition that Jean Petitot emerged but it was in England where he was the first to introduce enamel portrait painting, that he perfected his art. This novelty had become the leading fashion by the first half of the eighteenth century, until it was supplanted by another novelty – that of painting in watercolour on an ivory support. From the second half of the eighteenth and into the early nineteenth centuries, the art of the miniature on ivory attained new heights of excellence. Such artists as Richard Cosway (see cat. no. 81) and Richard Crosse (see cat. no. 82) used watercolour for flesh tones to take maximum advantage of the ivory's translucency. But although this technique may have dominated the market, it did not completely supplant the enamel, as the Gilbert Collection's examples by Henry Spicer, William Birch, Horace Hone, Denis B. Murphy and

Henry Bone and his sons demonstrate. During this so-called golden era of miniature painting, many of the artists worked, in fact, in a variety of media: enamel, watercolour on ivory and drawings. The fact that the enamelled miniature did not die out in England during this period shows how firmly it had become established and how essentially conservative English artistic taste was. When Henry Bone introduced a technique which enabled larger enamel plaques to be produced, he was making a specifically English contribution to an art form already established in Britain for more than a century.

The beginning of the portrait miniatures in England generally is equated with those produced by Hans Holbein the Younger, at the court of Henry VIII. From that moment miniature painting in England had enjoyed moments of glory in the art of limning, or portrait miniature painting, during the sixteenth and seventeenth centuries. The most notable of the exponents of it were Nicholas Hilliard (1547–1619), who had trained as a goldsmith, and Samuel Cooper (1609–72), a limner who painted with the broader strokes more associated with full-scale painting, who is thought to have been trained by his uncle John Hoskins (d.1664/5).

For Hilliard and subsequent limners, who painted in solid watercolour on parchment or vellum, the miniature could be a cabinet piece or incorporated into a piece of jewellery. An unusual and interesting example of this may be the oil-on-crystal (see cat no. 84) in the Gilbert Collection. This appears to be in a later frame but, judging from its size and the delicate detailing of the lace ruff depicted, it is an early piece in the small, oval locket or 'keepsake' tradition, for it might well have been set originally in a jewelled or enamelled pendant frame. Early miniatures in cabinet form often showed the sitter in a specific environment, like Hilliard's 'Young Man among Roses', c. 1587, in the V&A. Large miniatures, in particular, were seen as cabinet pieces for wall display, whereas the smaller ones could be worn, as well as hung. They were often made to be presented by the monarch to a courtier, whether to be given to friends, spouses or lovers.

When Jean Petitot arrived in England in the 1630s both 'keepsake' and cabinet miniatures were being painted thus. Perhaps the popularity of the cabinet miniature in England explains the fact that the miniatures that he made in Britain were larger in size than his later works in France. His enormous popularity undoubtedly had influence even on the great Samuel Cooper, who started to paint miniatures in a greater variety of sizes at this time, to include some small ones. Thus, as well as introducing the technique of enamel painting to England, Petitot also helped to maintain the fashion for the small oval portrait miniature concurrently with the rise in popularity of the cabinet piece.

In the second half of the seventeenth century 'cabinets of curiosities' became fashionable, both in Britain and on the Continent. Frederick III (r. 1645–70) of Denmark and Norway established one at Rosenborg Castle in Copenhagen in 1650, and collected many categories of items for it. By the time an inventory was taken in 1718, the cabinet was hung with jewellery, rock crystal, cameos, portrait miniatures, cameo-vessels, semiprecious stones and gems, as well as various tusks and ivory and boxwood items.[1] In Britain, as early as 1639, the inventory of Charles I's Cabinet at Whitehall Palace included paintings, miniatures, drawings, statuettes, busts, sculpted reliefs, antiquities, cameos and coins. Similarly, the Green Closet at Ham House in Richmond, London, was arranged with small cabinet paintings, miniatures and framed portrait drawings, according to the first inventory, made between 1677 and 1683.[2] The popularity of gems, hardstones and cameos in these cabinets suggests that enamels probably also would have been included.

Like most of the foreign-born enamel artists who followed him, Petitot did not come to England for religious reasons. It was undoubtedly the prospect of patronage that attracted him, as it did Charles Boit later. The reason why he was able to obtain commissions to paint Charles I, Henrietta Maria and the future Charles II apparently so soon after he arrived must in the first place have been the very novelty of the art of enamelling, but equally Petitot also had good introductions and allies at court.

George Vertue, the engraver and painter who chronicled the London art scene for the first half of the eighteenth century, stated that Petitot learned much about the properties of enamel from Theodore Turquet de Mayerne, physician to Charles I. Turquet de Mayerne wrote a technical description of enamelling on a gold ground entitled *Des Esmaulx* and suggested that enamels should be seen as 'unbreakable miniatures' which, having a hard

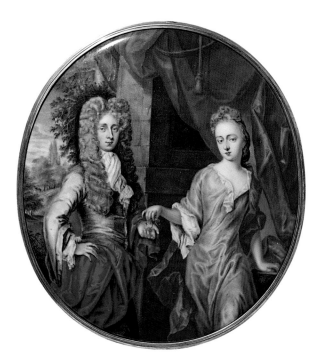

Fig. 6. Earl of Godolphin and his wife, by Charles Boit;
Stockholm Nationalmuseum.

surface, did not need protective glass. He is presumed to have worked with Petitot, which would explain the technical virtuosity that Petitot achieved in England. Jean André Rouquet (see pp. 98–99), the Swiss-born enameller who worked in London, wrote in 1755, of Petitot:

> Some happy discoveries furnished him with the means of executing with ease, such surprising things as, without the assistance of these discoveries, the most perfect organs, with all the dexterity imaginable could never have produced. Such are the hairs, which Petitot drew lightness surpassing the power of the ordinary instruments of preparations.[3]

Petitot left England at the outbreak of the Civil War and with the subsequent decrease in patronage, no other enameller stepped in to replace him. For most of the second half of the seventeenth century, almost the only enameller of any note working in England was Jean Petitot II (1653–1702), who was sent there by his father to learn limning from Samuel Cooper, prior to Cooper's death in 1672. The younger Petitot went back to France but returned to London to work for Charles II from 1677–82. He painted miniatures on vellum as well as enamels.

In 1687, Charles Boit arrived from Sweden to find a market in which larger portrait miniatures were seen as cabinet pieces, while Petitot's enamels were the principal fashionable representatives of the keepsake piece. Vertue says he came to Britain with the intention of being a jeweller 'haveing a good share of Ingenuity in enamell work.'[4] Boit probably was encouraged to use his enamelling skills in the field of portraiture by other Swedish or Swedish-trained artists in London, such as Michael Dahl, who, according to Vertue, advised him to pursue enamelling.[5] Dahl, who had arrived in 1682, already enjoyed extensive royal and aristocratic patronage. Boit appears to have reintroduced the art of enamelling to England thus reviving the fashion for the medium. He was probably able to gain access to important clients so quickly both because of Dahl's promotion and because he was working in enamel, a medium associated with the court of Charles I and Petitot's elite clientele.

The concept of painting enamel portraits from life – *ad vivum* – for enamel portraits, may also have resulted from the conjunction of English preference with Continental technique. Although no *ad vivum* works by Petitot are known, Boit probably did work *ad vivum*, as well as copying from paintings and engravings. What is probably a signed and dated self-portrait of 1694 appears to have been made from life. If so, it may be the very first *ad vivum* enamel portrait, made possibly in anticipation of painting clients in this manner. Clearly by the time Boit painted a large plaque of Emperor Leopold I and his family in Vienna, c. 1700, signing it *Carolus Boit ad vivum fecit* (although much of the surrounding is from engravings), he was at ease with *ad vivum* work, and not limiting it to the British market.

Boit's earliest English enamels are of the smaller 'keepsake' type (see cat. no. 5) and another enamel thought to depict Sarah Middleton, who married Robert Harley, 1st Earl of Oxford, as his second wife in 1694. If the latter identification is correct, the commission undoubtedly was the result of the profitable relationship which Boit established early in his English career with the Earl of Oxford, at least as early as 1693 when he signed the miniature '*C Boit p in Coiventry / 1693.*[6] The Earl of Oxford commissioned and collected numerous miniatures, particularly in enamel, many of which subsequently descended as a collection at Welbeck Abbey [7]. His enthusiasm for enamelling apparently was such that he asked Boit to train his librarian in enamelling. Although no works by him are known to have survived, Vertue states that 'Humfrey Wanley took lessons with Boit, but those lessons has ceased before 20 March, 1694–5, when Wanley wrote from Coventry: "Everybody here is glad to see me, and gladder that I have left Mr Boit".'[8]

In 1696, Boit was appointed Court Enameller, the title being changed from, rather than added to, that of limner. This implies that the court had taken to this medium as the principal form of miniature painting. In fact, after Boit's departure from England, his successor Bernard Lens was also known as Court Enameller for much of his tenure, even though he worked in body colour in the limning tradition.[9]

Boit was away on the Continent from 1700 to 1703. While he was away, another Swedish miniature artist, Christian Richter, arrived in London in 1702. Although he may well have been trained in enamelling in Sweden, Richter is described by Vertue as a limner who trained as a silversmith before coming to London. While no signed enamels by Richter are known, Vertue in commenting on his death (as 'Mr Christian Rechter') in 1732 states that the artist had noticed 'laterly that enamelling was much encourag'd and liked by persons of fortune and nobility he therefore set about the practice of if wherein tho' a beginner he succeeded so well that in time he might have arrived to great perfection'. [10] Whether he was painting in enamel or not upon his arrival in England, Richter's success with miniatures of English patrons may have encouraged Boit to return to England by the following year.

Despite having started out with small bust-size portraits of the type he painted for the Earl of Oxford, Boit soon aspired to create the ultimate cabinet piece – the enamel plaque. One of his earliest examples is of the Earl of Godolphin and his wife in 1697, now in the Nationalmusem in Stockholm.[11]. Interestingly, Lady Godolphin is shown handing a miniature of the smaller type to her husband. Boit was growing increasingly ambitious; his plaque of Emperor Leopold I with his family, of c. 1700, was a precursor of his largest commission which he received on his return to England in 1704: a plaque commemorating the Battle of Blenheim. He also executed one of Queen Anne and her consort, Prince George of Denmark, in 1706.

The large plaques enabled Boit to show off a flamboyant technical virtuosity and more ambitious subject matter which seem to have attracted the patronage that Boit sought. One such result is the enamel of John Churchill, 1st Duke of Marlborough, with the Battle of Blenheim in the background (see cat. no. 3). Clearly, this rectangular miniature is far grander than the mere head-and-shoulders previously accorded to most sitters and is an image commensurate with the Duke's standing around 1705.

The other significant consequence of Boit's attempt to produce the largest known plaque, was his invitation in 1706 to Christian Friedrich Zincke, also a goldsmith-trained enameller, from Dresden, to work on the plaque with him in his studio. Zincke was to become the dominant figure in English enamel portraiture, and indeed, along with Bernard Lens, in English miniature painting generally for most of the first half of the eighteenth century, especially following Boit's hasty departure from England because of his debts in 1714.

Zincke, who is so well represented in the Gilbert Collection, was central to the development of the English enamel miniature and, as Vertue clearly indicates, not only studied with Boit, but actually worked on the large enamel. Vertue, in referring to the plaque, states 'the piece in effect being too large ever to be accomplished, as he well knew & ownd since to Mr Zinke. Who then workt much for him and on this great work on the plate'.[12]

Thus Zincke understood the pitfalls and, perhaps as a result, shied away from producing large enamels. Lens, without the technical constraints, continued to produce some cabinet-size miniatures in watercolour on vellum, such as the one of Sarah Duchess of Marlborough of 1720.[13] Possibly as a result of Zincke's influence, Rouquet compared the latter to Petitot as a 'master of particular materials'. He was also of the opinion that 'enamelling is proper only for places in miniature'. Indeed, it may have been that the enormously successful Zincke's reluctance to paint large enamels was one of the principal reason for the near demise of the cabinet miniature during the second quarter of the eighteenth century.

Because of Zincke's extended involvement in Boit's studio, from his arrival in 1706 until Boit's departure in 1714, it can be hard to distinguish between some works by Boit and early ones by

Zincke. Boit's work is characterised by small strokes of the type seen in the enamel of Anne Countess of Sunderland (see cat. no. 4), while Zincke's later work features a red stippling, looking almost like measles, in the flesh tones. However, the Zincke miniatures of a gentleman (see cat. no. 64), formerly thought to be the Duke of Marlborough, and one that actually is of the Duke of Marlborough (see cat. no. 65) demonstrate a technique closer to Boit's because they are early works. A further example of this closer technique can be seen by comparing the three enamels of Sarah Duchess of Marlborough, formerly in the Spencer Collection (see cat. nos. 66, 67, 68). Catalogue number 67 is much closer to Boit than the other two and is particularly close to one signed 'C Boit pinxt', which is also after Kneller and was formerly in the Ashcroft Collection.[14] While this may be because both are copies after Kneller, it is also probable that catalogue number 67 is somewhat earlier than the other two and may have been painted when Zincke was in Boit's studio.

Whereas Zincke's work produced at the beginning of his career may be difficult to distinguish from Boit's, the work he produced at the height of his popularity is difficult to identify because he was to enjoy such extensive patronage that most artists had to subordinate their own individual styles to his to secure commissions. As a result many works have been wrongly attributed to Zincke. Without the signature on the back, one example might have been Abraham Seaman's miniature of Francis Lady Carteret (see cat. no. 48) which probably would have been attributed to Zincke. While some of its style may be owed to the orginal from which it is copied, of a portrait dated 1716, possibly by Kneller, it has a number of hallmarks characteristic of a Zincke studio piece. Moreover, the enamel of the sitter's husband, John Carteret, Earl Granville in the Spencer Collection (see London, 1889) was catalogued as by Zincke, whereas that of his wife was catalogued as 'A Leeman' in the same exhibition. This suggests either that Seaman may have been independent enough to sign his own name or that he had obtained this commission via the Zincke studio. Another miniature of an unknown gentleman,[15] which does not have the large eyes generally associated with Seaman's works, looks very much like a typical Zincke, yet it is signed on the reverse *A B Seaman*. While flattery is not unusual for portraiture, the fact that it was common and acceptable for enamellers to copy portraits also enabled a patron or artist to select portraits of differng periods as sources when commissioning pairs, such as spouses, thus enabling a wife to be depicted at a younger age than her husband.

Just because the dates of the costumes worn by the Granvilles in their miniatures by Seaman and Zincke differ does not mean that the works were not considered a pair. This same diversity of fashions is seen in the Zincke miniatures of a lady and a gentleman on a gold box (see cat. no. 74) and may also explain the differences in date of the lady and gentleman called Mr and Mrs Tilson by Zincke and Spencer (see cat. nos. 53, 71). The most obvious reason for this discrepancy which undoubtedly contributed to Zincke's enormous popularity may be in part have been due to his willingness to portray his patrons, especially women, in a flattering light and as more youthful than they were. Much fun was made at Zincke's expense by contemporaries indicating that he practised this form of flattery far more than most portrait artists. Vertue quoted this poem of 1734:

Love of fame. The universal passion by Dr. Young
Ye fair! to draw yourexcellence at length
Exceeds the narrow younds of human strenght,
You here in miniature your pictures see;
Nor hope from Zincks (a famous Enameller) more Justice, than fromme
My portraits grace your mind, as his your side,
His portraits will inflame, mine quench your pride,
He's dear, you frugal; chuse my cheaper lay,
And be you Reformation all my pay.[16]

Such flattery might be achieved, perhaps, by copying an earlier painting of the wife, while having the husband sit *ad vivum*, or, as the poem suggests, by straight flattery, making the subject appear younger in what was claimed to be an *ad vivum* likeness. Zincke's most notable examples of the latter are his enamels of Frederick, Prince of Wales, George II and Queen Caroline. Queen Caroline (see cat. no. 72) is also of this type.

According to Vertue, the Queen asked Zincke 'to be sure to make the King's picture young, not above 25 & the King commended his work and admonished him not to make the Queens picture above 28.'[17] As George II and Queen Caroline were both aged forty-four at their coronation, and forty-nine when the *ad vivum* series was commissioned, it is clear from looking at the miniatures in the Royal Collection, and at the Gilbert Collection miniature (see cat. no. 72) that Zincke obliged.

Such flattery is also evident in Zincke's miniatures of Frederick Prince of Wales in the Royal Collection (Walker nos. 41–4). In these, the Prince wears oak leaves denoting the victory of his father, George II, at the Battle of Dettingen in 1743. Yet he appears little older than in another miniature in the Royal Collection (Walker, 1992, no. 40) made fourteen years earlier in 1729. It is not surprising that Zincke was paid the substantial sum of 105 guineas for two years work, as Cabinet Painter to the Prince of Wales, as recorded in a document in the Royal Archive.[18]

Zincke's flattery should be seen in the context of the patronage of the day. Clients would visit artists' studios, as they might visit commercial galleries today, as a way of seeing artists' work and of deciding whether to patronise them, and to be seen to do so. Jean André Rouquet, in his *L'Etat des arts en angleterre* of 1755, commented on the London rage for patronising the most fashionable artist of the moment.

A portrait painter in England, makes his fortune in very extraordinary manner . . . His aim then is not so much to paint well, as to paint a great deal; his design is to be in vogue, one of those exclusive vogues which for a while shall throw into his hands all the principle portraits that are to be drawn in England. If he obtains this vogue, to make a proper use of it, he is obliged to work extremely quick, consequently he draws a great deal worse, by having a great deal more business. Fashion, whose empire has long ago subverted that of reason, requires that he should paint every face in the island, as it were, against their will, and that he should be obliged to paint much worse than he would really chuse, even by those who employ him. He thinks nothing but monopolizing the whole business.[19]

We cannot see that the public are really the dupes of all the puerilities which we have been here exposing; no, they are only dupes to the fashion which they follow, even with reluctance, it is the fashion that carries them to a painter of whom they have no great opinion, to engage him out of vanity to draw their picture, which they have no occasion for, and which they will not like when finished. But the women especially must have their pictures exposed for some time in the house of that painter who is most in fashion.[20]

This might be construed as a personal criticism of Zincke as the most fashionable painter of enamel miniatures. A popular artist would have numerous other artists working in his studio, just as Zincke and Otto Peterson, another enameller, had worked in Boit's. Boit clearly understood the importance of a fashionable address. He established himself in Mayfair, which both exemplified his extravagant lifestyle but also enabled him to receive the most elevated members of society there and paint their likenesses, especially necessary when working *ad vivum*. The names of his known sitters attest to the success of this plan.

One result of patrons both visiting and being seen in the artists' studios was the chance that this offered some of the studio artists to make contact with these 'people of quality'. In this way Zincke was launched from Boit's studio, and, in turn, William Prewett, Jeremiah Meyer and probably Abraham and Noah Seaman emerged from Zincke's. Only with the advent of the Society of Artists and, later, the Royal Academy exhibitions, which offered public forums for display, did artists' studios cease to be the primary places of contact between patrons and works of art, although they did remain so for sittings. In the field of enamelling, however, because of various technical demands, including the need for a kiln and a firing instruction, the studio maintained its importance for longer than for artists in other media.

The repeated firings needed for enamels would have made lengthy *ad vivum* sittings problematic. The studios, therefore, appear to have kept on hand engravings after portraits by famous artists such as Kneller. Vertue observed, 'no sooner is a picture painted by any painter of any remarkable person but presently he has it out in print also now or lately he has done some plates drawn from the life without the assistance of a painter.'[21] They also appear to have either borrowed or had to hand specific robes and accoutrements of office, such as the Lord Chancellor's robes, as worn by Sir Robert Walpole (see cat. no. 75), as well as fashionable dress and jewellery for female sitters. This procedure was not, of course, confined to enamellers and must have been similar to that employed by life-scale portrait painters, as described by Katharine Baetjer:

The most common practice, for which several meetings were typically required, was for the artist to paint a sketch of the head from life. As sittings are tedious, an artist who could converse with and entertain his client meanwhile may have had greater success. A drawing of the head with colour notes, which could be completed in a much shorter time, sometimes served the purpose instead. An influential painter might have a role in determining the costume to be worn. In the case of an exceptionally prominent or busy client, the clothes and jewels might be lent to the studio.[22]

The resulting correction of one artist to a specific costume, even one selected by the patrons, can help to identify unsigned works or to establish the original large-scale artist after whose painting an enamel was made. Examples of the repeated use of clothing include a group of miniatures by Zincke and his studio, which all include the white dress, bows and pearls shown in the miniature of a lady (see cat. no. 77). Other examples that depict this dress include two without a lace cape: one of a lady of the Booth family, in the Yale Center for British Art (now attributed to a 'follower of Zincke'), and one of an unidentified lady.[23] Two more, which do show the cape, depict Louisa Viscountess Weymouth née Carteret (daughter of the Lady Carteret portrayed by A. Seaman (see cat. no. 48) and Miss Campbell[24] (who has red bows). The frequency of such exact repetitions suggests that the studio would paint in the same dress and jewellery, which they either borrowed or kept drawings of, and helps to attribute works to Zincke's studio.

Although not known to have been a pupil of Zincke's, Gervase Spencer used the same procedure for clothing and jewellery. His first foray into miniature painting appears to have been as a copyist according to Edward Edward's account of 1818:

Jarvis Spencer

A miniature painter of much celebrity, and lived about the middle of the last century. He was originally a gentleman's servant, but, having nat- ural turn to the pursuits of art, amused himself with drawing. It happened to some one in the family with whom he lived, sat for their portrait to a miniature painter, and when the work was completed, it was shewn to him; upon which he observed, that he thought he could copy it. This hint was received with much surprize, but he was indulged with permission to make the attempt, and his success was such, that he not only gave perfect satisfaction, but also acquired the encouragement and patronage of those he served, and, by their interest, became a fashionable painter of the day.[25]

Although it is unclear where he learned the art of enamelling, Spencer acquired an elegant clientele for his miniatures on both ivory and in enamel, presumably due to his well-placed patrons. He too appears to have copied stock clothing or used clothes borrowed from one sitter for others. The miniature of a lady by Spencer (see cat. no. 54) wearing a black dress and a white lace collar with a blue central bow, a crimson cloak over her left shoulder, and pearl drop earrings, is almost identical with another miniature by him,[26] except that in the latter miniature the sitter wears pearls on her bodice as well.

Spencer's use of dress *à la Turque* seems to have originated with Jean Etienne Liotard (see pp. 82–3) whose pastel portraits of the Countess of Coventry, painted in London 1753–5, inspired a copy by Spencer in enamel dated 1757.[27] Spencer adapted the same pose and costume for enamels of Lady Mary Wortley Montague, now in the V&A, and of Elizabeth Montague, also dated 1757, in the Yale Center for British Art. The fact that these two works are in reverse suggests that Spencer used a print as his immediate source – possibly the mezzotint by Richard Houston.

The influence of Zincke and Spencer links the enamel miniatures of the first half of the eighteenth century with the subsequent history of miniature painting in general. This influence came primarily through the studios because patrons would seek something similar to what they had seen or heard about at Court; the more ambitious artists who worked in the major artists' studios often set up on their own, both adapting their masters' techniques and developing an independent style. Moreover, in the case of Zincke, the case of his failing eyesight and his overwhelming popularity must, in his later years, have resulted in his assistants playing a major role. In 1739 Vertue remarks:

> of late years since Mr Zincke Enameller has had so much employment amongst the Nobility & at Court and has raised his price from 10 to 15, or 20 guineas a small head, which is his price now – others have endeavourd to imitate and follow him close, particular, Rocquet Enameller has best succeeded, and now is much imployed – he is Swisse born, of French extraction and at this present 10 guineas ahead.[28]

By 1742, he claims:

> Mr Zinke told me he now had raisd his price of enamelling a picture to 30 guineas, and the reason he gives is that now he don't care to work so close as he used to and therefore is not undertaking much work.[29]

Thus Boit's studio produced Zincke, whose studio in turn may have produced William Prewett and Abraham and Noah Seaman and certainly Jeremiah Meyer. German-born Meyer was naturalised in 1762, and lived in Zincke's house. There, he was a founding member of the Royal Academy and held positions both as a miniature painter to Queen Charlotte and, from 1765, as painter in enamel to George III. He then took up painting both in enamel and on ivory, teaching Richard Collins, who worked in both media, and Diana Dietz who worked on ivory.

Seaman appears to have ventured away from the main artistic flow and set himself up as an enameller and as a vendor of enamelling colours in Birmingham, where so many enamel boxes and other enamelled metal table articles were produced. He advertised in Aris's *Birmingham Gazette* of 23 September 1751 thus:

> Abraham SEEMAN, Enamelling Painter, at Mrs Weston's in Freeman Street Birmingham, makes and sells all sorts of enamelling colours, especially the ROSE Colours, likewise all sorts for China Painters. N.B. Most of the eminent Painters of Birmingham, Wednesbury and BILSTON have made use of the above colours to their satisfaction.[30]

The fact that he describes himself as an 'Enamelling Painter' in an era when the Birmingham metalware artists were generally known as 'enamel manufacturers' or 'box painters'[31] suggests that he wished to emphasise his 'higher' professional status, while supplying other enamellers and China painters with properly prepared paints. No known portraits by him, however, survive from this period. Perhaps it was by chance that he became involved in painting on objects in the enamels industry, thus providing a link between the world of Zincke and portrait enamelling with the box industry.

Gervase Spencer seems to have been unusual in not learning the art of enamelling through a known studio. He was one of the first to work both in enamel and on ivory and trained a pupil, Henry Spicer (see p. 105–7 and cat. no. 56), who also worked in both media. Spicer, in turn, taught William Birch (see p. 49–50 and cat. no. 2), who exhibited both miniatures and enamel plaques at the Royal Academy and continued to work in enamel after moving to America in

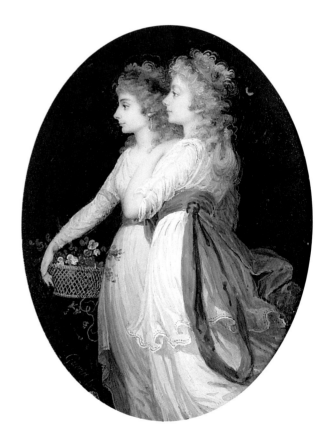

Fig 7. Georgiana, Duchess of Devonshire and Lady Elizabeth Foster, by Jean Guérin, 1791; Wallace Collection.

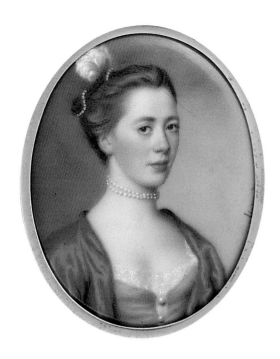

Fig. 8. Georgiana Poyntz, Countess Spencer, by Jean Liotard; Musée de l'Horlogerie, Geneva.

1794, very possibly being the artist to transmit the art of enamel portrait painting to America. The enamels of Spicer and Birch were popular when Henry Bone started to exhibit.

Thus, the history of portrait miniature painting in England passed directly through the enamellers rather than around them, and the art of painting enamel miniature portraits continued in an unbroken line from the arrival of Boit in the late seventeenth century to the Bone family in the nineteenth century.

A few enamel artists who are not represented in the Gilbert Collection also played a role in the history of enamelling in England. Otto Fredrik Peterson (1672–1729), the son of a Stockholm goldsmith, was a pupil and later an assistant to Boit in London and worked on the large unfinished plaque. Little of his work is known, although there is a signed enamel of the playwright John Gay, probably after Kneller, in the Nationalmuseum in Stockholm.[32] Other unsigned works probably go unidentified or are attributed to the circle of Zincke. The exclusivity of Zincke's success may explain why Peterson died, a debtor, in Marshalsea Prison.

Andreas Henry Groth (fl. 1739–55) was a German-born artist who was appointed Painter in Enamels in Ordinary to George II (1741–42). Horace Walpole refers to him as 'a German, painted in watercolours and enamel, but made no great proficience'.[33] Miniatures by him of Clemens August Elector of Cologne, Princess Elizabeth Caroline and Princess Louisa Anne and possibly Frederick Prince of Wales are to be found in the Royal Collection.

Two other artists whose surnames begin with 'G' apparently painted enamels although the coincidence of three surname initials may have led to some mistaken attributions. Theodore Gardelle (1722–61) came from a family of Geneva goldsmiths and jewellers. He worked in Geneva and Paris before arriving in London in about 1759. Although mentioned by Vertue, his career was short, because he was executed for murder in about 1761. The second, a Mr Gamble, may have been a pupil of Zincke's; his documented work consists of two enamels of the Annunciation after Guido Reni, which were exhibited at the Free Society of Arts in 1773.

Lucius Barber/Barbor (d. 1767 London), who may have been Swedish, exhibited at the Society of Arts from 1763–6 and painted full-scale works as well as miniatures, including enamels. His enamel of Lord Edward Bentinck is signed on the reverse *L. Barber ad Vivum Pinxt 1749*.[34] The Irish enamel miniature painter Rupert Barber (fl. 1736–72) is an unrelated Irish artist who painted enamels mainly in Dublin.

Samuel Finney (1718/19–98), an artist from Cheshire, is now principally remembered for his work in watercolour on ivory, particularly because he was appointed Miniature Painter to Queen Charlotte in 1763. However, he had also taken up enamelling in anticipation of rising competition. As early as 1761, 'A catalogue of the pictures now exhibiting by the Society of Artists at the great room in Spring Garden, Charing Cross' of that year lists no. 30 as 'Three miniatures; two ladies in watercolour, and a gentleman in enamel, – by Finny',[35] along with many other miniatures – some in enamel, including no. 111 Two Ladies by Spencer. Finney had some reason for concern about the rising competition from watercolour miniaturists. Among other names in Mortimer's Trade Directory of 1763 under 'Miniature Painters' were four young artists, Richard Cosway, John Smart, Richard Crosse and Ozias Humphry, whose names are now synonymous with the mastery of painting in watercolour on ivory, although Crosse painted well in enamel too.[36]

Finney's decision to work in enamel is recorded in

his memoirs where he writes that he 'decided to attempt this difficult art too without a Master' and describes the resulting miniatures as 'some bad, some tolerable, and some good'.[37] If there is a possibility that Finney was self-taught at painting in enamel, Spencer might have been too. Clearly the economics of painting in both media attracted Finney, Spencer and others. Some patrons, like the Colonel Graeme who introduced Finney to Queen Charlotte, requested miniatures in both media. The fact that Finney charged double – twelve guineas for an enamel, as opposed to six guineas for a watercolour miniature – reflected the greater difficulty of the technique and, possibly that, as Finney put it, 'little Durability was to be expected from his deceitful watercolour performances.'[38]

Dublin-born Nathaniel Hone (1718–84) was a founding member of the Royal Academy who painted full-scale oil portraits and miniatures both on ivory and in enamel. He exhibited an enamel miniature (exh. no. 57) at the first Royal Academy summer exhibition in 1769. His miniatures, dating from the late 1740s to the early 1770s, are generally small and are often incorporated into jewellery, especially bracelets. In 1771, no. 106 in the Royal Academy exhibition is described as 'A portrait of a lady in enamel, for a ring'. The National Portrait Gallery possesses his enamel miniature self-portrait.[39]

Although it is unclear where he acquired his knowledge of enamelling, he is presumed to have taught his son Horace Hone (see p. 73 and cat. no. 25), who also worked in both enamel and watercolour. Horace Hone enjoyed substantial important patronage in the late eighteenth and early nineteenth centuries, connecting the era of his father with that of Henry Bone. Although born and trained in England, Hone based his miniature of Georgiana Duchess of Devonshire (see cat. no. 25) on another by a French artist, Jean Guérin, painted in Paris about twenty years earlier (see fig. 7). He extracted the single figure of the Duchess from a double portrait in watercolour on ivory, which demonstrates that both recent past and contemporary art were deemed suitable for copying in enamel by artists who exhibited at the Royal Academy.

In addition to these British-born artists, other foreign-born figures known principally for their enamelling continued to be attracted to England during the third quarter of the eighteenth century,

presumably by the prospects of patronage. Among the most notable was Jean-Etienne Liotard (see p. 82), who exhibited five pastels at the Royal Academy in 1773 and an oil in 1774, but was in considerable demand for his finely executed enamels such as those of John, 1st Earl Spencer (see cat. no. 35), and his wife Georgiana Poyntz (see fig. 8). Liotard gained the friendship of the Earl of Bessborough and accompanied him on his travels through Europe, which eventually took them as far as Constantinople in Turkey. The Earl became Liotard's patron, and introduced him to many of his friends.

Another well-known foreign-born artist was Johann Heinrich Hurter (see p. 76) who probably studied with Liotard and whose miniatures of Queen Charlotte (see cat. no. 30) and Georgiana Duchess of Devonshire (see cat. no. 29) show that enamels continued to be fashionable in the highest circles. Hurter and his son Carl Rudolph both exhibited at the Royal Academy, the father being described as 'enamel painter' and the son as 'miniature painter'.

In 1772, the French artist Pierre Pasquier exhibited nine miniatures at the Royal Academy, at least seven of which were enamels. The subjects ranged from Rinaldo and Armida (the same subject was also exhibited by Cosway that year) to 'the King from memory' to 'Voltaire from the life', and one of a lady, for inclusion in a ring. While Liotard and Pasquier can be treated as influential visiting foreign artists, others, like the Hurters, established themselves in England with extended stays or took up residence.

Another enameller who regularly exhibited at the Royal Academy during the 1770s was John Howes (fl. 1770–93). He received early laudatory press in 1777 for a medal made for presentation to the actor David Garrick 'which does Mr Howes as much credit as an enamel painter as the presenting it reflects in the actors.'[40] Since Howes' initials are 'JH', some of his works may have become confused with those of Johann Hurter.

An artist not represented in the Gilbert Collection but deserving of mention is William Hopkins Craft (or Croft) (fl. c.1730–5, d. 1811). Craft specialised in large plaques of notable people, including George III and Queen Charlotte in 1773, and another series of contemporary naval heroes of c.1798. Some of his plaques were landscapes and clock-faces, which places him more in the craftsman-artist tradition than as a painter in enamels. The newspapers of the day thought the same, as a review of the Royal Academy exhibition of 1774 indicates:

> William Craft. No. 49. Power, No. 50. Urbanity, (enamel) No. 51, A frame containing several pieces of Enamel. The designs of the two first have some degree of fancy, but the colouring, proportion, and general execution, are almost beneath observation.[41]

William may have been the brother of the Thomas Craft who was a painter at the Bow Factory. If so, this provides another link between a portrait enameller and the world of porcelain enamelling suggested by Abraham Seaman's advertisement and certainly by the training from which Henry Bone later emerged. Henry Bone (see p. 53) was not, therefore, the first to reintroduce the enamel plaque, although he certainly improved its techniques and expanded its popularity.

It is possible that the larger enamel miniatures and plaques produced in the later eighteenth century resulted from the inclusion of miniatures as wall hangings at the Royal Academy from its inception in 1769. The hanging of miniatures on the walls at the Academy encouraged the perception of miniatures as cabinet pieces once again, while maintaining their alternative role as presentation works and intimate keepsake gifts. The more personal nature of the miniature mounted on a snuffbox, especially one given as a keepsake, made it inappropriate for display in a public forum such as the Royal Academy. The boxes were considered objects, not paintings, but some of the smaller miniatures, including those set in jewellery, could be exhibited together, individually framed and then mounted as a group within a single larger frame. Strict rules about the number of miniatures allowed per frame seem to have existed, ranging from three or four in the earlier years to five by 1776. By 1778, Horace Hone exhibited in one frame a group set for bracelets, in enamel. By 1796, this group hanging was even more common.

With the founding of the Royal Academy in 1768 and the inclusion of miniatures in its exhibitions, the nature of patronage, of an artist's reputation, and the way in which miniatures were perceived, changed, just as they did for full-scale painting. As early as 1767, in fact, the *Gazetteer*, an artist's critique of the exhibitions at the Great Room in Pall Mall, cites a miniature by James Scouler 'no 224 this miniature is well executed' – something more than the mere listing of works of art including miniaturists provided for the Society of Artists Exhibition in 1761.

One can gather a good deal about the exhibition of miniatures from studying the list of works exhibited in the Royal Academy, from mentions of miniatures in contemporary press accounts and from images such as the engraving by Martini after the painting by H. Ramberg of 1787, which shows both large numbers of spectators and the miniatures hung around the fireplace.

Of the founding members of the Royal Academy, Nathaniel Hone and Jeremiah Meyer painted miniatures. Both worked in enamels and in watercolours, and Hone in full-scale oils (his name was added to the list of founders at George III's suggestion).[42] Meyer was unusual in being singled out in the press at an early date for comment rather than mere listings and his miniatures. In the Royal Academy Exhibition of 1774, Meyer is praised for his miniatures (nos. 181, 182) of the Prince of Wales and the Bishop Osnabrück:

> These Miniatures excell all others in pleasing Expression, Variety of Tints and Freedom of Execution, being performed by hatching, and not by stipling as most Miniatures are. – Indeed in this Branch of the Art Mr. Meyer seems to stand unrivalled, and I believe he may justly be reckoned the first Miniature Painter in Europe.[43]

Again in the 1777 Exhibition of the Royal Academy, Meyer is referred to as:

> Jeremiah Meyer, R.A. Painter in Enamel and Miniature to his Majesty, Tavistock row Covent garden. 236 Portrait of a Lady in miniature. 337 Ditto This artist's superior merit, in the enamelling style, has been long, and justly acknowledg'd; the two miniature portraits here exhibited, do not discredit that reputation.[44]

Nathaniel Hone was also cited, but usually for his full-scale works. Although the Royal Academy did not feature miniature painting in its stated objectives or its teaching, it did not exclude it. In fact, the number of miniatures grew every year. It is hard to make a precise count, or to be certain whether something was actually in enamel, especially as, in the early years, works were listed by artist and neither the word 'miniature' nor 'enamel' was included with any consistency. Thus for an artist such as Nathaniel Hone who worked in various sizes and media it is hard to determine the size or the relevance of the location of his works. It was not until 1780 that a separate miniatures section was initiated, presumably reflecting their placement as a group around the fire-place. In 1780, numbers 226–99 were listed as miniatures (including waxes) out of a total of 489.

Initially, the critics described just a few of the full-scale works at the Royal Academy exhibition. Each year, the amount of commentary in the press grew, and occasionally comments about miniatures, or artists working in miniature, would be included:

> I did not intend saying any Thing of the Miniatures, as I do not like see the Human Shape so much diminished, and to be obliged to pull a magnifying Glass to view, what I can see every moment of my Life, with my naked Eye; but I cannot help mentioning 236, the Portrait of a Lady, by Mr. Meyer, as soaring above the rest, and leaving them at an amazing Distance. It is rather large for a Miniature. Every Part of it is well drawn, well painted very noble and graceful.[45]

This passage, as well as being a critique of a work by an artist not known for full-scale work, notes the large size of the miniature perhaps, in part, as justification. A defence of some children's portraits by Cosway was just above this comment. However, those must have been larger-scale works as the defence refers to a negative review in the *Morning Post*:

> 66. Lord Cork's little family: but coloured in so languid a manner, as to confirm us in our former opinion, that this style is not Mr. Cosway's forte . . . 67 Portrait of a Lady in miniature. In this line he excels, as above portrait clearly demonstrates.[46]

The numbers of miniatures continued to grow steadily. A drawing in the Royal Academy (52.10) from 1792 shows the chimney wall of the Great Exhibition Room with small full-scale paintings around them, including two by Ozias Humphry. The following year, 1793, the miniatures, now numbered 346–491, were listed as being in the library. From 1803 to 1805, they were in the Council Room, although it is interesting to note that the enamels, presumably large ones, by Henry Bone were largely separated from the works listed as miniatures, which they had not been before. This was probably part of a strategy by Bone to exhibit outsized enamels so the Royal Academy would not regard him as a miniature artist when they voted on membership. A look at the voting for miniature artists shows that they inevitably lost out to full-scale artists when there was competition for a place. Cosway, possibly because he presented himself as a full-scale draughts-man as much as a miniaturist, had managed to be elected as an associate in 1771 and a full member in 1775. After that, despite regular exhibitions, minia-ture artists – whether watercolour or enamel painters – feature mainly as 'also-rans' in the Royal Academy. Horace Hone was elected an associate in 1779, but never managed full membership. Throughout the 1780s and into the early 1790s, his name, like that of miniaturist James Nixon (who was elected an associ-ate in 1778), was listed as under consideration for full membership, but usually gained few or no votes, languishing from competition with full-scale artists.

Henry Bone was only elected to the Royal Academy in 1811 after about thirty years of exhibit-ing, ten years as ARA and considerable patronage by the Prince of Wales. His early career as a porcelain painter may have damaged his standing with the Royal Academy artists, but the critics' high esteem for his work may have helped to convince them that to keep him out would not be popular. Reviewing the Royal Academy exhibition, the *Examiner* of 30 April 1809 stated:

> Bone has many beautiful enamels; he has been deservedly appointed Enamel Painter in ordinary to his Majesty.

His good notices no doubt encouraged other enam-ellers, like Denis Brownell Murphy, who exhibited an enamel of the Earl of Moira (1809) as well as various historical works such as Pope Innocent IX after Velasquez (1806). Henry Bone created a series of plaques of figures of the Elizabethan period – one example of which is the portrait of Hugh Myddleton (see cat. no. 12). In his son William's miniature portrait of him, now at the National Portrait Gallery, Henry Bone is depicted with this series of plaques arranged in his private gallery. Clearly Denis Brownell Murphy was working in the same vein when he created his series (see cat. no. 42) of the monarchy from a Scottish viewpoint from James VI of Scotland to Charles Edward Stuart (Bonnie Prince Charlie). Bone exhibited some of his series privately, but included plaques of historic subjects in Royal Academy exhibitions.

These series were part of a broader enthusiasm for historicism in the arts. They were initiated soon after the creation in 1790 of the 'Shakespeare Gallery' in Pall Mall, where works of art illustrating subjects from Shakespeare were exhibited, and then published by John Boydell. With time, it became clear that Bone's oversized enamels were his ticket away from being associated exclusively with miniatures. He was often able to have them exhibited individually at the Royal Academy as the 1804 exhibition attests.

That a distinction was drawn between these is not only apparent from the location of the works, but also from the press of the day. *The National Register* of 29 April 1810 remarked 'There are many beautiful miniatures and some exquisite enamels by Mr Bone.' However, Bone did not abandon miniature painting while he was making large plaques. An 1813 review praised A.E. Chalon for his 'fancy subjects in Miniatures' and followed by commenting on H. Bone, RA, 'Whose Enamels after the old and modern Masters are in his well known richly coloured and highly delicate style.'[47] This sort of review continued throughout the Regency period, although a review of 1818 also complained about the Royal Academy display in the Antique Academy in these terms:

In the Antique Academy we have great objection to the way in which the pictures have been disposed. Enamels, paper-drawings, miniatures, fancy-pieces, &c.&c. are huddled together without order or method, and so ill an effect that each particular branch is injured by the rest. For the Miniatures at least we would claim a separate allowance of wall-room, since altogether they do not occupy so much space as one of the prodigious portraits upstairs. But some are at a height to be invisible, others so low as to be unseen and we think the less excusable because in the very middle of the place assigned to them the chief parts are usurped to their exclusion by favoured

water-colour drawings. This seems to be neither just towards the artists nor the public.[48]

Bone found a ready audience both for his copies of works from the distant past, as well as for those with very recent sources – the latter a practice started by Petitot:

No. 577 Portrait of Mrs. Hope in enamel after G. Dawe, A. by H. Bone R.A. – we recollect with pleasure the portrait of this aimiable lady in last year's exhibition, and we are happy to find that the enamel painter has translated all the beauties of the original and the careful and high finishing of every part.[49]

Despite a positive press for the quality of Bone's work especially the exhibition conditions seem not to have improved:

Antique Academy: In this inconvenient and crowded room where many pictures are hung and few are seen and in . . . The enamels by H. Bone are in his usual style of ease and finish, exhibiting at once the varied characters of the different schools and ensuring to posterity their lasting record by means of enamel painting of which hazardous and tedious process it is but justice to say that the improvement was first begun and preserved in, till reached the high and perfect state which it has now attained by this eminent artist.[50]

In fact, Bone's career had mixed financial success. Because of his enthusiasm for historic portrait series Bone appeared to be in the vanguard of the nineteenth-century historicism. In fact, enamels were an ideal medium in which to adapt works of art of varying periods into a harmonious group in a single different medium and format. They were an important agent in the continuation of historicism in portraiture in England through into the mid-nineteenth century. Historicism plays a strong role in English portraiture in general, including well before the nineteenth century, and is one of the principal themes of enamel painting in England, which may be one reason for the long popularity of enamelling there.

Earlier historically minded patrons had included the 1st Earl of Oxford, who collected enamels, miniatures and full-scale paintings not only of himself and his family but also of famous figures from history. About a century later, Johann Heinrich Hurter's patron, the Earl of Dartrey, commissioned numerous enamels both of his own family and of well-known historical figures, such as Charles I (cat. no. 31, for example). Both patrons were genuine art collectors, the Earl of Oxford amassing 532 paintings, many of which were miniatures. Nevertheless, portraiture also validated their social positions. Both had been ennobled and commissioning enamels of other august personages, both past and present, to hang alongside their own portraits to bolster their status.

Whereas the snuffboxes of the early eighteenth century generally held miniatures of contemporary figures, although sometimes depicted in earlier period costume, historicism appears more significantly on snuffboxes of the late eighteenth and early nineteenth centuries, which were often adorned with enamels by Petitot and copies after his work or other historical subjects. It is interesting to compare three English snuffboxes of the early nineteenth century in the Gilbert Collection: cat. nos. 8, 17 and 19. One is mounted with two miniatures of eminent seventeenth-century French figures, the other two are set with contemporary Bone enamels – one of an earlier English subject, probably Anne Boleyn, and one of a contemporary one, the Countess of Conyngham. Similar snuffboxes with variant miniatures of George IV are known (like cat. no. 11 by Henry Bone) which were, in many cases, presentation pieces, much like their seventeenth-century counterparts, thus reinforcing the historical connection.

As Henry Bone grew increasingly blind and then ill, his influence continued with his 'dynasty' of sons and grandsons, particularly Henry Pierce Bone, who continued to work in his manner. Later artists who worked in enamel include William Essex (1784–1869) who, like Bone (see cat. no. 11), also made enamels of George IV after Sir Thomas Lawrence.

After Henry Pierce Bone's death, an estate sale was held of his sizeable collection of his own enamels at Christie's, London (13–14 March 1856). His ownership of so many enamels at the time of his death may indicate more than just an enthusiasm for the subject. The market may not have been as vigorous as his production. Although miniatures on ivory suffered a marked decline in popularity with the advent

of photography, enamels maintained some popularity for longer, especially if set in jewellery and objects of vertue, but their market, too, suffered.

An unpublished petition presented by a group of miniature painters to the Royal Academy in 1834, the year of Henry Bone's death, survives in the Soane Museum. It champions newer techniques and complains of the decline in recognition for miniaturists and enamellers, in contrast to the situation at the founding of the Royal Academy:

> This art is now practised on a scale capable of producing works more comprehensive in subject, with all the force, richness, purity, and durability of oil colours . . .

> In the lines of Charles the 1st & 2nd, Miniature Painting was carried to a considerable degree of perfection, upon the most stubborn & opaque material, (viz), parchment, by the Ollivers, Cooper, & others – When ivory was first adopted as substance to paint upon, the Fine Arts, generally had greatly declined, & Miniature Painting at length degenerated into an imitation of the worst features of Cosway's style, by men who possessed none of that fascinating taste and elegance which stamped him a man of genius imagination. In short this Art sunk so low, that we have heard it was at one time in contemplation to exclude Miniatures from the Exhibition altogether . . .

> When the Royal Academy was founded & long after the number of Artists were small compared with those of the present day & Miniature as well as Enamel Painters were practically eligible to its honour, but we have seen with extreme regret, that notwithstanding Miniature Painting has become more worthy of distinction from the Royal Academy, when vacancies have occurred in this department, they have not been supplied by the same branch of the arts, thus virtually excluding Miniature Painters from the former participation in the honours of the academy.[51]

The techniques being promoted as admirable in this letter included the use of larger plaques of ivory and stronger colours, suggesting that the popularity of enamels had caused the miniaturists on ivory to try to emulate the depth of colour achieved in enamels in an attempt to foster interest in their art. Certainly, strong colouring was something that early photography could not offer, but it was another novelty of similar size which contributed to the decline in portrait miniatures.

In an attempt to revive and promote interest in these arts, the South Kensington Museum, later the Victoria and Albert Museum, included miniatures and enamels in its 1862 exhibition and then held 'an exhibition of Portrait Miniatures' in 1865. A further exhibition of approximately 375 miniatures was held at Leeds in 1868. The 1862 exhibition included works by Nicholas Hilliard, Samuel Cooper and Hans Holbein II, along with enamels by Petitot, Boit and Henry Bone from those lent by S. Addington. The Duke of Buccleuch lent two of Oliver Cromwell by Samuel Cooper (including the famous unfinished one) and the Earl of Spencer lent two (nos. 2655, 2656) of Sarah Duchess of Marlborough by Zincke (very probably two of the three now in the Gilbert Collection) as well as one of an unknown Gentleman by Zincke and a Petitot.

A subsequent revival of interest in miniatures and enamels was stimulated by the important 1889 Burlington Fine Arts Club exhibition. This exhibition featured many miniatures lent by the major private collections – including those of the Earl of Spencer (several of which are now in the Gilbert Collection), and of the Earl of Dartrey (which had descended from Hurter's patron), as well as of the Duke of Devonshire, W.W. Aston and other more recent collectors. Further turn-of-the-century exhibitions fuelled a renewed interest in miniatures, but the actual revival of the practice of miniature painting occurred principally in watercolour on ivory.

Today, miniature paintings in enamel continue to be popular with collectors, although not with artists. The experiences and behaviour of some of the enamellers of the past suggest that enamelling may be an unhealthy practice, perhaps because it involves firing toxic materials. Whereas some of its practitioners were merely extravagant in the extreme – Boit, Peterson and Nathaniel Hone to name but a few – Zincke and Henry Bone both suffered from blindness. Gardelle committed a gruesome murder and attempted suicide, Rouquet died in an insane asylum and Horace Hone suffered from extreme depression. Even without these possible deterrents, artists of the modern era have shied away from combining the arts of enamelling and portraiture. However, the longevity of this medium, with its durability and ability to retain its vivid colours, enables us to see the sitters generally just as they wished to be seen, unfaded either by memory or by the bleaching action of the sun.

1 From Jorgen Hein 'Precious Objects from the Green Cabinet at Rosenborg Palace', International Fine Arts Fair, NY, 1993, Catalogue, pp. 26–30.

2 Christopher Rowell, 'A Seventeenth Century Cabinet Restored', The Green Closet at Ham, *Apollo*, April 1996, pp. 18–33.

3 Jean André Rouquet, *L'Etat des arts en angleterre*, Paris, 1755, translated as *The Present State of the Arts in England*, London, 1970.

4 From Vertue III, vol. V, p. 19, BM, 18b, 1726 Walpole XVII, 1734, p.25.

5 Ibid.

6 Collection of the Duke of Leeds sold at Sotheby's London (3 July 1961, lot 97).

7 Goulding, 1916.

8 Vertue I, Walpole Society, vol. IV, p.18.

9 Vertue, 1731, vol. V, m BM 32b.

10 Thus the attribution when the miniature was sold from the Clore Collection at Sotheby's, London (10 November 1986, lot 59).

11 Cavalli-Bjorkman, 1981, p. 41, illus. 15, p. 40.

12 Vertue II, vol. 20, BM 20b.

13 In the V&A, illustrated in Coombs, 1998, p. 79, pl. 52.

14 Sold at Sotheby's, London (7 May 1946, lot 21).

15 Sold at Sotheby's, London (9 July 1986, lot 104).

16 Vertue III, vol. 53, BM 35 b, 1734.

17 Vertue, Notebooks, III p. 58.

18 Walker, 1992, p. 18, (WRA. Geo 54020).

19 Rouquet, 1755, p. 38.

20 Rouquet, 1755, p. 41.

21 Vertue III, vol. 17b, BM21b, 1742 BM, Walpole, 1934, p. 109.

22 Baetjer, *British Portraits in the Metropolitan Museum of Art*, New York, 1999, p. 3.

23 Sold at Sotheby's, London (24 February 1969, lot 116, property of Mrs Walter Raleigh Gilbert as by Zincke); sold at Sotheby's (26 June 1979, lot 36).

24 Sold at Sotheby's, London (24 November 1983, as by Zincke); sold at Sotheby's, London (2 February 1970, lot 30, as a Zincke).

25 Edward Edwards, *Anecdotes of Painting*, London, 1818, p. 18.

26 Sold at Sotheby's, London (16 December 1974, lot 29).

27 Sold at Christie's, London (11 May 1994, lot 35).

28 Vertue III Vb, BM10, 1739, Walpole XXII, p. 96.

29 Vertue II, V 17b, BM21b, Walpole XXII, p. 109.

30 Watney/Charleston, 1966, p. 70

31 Benton, 1970, p. 166.

32 Cavalli-Björkman, 1981, p. 46 illus. 19.

33 Walpole, Anecdotes, vol. IV, p. 93; Walker, 1992, p. 53.

34 Goulding, 1916, illus. no. 211.

35 From The Public Ledger, 11 May 1761, p.1.

36 Indications of how highly these artists were soon to be regarded is available from the contemporary press. A review from the *General Advertiser and Morning Intelligenser*, 28 April 1778, p. l, on the exhibition at the Society of Artists lists first '207 Seven miniatures in a frame, by J. Smart excellence of this artist so well known, that it would be as a tale twice told to enumerate his miniatures. These miniatures possess that bold vigorous effect for which he stands in that line unrivaled'; *Morning Post and Daily Advertisement*, 30 April 1778, p. 2, 'Royal Academy Exhibition 'Richard Crosse'.

37 Coombs, 1998, p. 89.

38 For a full discussion of Samuel Finney, his role as a miniaturist and the information gathered from his previously unpublished memoirs, see Coombs, 1998, pp. 87–92.

39 Walker, 1998, p. 15, fig. 15.

40 *Morning Chronicle*, 26 April 1775, p. 2.

41 *Morning Chronicle*, 30 April 1774, p. 2

42 Joseph Farrington's Diary

43 *Public Advertiser*, 3 May 1774, p. 2.

44 Guido, *Morning Post and Daily Advertiser*, 30 April 1777. p. 4.

45 Gaudenzio, St James Chronicle, 3 May p. 2.

46 *Morning Post and Daily Advertiser*, 26 April 1777, p. 4.

47 *Examiner*, 13 June 1813.

48 *Literary Gazette and Journal of the Belles Lettres*, 1818.

49 National Register, 30 May 1813.

50 *Literary Gazette and Journal of the Belles Lettres*, 1820.

51 Unpublished letter in the Soane Museum, London, Private Correspondence, 1834 (Watermark), 'To the Members of the Royal Academy'. We are grateful to Anne Puetz for drawing our attention to this document and the Soane Museum for permission to publish extracts.

NOTE TO THE READER

This catalogue lists the enamels alphabetically by
the name of the artist, attributed artist regardless of
country, or enamels by country without artistic
attribution. The last section lists alphabetically
miniatures which are not enamel.

Dimensions of the miniatures without frame are
provided as height by width.

Inventory numbers are provided for each catalogue
entry, and comprise the Museum's accession number
followed in brackets by Sir Arthur Gilbert's
personal inventory number.

Short citations for sources are provided in the text; a
complete listing of references can be found in the
Bibliography. Similarly, a short form for exhibitions
has been provided, where applicable, in the entries;
a complete exhibition history follows the
Bibliography.

When known, life dates are provided.

Abbreviations for some of the exhibition locations,
museums, and documentary sources referred to in
the text are as follows:

Heinz – Heinz Archive, National Portrait Gallery,
    London
Metropolitan – Metropolitan Museum of Art,
    New York
NPG – National Portrait Gallery, London
RA – Royal Academy, London
SA – Society of Artists, London
Uffizi – Galleria degli Uffizi, Florence
V&A – Victoria and Albert Museum, London
Witt – Witt Library, Courtlaud Institute

Portrait Miniatures in Enamel

JOSIAS BARBETTE (1657–1732)

Josias Barbette was born in Strasbourg and was trained by his father, the goldsmith and enameller Frédéric Barbette. Like many other Protestant artists, Barbette had to leave France upon the Revocation of the Edict of Nantes in 1685. He is said to have stayed for some time in Geneva and Kassel and is thought to have worked for Landgrave Charles of Hesse-Kassel, the subject of the miniature below. It has been suggested that the Landgrave recommended Barbette to his sister, Queen Charlotte Amalie of Denmark. Certainly, by 1690 Barbette was recorded in Copenhagen. He painted numerous enamel portraits of the Danish kings Christian V and Frederick IV and other members of the royal family. His enamels are often confused with those of his father, who signed his name as *F.N. Barbette*. Nevertheless, the works of Josias are much finer and more accomplished than those of his father. Their harmonious pastel colours and their soft handling contrast sharply with the hard and rather naïve portraits produced by his father. Barbette, who was a prolific artist, also painted heraldic and allegorical enamels. He was one of the best enamellers active in Scandinavia.

Enamels by Barbette are to be found not only in Denmark, particularly at Rosenborg Castle and Frederiksborg Castle, but also in the Nationalmuseum in Stockholm, the Atheneum in Helsinki, the Bayerisches Nationalmuseum, Munich and the Landesmuseum, Kassel.

1 *Landgrave Charles of Hesse-Kassel*

Josias Barbette
Kassel or Copenhagen, c. 1690
Enamel on gold, 3.2 × 2.7 cm (1¼ × 1¹⁄₁₆ in), oval
Open gold rim frame, enamelled on reverse with interlaced mirrored Cs below the coronet of a German landgrave surrounded by scrolls
1996.782 (MIN17)

PROVENANCE: Countess Charlotte Sophie Bentinck and William, 1st Count Bentinck of Rhoon and Pendrecht in Holland and Terrington St Clements in Norfolk; their eldest son, Christian Frederick Anton, Count Bentinck, husband of Marie Catharine van Tuyll van Serooskerken; by descent to Timothy Bentinck; the sale of his family miniatures, Sotheby's, London (30 June 1980, lot 226, erroneously as by the Huaud brothers, sitter unidentified); S.J. Phillips, London (1980).

DESCRIPTION: The sitter wears a dark brown wig, lace, red knotted cravat, with armour and the blue sash of the Royal Danish Order of the Elephant.

COMMENTARY: Landgrave Charles (1654–1730), son of Landgrave William VI of Hesse-Kassel married Hedwige-Sophie of Brandenburg and succeeded his elder brother William VII in 1670. He became the archetypal German baroque prince, fond of pomp and splendour. He collected and travelled extensively and built a magnificent baroque garden in Kassel. Through a clever marriage strategy, he succeeded in allying his family with the most important courts of

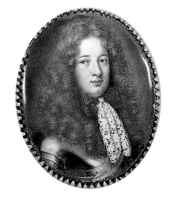

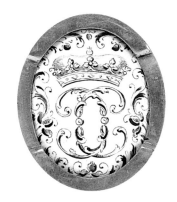

central and northern Europe. His two sisters were married off to the King of Denmark and the Elector of Brandenburg and his daughter to Prince Johan Friso of Orange. His son and heir married first the daughter of the first King of Prussia and later became King of Sweden through his marriage to Queen Ulrika Eleonora of Sweden. The identities of artist and sitter are confirmed by a slightly smaller version of this miniature, paired with one of the sitter's wife, in the Treasury, Stockholm (Treasury no. 646 and 648), on loan to the

Nationalmuseum, Stockholm.[1] A portrait of the Landgrave at Fasanerie Castle, Fulda, depicts the sitter three-quarter length wearing a blue sash, as in the present miniature, but with the jewel of the Order of the Elephant clearly visible at the sitter's right hip. The identities of the sitter and the artist have also been confirmed by Halgard Kuhn, Hanover (letter dated 13 October 1999).

[1] Inv. no. NMB 2160–2161, illustrated and discussed in Colding, 1991, I, pp. 44, 188 note 69, II, p. 48, nos. 97 and 98, and again in Colding, 1994, pp. 80–1, figs. 39–40.

WILLIAM BIRCH (1755–1834)

William Birch, born in Warwick, exhibited two mythological enamels in 1775 at the Society of Artists while he was a pupil of Henry Spicer. He showed at the Royal Academy from 1781 until 1794, when he left for America. There he stayed, principally in Philadelphia, until his death in 1834. In London, in addition to creating his own compositions, he copied the works of various artists, both in enamel and in engravings. Most notable were his copies after Sir Joshua Reynolds (1723–92), including, in 1792, one of Reynolds's self-portraits. In America, he had considerable success making copies of Gilbert Stuart's portraits of George Washington. His son, Thomas Birch, emigrated to America with him and produced enamels and engravings.

His works are in major museums including the Ashmolean Museum, Oxford and the V&A.

2 Charles Watson Wentworth, Second Marquess of Rockingham

William Birch
England, 1786
Signed on front *WB / from J R / 1786*
Enamel on copper, 5.7 × 4.5 cm (2¼ × 1¾ in), oval
Gold frame with glazed reverse, set with scrolled and woven hair underneath; engraved on reverse of frame *Chas. Watson Wentworth 2nd and last Marquis of Rockingham died July 1782*
1996.774 (MIN9)

PROVENANCE: Christie's, London (19 March 1980, lot 17).

EXHIBITION: Possibly exhibited in London, 1889, as lent by Jeffery Whitehead Esq., case XVI, no. 28 (p. 49).

DESCRIPTION: The sitter is shown almost in profile, dark brown hair *en queue*, blue peer's cape, red jacket, chain with the Order of the Garter and another not visible.

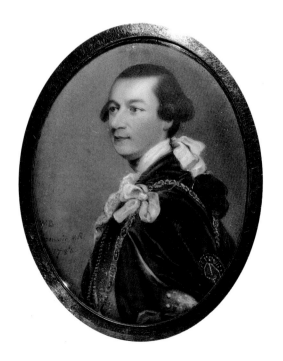

COMMENTARY: Charles Watson Wentworth (1730–82) was the fifth but only surviving son and heir of Thomas Watson Wentworth (1690–1750); created Viscount Higham, Earl Melton in 1733, Baron Wath and Baron Harrowden in 1734; Marquess Rockingham in 1745. He served as a volunteer under the Duke of Cumberland during the Jacobite rebellion of 1745–46 and was Lord of the Bedchamber to George II and George III. He was Prime Minister in 1765–66 and in again 1782. He took his seat in the House of Lords in 1751 and was appointed Lord Lieutenant of the North and East Ridings of Yorkshire. A Whig, he resigned from his post as Lord of the Bedchamber in 1762 shortly before the Peace of Paris preliminaries. He died a few weeks after becoming prime minister in 1782, leaving no heirs from his marriage to Mary, the daughter and heiress of Thomas Bright, and his titles became extinct (cf. *Memoirs of the Marquis of Rockingham and his Contemporaries* by George Thomas, Earl of Albemarle (2 vols., 1852).

The inscription indicates that this miniature was made during the period when Birch was exhibiting at the Royal Academy and after the subject's death. The original painting after which this miniature was taken would appear to be the full-length portrait by Reynolds now in the Royal Collection. This or a similar enamel was sold at Sotheby's on 11 December 1969, lot 89, where it was stated to be another version of lot 82 in the same sale.

CHARLES BOIT (1662–1727)

Charles Boit was born in Stockholm to French parents. Initially apprenticed to a goldsmith in Stockholm from 1677 to 1682, he then travelled to Paris, returning to Stockholm by 1685. He may have studied with the enameller Signac, or with Elias Brenner and Andreas von Behn.[1] The year after the accession of William of Orange and Mary Stuart to the English throne in 1688, Boit became court enameller to William III. By 1700 he was in Bonn and Düsseldorf and then Vienna, painting a large enamel portrait of the Imperial family.

By 1703 he was back in England, where he received a commission from Prince George of Denmark, consort of Queen Anne, for a very large enamel commemorating the Battle of Blenheim (August 1704). It was to be '22 (24) Inches by 18 (16) Inches which certainly is the largest plate known to be enamelled in Europe', according to George Vertue, who based his account on that of 'a Mr Peterson an Enameller who then workt with Mr Boit as also Mr Zinke. It was to depict the Duke of Marlbro introduced by Victory to the Queen and her court, with Prince Eugene at his side. He received an advanced payment of a thousand pounds with which he took a convenient spot of ground in Mayfare and there he built a furnace.'

Boit lived grandly and presumably received numerous smaller commissions on the strength of his royal patronage and on that of the great collector Robert Harley, Earl of Oxford. The Prince of Denmark came privately to see the execution of the work but died soon afterwards, which put a temporary halt to further funding. In order to receive further advances, Boit executed watercolours of his proposed design, which Vertue says 'were to deceive the piece in effect being to large ever to accomplish as he well know and owned since by Mr Zinke who then workt much for him and on this great work. Boit did request and receive 700 pounds more to go on with it this made a prodigious noise about the Court and quality that brought with in a Multitude of Busines to him.' Then the Queen changed her court favourites, which necessitated alterations to the composition in the drawing phase and led to further problems.[2]

In 1714 Boit, having run into debt and, having had his effects seized, fled to France. There he had considerable success, gaining the patronage of the Regent Duke of Orleans. Nevertheless, he died in Paris in poverty, leaving a wife and five children.

His works are in major museums, including the Ashmolean Museum, Oxford and the V&A.

[1] Walpole vol. IV, p. 18.
[2] George Vertue, notes relating to the *Time Arts* p. 725–31 vol. III, fol. 20 Add. Ms 23070, collection Vertue, Archives of British Museum, pp. 30–1.

3 *John Churchill, First Duke of Marlborough*

Charles Boit
England, c. 1705
Signed *C Boit pinx* on counter enamel (faint)
Enamel on copper, 9.2 × 7 cm (3⁵/₈ × 2³/₄ in), rectangular
Silver-gilt rectangular frame with moulded surround; later inscribed on reverse of frame *John Duke of Marlborough*, inventory no. H547
1996.769 (MIN5)

PROVENANCE: The Earls Spencer, Althorp, Inventory H547 '6th frame'; S.J. Phillips, London 1979.

LITERATURE: Spencer, 1831, p. 31, no. 455

EXHIBITIONS: London, 1865, cat. no. 954 (as by Zincke); *Painting and Sculpture in England 1700–50*, Liverpool, 1958 (as by Zincke).

DESCRIPTION: The subject stands three-quarters length, in armour, a blue sash with the Order of the Garter, ermine and a red cloak, with his field marshal's baton, in front of a battle scene lower right.

COMMENTARY: The subject matter suggests that this may have been a private commission from the duke (1650–1722) or one from the king to commemorate his victory. Through this miniature Boit may have helped to promote the status of the large enamel by depicting the Battle of Blenheim.

Several full-scale portraits with similar poses by Sir Godfrey Kneller and Michael Dahl survive. This appears to be based on one previously thought to be by Kneller and now attributed to Dahl, which was formerly in the Foley-Grey Collection, Enville Hall, sold at Christie's, London (15 June 1928, lot 40), bought by the Hudson Bay Company c. 1928.[1] The same subject by Zincke is depicted in catalogue number 65.

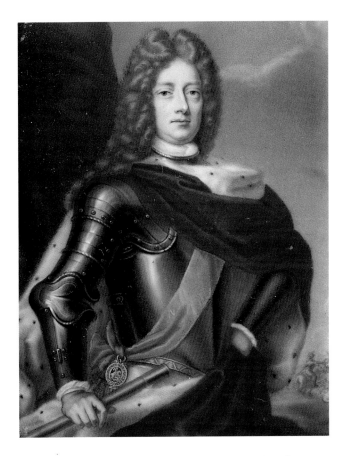

[1] Previously exhibited Manchester, 1857, no. 242 from the collection of the Earl of Stamford and Warrington, (photo the National Portrait Gallery, Heinz Archive, no. TSB II 56).

4 *Lady Anne Churchill*

Charles Boit
England, c. 1710
Unsigned on front
Enamel on copper, 6.8 × 5.6 cm (2¹¹/₁₆ × 2³/₁₆ in), oval
In gold frame with engraving on reverse; back of gold frame engraved *The / Lady Anne Churchill / & Daughter to John Duke of / Marlborough & Sarah Jennings / Duchess of Marlborough. Wife to / Charles Spencer 3rd Duke of Sunderland / and mother to / Charles Spencer 2nd Duke of / Marlborough to the Hon / John Spencer to Diana Dus / of Bedford & to Lady Bateman* [?], also with Althorp E-10 tag
1999.54 (MIN71A)

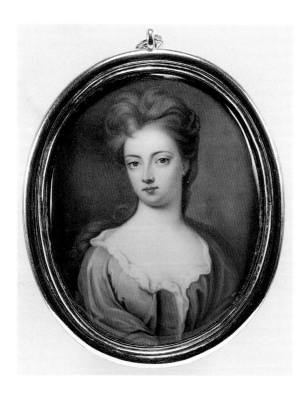

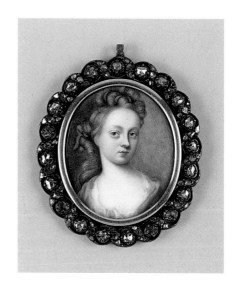

5 *A Lady*

England, c. 1720
Signed on counter enamel C. Boit
Enamel on copper, 3.5 × 2.9 cm (1 ¼ × 1 in), oval
Oval gold rim frame with diamonds in guilloch
garland surround
1996.485 (MIN29)

PROVENANCE: D. S. Lavender, London (October
1881).

DESCRIPTION: She is shown bust-length with long
light brown hair tied with a ribbon and a white dress
with a rose shawl.

COMMENTARY: This is typical of Boit's style with
large-eyed faces, less stippled than Zincke's were to
become.

PROVENANCE: Spencer Family, Althorp; S.J. Phillips,
London (August 1997).

LITERATURE: Spencer, 1831, p. 31, no. 456.

EXHIBITIONS: London, 1865, no. 968; London,
1889, p. 94 case XXXII no. 75, lent by the Earl
Spencer.

DESCRIPTION: Shown facing forward in a gold gown
and red shawl.

COMMENTARY: Lady Anne Churchill (d. 1716), the
second daughter of the Earl (later Duke) of
Marlborough, married as his second wife Charles
Spencer, 3rd Earl of Sunderland (1674–1722), in
January 1700. It was a great political event.
Although initially political opponents, Spencer later
drew the Marlboroughs towards the Whigs.

This miniature is undoubtedly the one listed in
the Althorp inventory of 1831, no. 456 as 'Ann,
Third Countess of Sunderland', with Boit named as
the artist.

Henry Bone (1755–1834)

Henry Bone, the best-known English enameller, was born in Truro. Son of a woodcarver and cabinet-maker, he produced a dynasty of enamellers which included Henry Pierce Bone and William Bone. As a child he was taught art and at sixteen had been apprenticed to a porcelain manufacturer in Plymouth, painting landscapes and floral scenes.

By 1779, he had settled in London apparently working in an enamel workshop, painting decoration for watches and jewellery. Here he would have been introduced to working on metal. In 1781 he exhibited his first enamel portrait miniature at the Royal Academy, where he continued to show regularly until 1831. He also exhibited at the British Institute and the Society of British Artists.

Most of his works were on enamel, but he did make a few miniatures on ivory early in his career. His enamels were usually copies after full-scale paintings, although a few were *ad vivum*. He made some series, including an important group of figures from the Elizabethan era.

Bone experimented with enamelling techniques and, with larger plaques, often inscribed on the reverse detailed information about the original painting, as well as his signature and the date.

His are works are in major museums including the Metropolitan and the National Portrait Gallery.

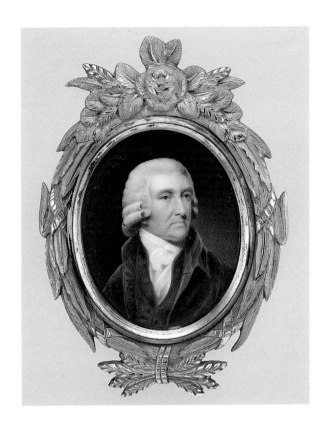

6 *Thomas, 1st Baron Dimsdale*

Henry Bone
England, 1800
Signed, dated and inscribed on counter enamel
Henry Bone pinxt. / June 1800, after a / miniature by A. Plimer
Enamel on copper, 7.1 × 5.9 cm ($2^{13}/_{16}$ × $2^5/_{16}$ in), oval
Ormolu frame with laurel and sheaf of wheat surmounted by flowers, probably original (formerly with a black wood surround, removed between 1980 and 1994)
1996.819 (MIN51)

PROVENANCE: Robert L. Bayne-Powell, Sotheby's, London (11 October 1994, lot 51) through S.J.

Phillips. This would appear to be the miniature previously sold at Christie's, London (3 March 1971, lot 62), which had as provenance 'Sir John Dimsdale Bt' and which appeared subsequently in a sale at Christie's, London (26 June 1980, lot 86, with wood frame).

LITERATURE: Walker 1999, no. 160.

EXHIBITION: Portland, 1994–95.

DESCRIPTION: Sitter with powdered hair *en queue*, plum-coloured jacket and waistcoat, with a white cravat.

COMMENTARY: A drawing for this miniature inscribed '1800 Baron Dimsdale' exists in the National Portrait Gallery, London, (vol. III, 5G); a photograph of a miniature stated to be by C.F. Zincke of the same subject, shown wearing a brown coat, H 4.5 cm ($1^3/_4$) in oval, is in the Witt Library as being from Private Collection LXXVI, no. 224.

Thomas Dimsdale (1712–1800) was an eminent physician who published a *Tract or Inoculation* in 1767. The treatise impressed Empress Catherine II of Russia at a moment when a severe epidemic of smallpox was sweeping through Russia. She was determined that she and her son, Grand Duke Paul should receive the inoculation. Dr Dimsdale, accompanied by his son Nathaniel, visited Russia in 1768 and performed successfully the potentially dangerous treatment. The Empress and the future Paul I were liberal in their gratitude to the doctor and created him a Baron of the Russian Empire. They also presented Nathaniel with a magnificent four-colour gold snuffbox, sold at Sotheby's, Geneva (16 November, 1989, lot 176), and now also in the Gilbert Collection (see Truman, 1991, pp. 368–371, cat. no. 128).

7. Captain John Whitby

Henry Bone
England, 1806
Signed and dated on front *HBone*
Enamel on copper, 9.6 × 7.9 cm (3$^{13}/_{16}$ × 3$^1/_8$ in), oval
Gold case with black enamel, trailing leaf border in front, hinged reverse centred by enamelled double anthemion and scroll border; engraved on reverse *Captn John Whitby / second son of the Rev Thos. / Whitby, of Creswell Hall in / The County of Stafford, and of / Mabella, Sister of John Turton / Esq.r of Sugnall Hall in the same / County. born Octr 7th 1774 made Post Capt / in the Royal Navy April 20th 1793 / married the 13th Octr 1802. Mary / Anne Theresa Symonds. died / April 7th 1806, leaving issue one / Daughter Theresa, born / May 1, 1805 / Henry Bone ARA pinx / May 1806*; memorial poem and lock of hair inside the hinged reverse
1996.788 (MIN23)

PROVENANCE: D.S. Lavender, London (1980)

LITERATURE: Walker, 1999, no. 546.

DESCRIPTION: Sitter shown bust-length with powdered hair, in naval uniform with gold buttons, trim and epaulettes.

COMMENTARY: This is presumably the Captain

Whitby identified as the sitter for a drawing by Bone in the National Portrait Gallery, called Clement or Henry Whitby by Walker (1999, vol. I, 93f). The drawing is inscribed '*late Captn. Whitby – for Adml Cornwallis April – 1806*'. Although this appears to be an *ad vivum* portrait, bearing a posthumous date, it may have been done as a death portrait or as an unidentified painting.

An apparently contemporary memorial poem was found inside the frame. As the enamel was painted in the year of the subject's death, it is reasonable to assume that the poem memorialised him. It reads:

> He was a man take
> him all in all, the like
> of whom I ne'er shall see again
> 'Sweet in Manners, fair in favour
> in Temper, fierce in fight
> Warrior Nobler, gentler, braver
> Never shall behold the light'
> He was too good for this
> world, therefore God
> in his Mercy has
> taken him to himself

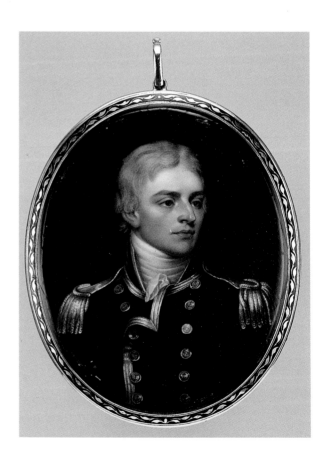

[page 2]

Forgive blest shade the tributary Tear
That mourns thy absence from a world like this
Forgive the wish that would have kept thee here
And stay'd thy progress to the seats of bliss
No more confined to groveling scenes of night
No more a Tenant pent in mortal clay
Now should we rather hail this glorious flight
And trace thy journey to
the realms of day.

8 *Probably Countess of Conyngham*

Henry Bone, probably after Peter Eduard
Stroehling (1768–1826)
London, c. 1810
Signed *HBone* in black, right edge
Enamel on copper, 9.7 × 7.5 cm (3 $^{13}/_{16}$ × 2 $^{15}/_{16}$ in),
oval
Mounted on lid of gold snuffbox by Alexander
James Strachan, London, 1812; box engraved
Rundell, Bridge & Rundell, Fect. 1812.
1996.503 (GB155)

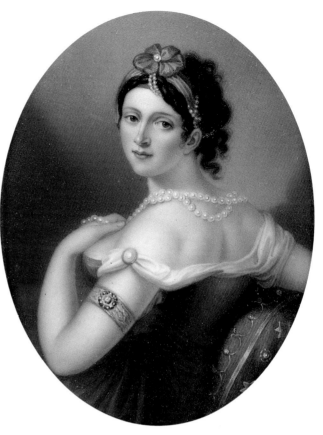

PROVENANCE: Enrico Caruso, sale of Caruso's
property by his daughter, Mrs Murray, Parke
Bernet, NY, (15–16 March 1949, lot 66); Christie's,
Geneva, (14 May 1980); Sotheby's, New York, (15
December 1989, lot 54); S.J. Phillips, London (18
January 1990).

LITERATURE: Truman, 1991, pp. 332–34, cat. 117;
Christie's Review, 1980, p. 326; *Orient Express
Magazine*, vol. 13, no. 4, 1996, *Gilbert's Gold*, pp.
20–4, ill p 23.

EXHIBITIONS: Los Angeles/Memphis 1991–92; San
Francisco 1996.

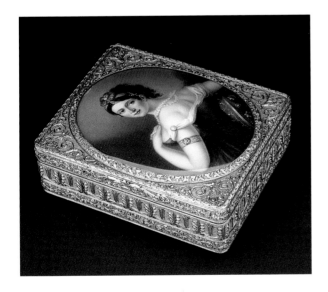

DESCRIPTION: Sitter shown half-length from the
rear, looking back over her left shoulder, wearing a
red dress with tiny white sleeves, and shawl held
with pearl clips at the shoulder, with a red ribbon in
her hair, long pearls around her neck and a jewelled
armband.

COMMENTARY: Elizabeth, 1st Marchioness of
Conyngham, (c. 1774–1861) married in July 1794
Francis, 2nd Baron Conyngham, created Earl and
subsequently in 1816 Marquess. Close friends of the

Prince Regent, later George IV, the Conynghams lived with him at Windsor and Brighton. Lady Conyngham acted as mistress of the King's household and received numerous gifts from him. She bore two sons and two daughters and died on 10 October 1861.

Stroehling styled himself 'Historical Painter to the Prince Wales'. Several oils by him of George IV are mentioned in the Prince's papers from 1808 to 1822. The last of these, painted on copper and showing the Prince in uniform on horseback, was given by the Prince to Lady Conyngham (Walker, *Regency Portraits*, London, 1985, vol. I, p. 209). His painting of Princess Elizabeth in the Royal Collection shows similar treatment of hair and pearls, adding credence to Stroehling's authorship of the source painting.

Interestingly, Stroehling painted a small picture of Mary Robinson (1758–1800), known as 'Perdita', an actress who was another mistress of the Prince of Wales, in a similar pose. It was probably painted on copper to match the series of royal princesses already in the Royal Collection. It shows her, in swarthy make-up, in the Shakespearean role of Volumnia, mother of Coriolanus, reclining on a couch by a fountain (Walker, op cit., pp. 418–19, vol I). Bone's drawing for this enamel is in the National Portrait Gallery (Walker, 1999, no. 69, p. 316; NPG, vol. III 20f.). It is inscribed as *Mrs. Brown* [More crossed out] *after Stroehling for Lord Mountjoy 1811*. This confusion over the name of the sitter may have resulted from Bone's uncertainty about which name to use for the sake of discretion.

9 *Francis Rawdon-Hastings, 2nd Earl of Moira*

Henry Bone
England c. 1817
Unsigned on front
Enamel on copper, 8.1 × 7 cm (3³/₁₆ × 2³/₄ in), elongated octagonal
Conforming silver-gilt frame with glass.
1996.789 (MIN24)

PROVENANCE: D.S. Lavender, London (1980).

DESCRIPTION: The sitter is shown bust-length, turn-

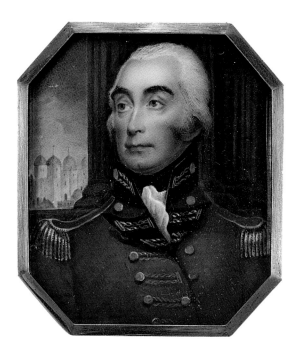

ing slightly left, in a white wig and red uniform with blue trim, gold braid and epaulettes, in front of green columns and Indian fortress – a loose interpretation of Fort William – with a sunset and pink clouds in the sky.

COMMENTARY: While in India, Rawdon-Hastings (1754–1826) sat for George Chinnery several times, both upon his appointment as Governor-General in 1813 and afterwards, including one sitting in the Bengal Artillery mess room at Dum Dum in 1823, a work which was subsequently engraved. For a detailed account of Chinnery and the Rawdon-Hastings commissions, as well as further biographical information on the latter, see Patrick Conner, *George Chinnery 1774–1852: Artist of India and the China Coast*, Suffolk, 1993. Rawdon-Hastings was Governor-General of Fort William from 1813 to 1823. For an almost full-length painting by Chinnery, c. 1818, of similar composition, see Mildred Archer, *India and British Portraiture 1770–1825*, London, 1979, pp. 330–1 illus. However, this miniature does not appear to be based on a known work by Chinnery.[1]

[1] We are grateful to Patrick Conner for this comment and help with the background conversation.

10 *George IV as Prince Regent*

Henry Bone, after Sir Thomas Lawrence
(1769–1830)
England, 1819
Signed and inscribed on reverse *May 1819 by Henry Bone R.A. Enamel Painter in Ordinary to His Majesty & Enamel Painter to H.R.H. The Prince Regent after the Original by Sir Thomas Lawrence R.A.*
Enamel on copper, 17.2 × 12.9 cm (6³/₄ × 5 in), oval
In gilt wood and gesso frame
1996.818 (MIN50)

PROVENANCE: Kugel, Paris (September, 1994).

LITERATURE: *Connaissance des Arts*, October 1996, p. 76; Walker, 1999, p. 218.

EXHIBITIONS: Portland, 1994–95.

DESCRIPTION: George IV as Prince Regent after Lawrence, with dark curling hair, in red field marshal's uniform with gold braid epaulettes and shoulder knots, wearing the insignia of the Order of the Golden Fleece pendant from his high black cravat and the star of the Order of the Garter, and insignia of the Orders of the Holy Spirit, Black Eagle and St Andrew.

COMMENTARY: A miniature of this description appeared in the H.P. Bone estate sale at Christie's, (13–14 March 1856, lot 75). Lawrence's original 1814/15 portrait, the first version of which was painted for Lord Charles Stuart in 1814, was exhibited at the Royal Academy in 1815 and sold at Sotheby's, London (16 November 1988, lot 73).

A full-length pencil sketch by Bone in the National Portrait Gallery after Lawrence's original was dated 1816, vol. I, no. 18 (Walker, 1999, no. 218). Walker (1992, p. 281) cites earlier examples, including one in the Princess Royal sale, Christie's, London (26 June 1966, lot 1815), dated November 1815, indicating that the demand for copies for presentation or otherwise must have started at the time of the Royal Academy exhibition. No fewer than ten enamels by Bone of George IV when Prince Regent after Lawrence are in the Royal Collection (see Walker, 1992, pp. 280–4 no. 8, 756–65).

The Prince Regent was a great patron of Henry Bone until the second decade, when he planned to rearrange the Painting at Carlton House with Lawrence's help, including removing the Bones. Lawrence, who earlier had not been favourably disposed towards Bone's work, played a major role in convincing the Prince to keep them in a position of prime importance.

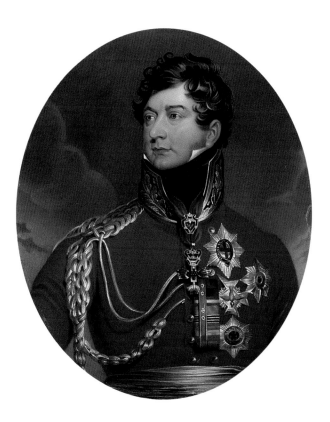

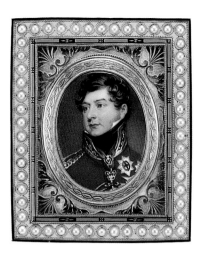

11 *George IV*

Henry Bone, after Sir Thomas Lawrence
(1769–1830)
England, 1821
Signed on counter enamel *His Majesty / London Oct.
1821 / Painted by Hy Bone / RA En. painter / to the
King &c.*
Enamel on copper, 3.3 × 2.7 cm (1⁵/₁₆ × 1¹/₁₆ in), oval
Oval contemporary gold, enamel and pearl-set
ormolu frame
1996.821 (MIN53)

PROVENANCE: Christie's, London (15 May 1990, lot
251); Au Vieux, Paris (3 November 1994).

LITERATURE: Clouzot; Schidlof; Walker, 1999,
no. 220.

EXHIBITION: Portland, 1994–95

DESCRIPTION: Head and shoulders, red uniform
with the Star of the Order of the Garter, green
background.

COMMENTARY: An identical miniature is in the Royal
Collection. Although dating from after the sitter's
accession to the throne in 1820, this miniature
appears to be based on Lawrence's earlier painting
from the Regency period. This image is bust-length
and much smaller, showing the Star of the Order of
the Garter but cutting off the pendant insignia of
the Golden Fleece. It most closely relates to no. 760
in the Royal Collection (see Walker, 1992, p. 282).

12 *Sir Hugh Myddleton*

Henry Bone, after Cornelius Jansen (1593–1661)
England, 1822
Signed and dated on counter enamel with
inscription *Sir Hugh Myddleton, Knight & Baronet /
Compleated the Newn River, A.D. 1613 / He was an
able Engineer, &&–Oct. 1613. / Painted by permission
of the Worshipful / Company of Goldsmiths, by Henry
Bone / R.A. Enamel painter to His Majesty & / Enamel
Painter to H.R.H. The Duke of York / from a picture by
Cornelius Jansen in the / Goldsmiths Hall, London /
London / Aug.–1822;* inscribed on matte *Enamel
HBone R. A.*
Enamel on copper, in original gilt-matte, 21.2 ×
16.9 cm (8³/₈ × 6¹¹/₁₆ in), rectangular
In later gilt gesso and wood frame with glass setting
1996.775 (MIN10)

PROVENANCE: Trustees of the Earl of Lonsdale;
Christie's, London (19 March 1980, lot 39).

LITERATURE: Walker, 1999, no. 372.

EXHIBITION: British Institute, 1835 (no. 82).

DESCRIPTION: Facing right, in black and brown coat
with jewelled buttons, white ruff and cuffs, black
gown, gold-linked chain with medallion suspended

COMMENTARY: Hugh Myddleton (c. 1560–1631) was
born in Denbigh, North Wales, the sixth son of
Richard Myddleton, MP. He married firstly Anne,
widow of Richard Edwards, and secondly Elizabeth,
daughter and heiress of John Olmested; he fathered
sixteen children. He was sent to London to learn the
goldsmiths' trade, which incorporated banking; he
became friendly with Sir Walter Raleigh and traded
by sea. He obtained a charter of incorporation for
Denbigh in 1596; he was elected first alderman 1597
and appointed recorder and MP in 1603.

The National Portrait Gallery (Walker, 1999,
no. 372, p. 337) has a drawing for this miniature
(vol. I, 26A) inscribed 'Sr Hugh Myddleton Bart
after original in Goldsmiths' Hall London 1822'.
There is also an entry by Bone in the Goldsmith's
Company Court Book for 9 April 1822, referring to
the loan of the portrait of Sir Hugh Myddleton,

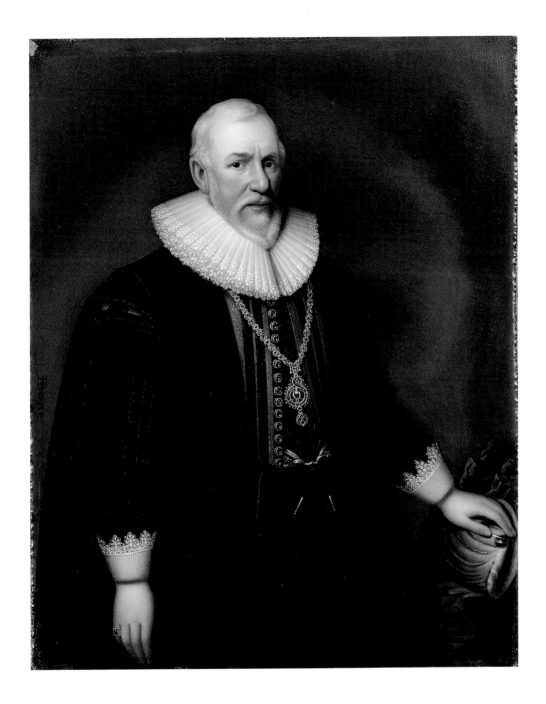

with Bone's letter to the meeting of the Court of
Assistants of 7 October 1822 about its return,
indicating that the enamel was to be part of Bone's
series entitled 'The Reign of Queen Elizabeth'.

The original painting by Jansen is owned by the
Goldsmiths Company and includes armorials and
motto on the right side.

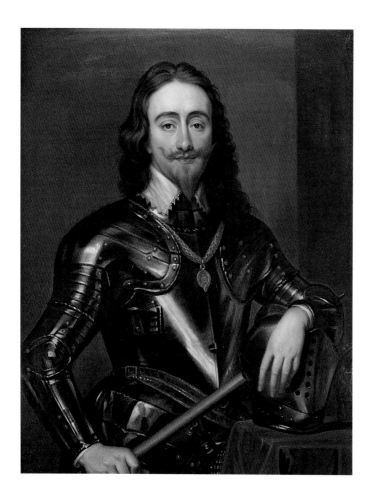

13 *Charles I*

Henry Bone, after Sir Anthony van Dyck (1599–1641)
England, 1825
Inscribed on the counter enamel *Charles I King of / Great Britain &c / London / March 1825 / Painted by Henry Bone, R.A. / Enamel Painter To his Majesty / &c Enl. painter to H. R. The / Duke of York after The Original / by Van Dyck in the Collection / of the Earl of Surrey / Worksop / Notts.*
Enamel in copper, 18.8 × 15 cm (7⁷/₁₆ × 5¹⁵/₁₆ in), rectangular
Gilt-matte surround with *Enamel HBone. RA* in glazed hinged door frame with foliate and arabesque gilt-gesso wood surround
2000.22 (MIN74)

PROVENANCE: Christie's, London (25 November 1980, lot 26); Private Collection, England; Bonham's, London (25 November 1998, lot 105).

LITERATURE: Walker, 1999, no. 106, p. 319

EXHIBITION: Royal Academy, 1825, no. 445.

DESCRIPTION: Charles I in armour, hand resting on helmet, holding baton, wearing a gold chain and the Order of the Garter, with an olive background.

COMMENTARY: Another Bone enamel of Charles I is in the V & A, signed on the back 'May–1825 / Painted by Henry Bone R.A. etc.' (4871–1901).

The drawing by Bone for this enamel is at the National Portrait Gallery (vol. I, 74a) and the original by Van Dyck is at Arundel Castle.

14 *George Washington*

Henry Bone, after Gilbert Stuart (1755–1828)
England, 1825
Signed *HBone* and dated on front; inscription on counter enamel in magenta on a background of speckled robin's egg blue reads *General George Washington / President of the United States / of America / London / 1825 / Painted by Henry Bone R.A. / Enamel painter to His Majesty and / En.L painter to His R.H. The Duke of York / &c&c After the Original painted / in America by Gabriel Stewart, and / now in the possession of – Williams Esq.r / of Finsbury Square – London. / N. B. – Cracked in the 5th fire / & finished by the permission of / Mr. Williams from the Original / picture.'*
Enamel on copper, 30.9 × 20.7 cm (12³/₁₆ × 8¹/₈ in), rectangular
Ormolu frame with gilt-matte; inscription on gilt-matte reads, *Enamel HBone R.A.*
1996.776 (MIN11)

PROVENANCE: Bone sale (1832, lot 58); Christie's, London (19 March 1980, lot 48).

LITERATURE: *Connaissance des Arts*, October 1996, p. 77; Walker, 1999, p. 348 (nos. 535–6).

DESCRIPTION: Washington is shown full-length in a black suit and frilled cravat, his right hand out-stretched, his left holding his sword, standing beside a table with books, a silver inkwell, a scroll and black

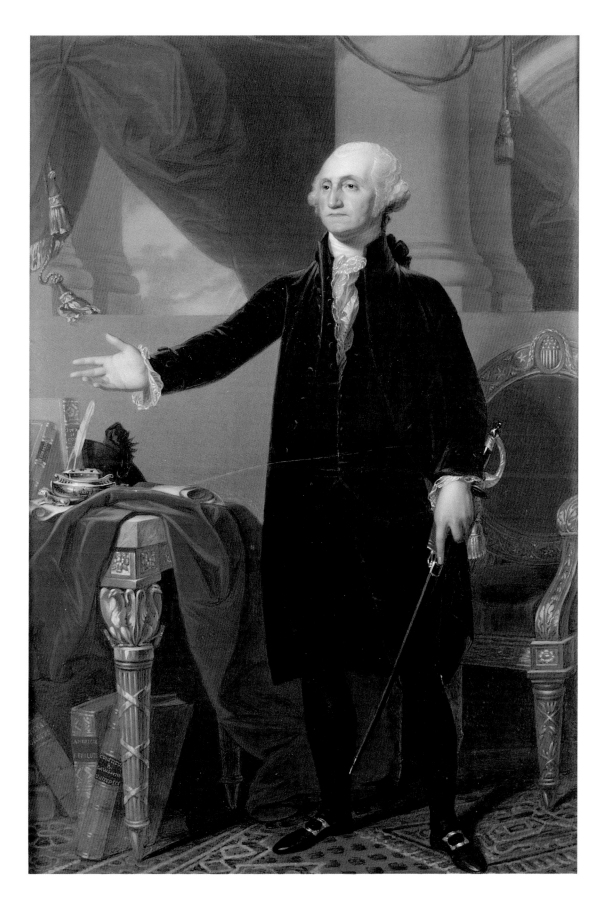

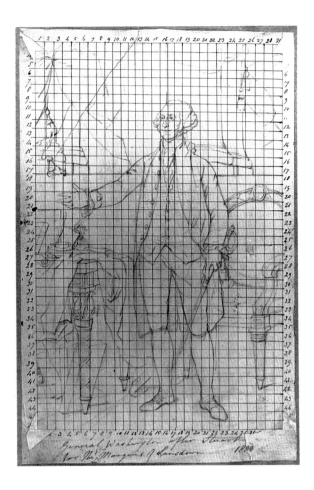

hat, other volumes beneath, red velvet chair to right, pillar and red curtain background.

COMMENTARY: George Washington (1732–99) was the first President of the United States of America from 1789 to 1797 (he refused a third term). He was Commander in Chief of the Revolutionary Army in the American Revolution from 1775 to 1776 and was called 'the Father of His Country'. Born in Virginia, he married in 1759 Martha (1731–1802), wealthy widow of Daniel P. Custis.

This miniature of Washington after the Lansdowne portrait is one of three commissioned by William Bingham of Philadelphia from Gilbert Stuart (not Gabriel as Bone incorrectly wrote) which was sent to the Marquess of Lansdowne by Bingham as a gift. It is now on loan to the National Gallery, Washington. Another version is in the White House and a third, that owned by Bingham, in the Pennsylvania Academy of Fine Arts. This appears to be one of four known enamels by Bone

after the Landsdowne portrait. It would seem that Bone executed the first version of this enamel in 1800. This is possibly the version sold at William Doyle Galleries, New York (1 December 1999, lot 336), signed and dated on the front '1800' and fully inscribed in the counter enamel with the same error in Stuart's name of Gabriel. The counter enamel reads *General George Washington, / President of the United States / of America / Born Feb. 22. 1799 / Died Dec 14. 1799 / Painted in London in the Year 1800 / by Henry Bone, Enamel Painter to His / Royal Highness the Prince of Wales, / after a Picture Painted in America by / Gabriel Stuart in year 1797.* It was probably the enamel which was exhibited by Bone at the Royal Academy in 1801 (no. 574) as 'The late General Washington'. This would be in keeping with the practice of exhibiting works of important subjects shortly after their deaths.

The National Portrait Gallery had a drawing by Bone listed as in vol. II 22B (Walker, 1999, p. 536) with the date 1800. The drawing (see left) is inscribed 'Genl. Washington after Stuart for Mr Kinder[sley?]' and there is also a faint inscription 'for Lord Landsdown Feby 1825'. There is a note in Bone's subject register (vol. II, p. 12) 'General Washington for Marquess Landsdown [subjects column]'. Another entry on p. 48 lists 'General Washington, for Mr Kinder [subjects column] Stuart [in masters column]'. This enamel appears to relate to Walker, 1999, no. 536, rather than no. 535, as this enamel is dated 1825, and it is the one sold at Christie's, London on 19 March 1980 which is listed as the enamel related to no. 535. The enamel related to no. 535 done in 1800 must be the one in the Doyle auction. It would appear that the drawing no. 536 was used twice: possibly the first version was for a Mr Kinder (or Kindersley as listed in Walker, 1999) and the 1825 version for Lord Lansdowne after the full-scale portrait commissioned for him. The identity of the Mr Williams who owned the full-scale painting and figures in the inscription on the counter enamel is not clear.

An apparent third version was sold from the Henry Symons Collection sale at the Anderson Galleries, New York, (27 January–3 February 1923, lot 1118, pp. 236–7, illus.). Although no mention is made of a signature on the front, the photograph shows the plaque to be signed 'Hbone' and dated

1809. No dimensions are given and the counter enamel is stated to be inscribed *Henry Bone / Hanover Street, Hanover Square / Enamel, London / Enamel Painter to His Royal Highness, The Prince of Wales.*

A fourth, oval, version is in the Holburne Museum, Bath, and relates to another drawing of Bone's (Walker, 1999, no. 537, (National Portrait Gallery, vol. 1).

HENRY PIERCE BONE (1779–1855)

Henry Pierce Bone, born in Islington, London, was the son of Henry Bone. He entered the Royal Academy Schools at sixteen in 1796 and exhibited at the Royal Academy and British Institute from 1799 to 1855. Like his father, whose style he emulated, many of his enamels were copies of full-scale paintings, including some of the 'Elizabethan' series which he undertook to finish after his father's death. He was appointed enamel painter to Queen Caroline, consort of William IV, the Duchess of Kent, Princess Victoria in 1833 and Prince Albert in 1841.

He was the father of the miniaturist Charles Richard Bone (1809–c. 1880) and enamellers Louisa Bone (fl. 1844) and William Bone Jr (fl. 1827–51).

Numerous works by Bone were lent to the South Kensington Museum in 1865. His works are in major museums, including the V&A and the Ashmolean Museum, Oxford.

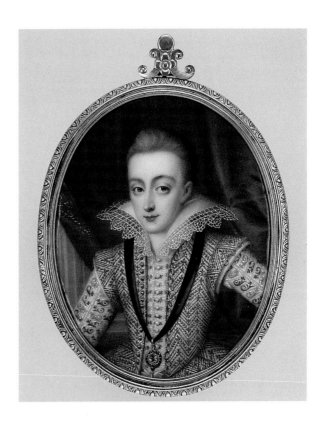

15 *Henry, Prince of Wales*

Henry Pierce Bone, after Robert Peake (d. 1626)
England, 1845
Signed, inscribed and dated on the counter enamel *Henry Prince of Wales / Son of James I.st / London Oct. 1845. Painted by / Henry Pierce bone. Enamel / Painter to Her Majesty & H.R.H. / Prince Albert &c From the Original by Vansomer in the / Collection of the Earl of / Craven, Combe Abbey.*
Enamel on copper, 10.2 × 8.1 cm (4 × 3³/₁₆ in), oval
In gilt frame with egg and dart border and scrolling surmount
1998.27 (MIN72)

PROVENANCE: Sotheby's, London (12 March 1984, lot 52), Christie's, London (21 April 1998, lot 25).

DESCRIPTION: The subject is shown facing left in a red, yellow and blue embroidered white doublet with lace bordering, standing white ruff, red and blue embroidered jerkin, wearing the Order of the Garter on a blue ribbon, with a pillar and curtain background.

COMMENTARY: Henry, Prince of Wales, eldest son of James I, was born in 1594 and died of typhoid fever in 1612, several years after being created Prince of Wales. The miniature appears to be a copy of the full-length portrait by Robert Peake, c. 1610, in the National Portrait Gallery.

16 *Frederick Henry, Prince of Orange, Count of Nassau*

Henry Pierce Bone
England, 1852
Signed and dated on counter enamel
Enamel on copper, 21.2 × 17.0 cm (8³/₈ × 6¹¹/₁₆ in), rectangular
Later gilt-wood frame; the inscription on the counter enamel of the miniature incorrectly identifies sitter as *Gustavus Adolphus of Sweden / Sept 1852 Painted by Henry Pierce Bone from a picture / in the Gallery of the Earl of Craven Combe Abbey / Warwickshire* and repeats the error caused by the misnaming of the oil painting from which it was copied while in the collection of the Earl of Craven. 1998.38 (MIN67)

PROVENANCE: ?H. P. Bone Estate Sale, Christie's, London (13–14 March 1856, lot 142? described as Gustavus Adolphus, as was lot 97); Christie's, London (15 April 1997, lot 145).

EXHIBITION: Royal Academy, London 1854, no. 666.

DESCRIPTION: The subject is shown three-quarter length in armour, with the Order of the Garter and holding a helmet in front of red drapery swag, with fluted column and landscape as a background.

COMMENTARY: The subject, Frederick Henry, was the son of William I of Orange and his wife Louise of Coligny. In 1625, he married Princess Amalia of Solms-Braunfels. Frederick Henry, something of an art collector, ordered that the miniaturist Alexander Cooper be paid 100 florins for a commissioned work in 1645 (Long, 1929, p. 79). Cooper, brother of the famous Samuel, subsequently went to Sweden and was the official limner to Queen Christina. He also received commissions from the King of Denmark and was therefore in a position of influence, directly or indirectly, for other artists working in Sweden

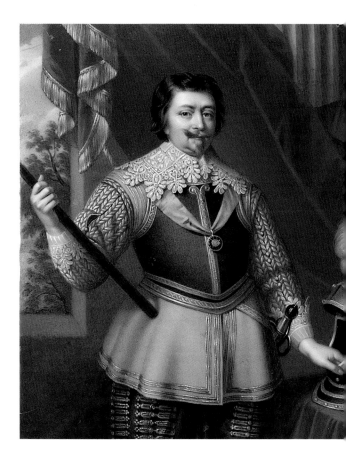

and Denmark, such as Boit and Richter. Thus this much-later work of Henry Pierce Bone celebrates a figure critical in the earlier history of miniature painting. Although Bone's motives were undoubtedly historical, especially as he appears to have misidentified the subject, the viewer can appreciate the added relevance of the true subject to earlier works in this collection.

The error in identifying the subject and the mis-naming of the oil painting was noted by Dr M. Loonstra and M. Tiethoff-Spiethoff of the Orange-Nassau Museum – where a miniature of Frederick Henry after Honthorst exists – and revised by the Hague when the plaque was sold at Christie's in 1997.

WILLIAM BONE SENIOR (FL. ?1810–43)

William Bone Senior, son of Henry Bone, worked with his father and in a similar manner, but with less subtlety of depiction. He exhibited at the Royal Academy 1815–43, but presumably worked at least in his father's studio, if not also on his own, for some time before that. Generally his enamels were copies, but he also worked on ivory including one of his father in front of his gallery with Elizabethan subjects, in the National Portrait Gallery. His works are in other major museum including the Royal Collection, the V&A and the Wallace Collection.

17 *Probably Anne Boleyn*

Attributed to William Bone Senior / ?Studio of Henry Bone
London, c. 1808
Unsigned on front
Enamel on copper, 6.5 × 4.6 cm (2⁹/₁₆ × 1¹³/₁₆ in), rectangular
Set into the cover of a gold and enamel snuffbox.
1996.515 (GB166)

LITERATURE: Truman, 1999, p. 67, cat. no. 40

PROVENANCE: Sotheby's, London (12 February 1981, lot 8); Hakim, London, formerly GB102; sold to Shrubsole; bought back from S. J. Shrubsole on 14 April 1992.

DESCRIPTION: The subject is shown bust-length facing slightly left, with blue bodice, white dress, white-bordered red cap, and a cross at her throat.

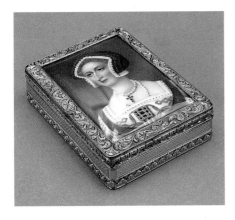

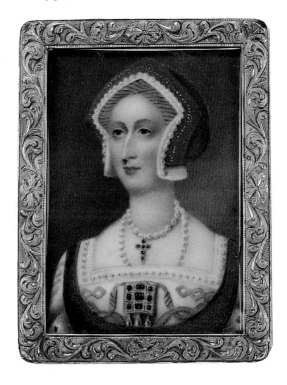

COMMENTARY: Anne Boleyn was married to Henry VIII, as his second wife, in January 1533 and was executed in 1536.

A firm identification of the subject is difficult as the costume type was used for portraits of Henry's other wives as well, and the faces frequently were stylised by subsequent copyists. A miniature of Anne Boleyn (formerly entitled *Catherine of Aragon*) by Lucas Hornebout in the Buccleuch collection (see Lloyd, 1996, p. 32 pl. 5) shows her in similar attire, although not with the cross, which is worn by Jane Seymour in a miniature by Hornebout (see Strong, 1983, p. 41 no. 17). Another miniature of Jane Seymour, somewhat similar to this subject and previously ascribed to Holbein, from the Stowe 1822 sale and exhibited London, 1865, no. 1645, was at Christie's, London (25 July 1967, lot 91 illus.) and described as being by Hornebout.

Given the date of 1808 for the box, this miniature may well have been painted by William Bone, while working in the studio of his father. Certainly, Henry Bone is known to have painted the wives of Henry VIII and some were in his estate sale in 1856.

JACQUES BORDIER (1616–84)

Jacques Bordier was the brother-in-law of the enameller Jean Petitot and worked closely with him. It has been suggested that some of the enamels by Petitot are in fact by both Petitot and Bordier. Bordier was also the Agent of the Council of Geneva at the Court of Versailles from 1668 until his death. Miniatures signed by Bordier's own hand are extremely rare.

18 *The Printer Antoine Vitré in Grey Coat*

Jacques Bordier
Blois, 1651(?)
Signed with monogram and dated, lower right, in gold *JB / 1651* (the last digit hidden under bezel)
Enamel, 4.8 × 3.9 cm (1⁷/₈ × 1⁹/₁₆ in), oval
Mounted since 1852 on an enamelled gold snuff-box, created for this enamel by Alexandre Leferre on behalf of the Court goldsmith Jules Fossin, Paris, for his client Prince Anatole Demidoff
1996.437 (GB86)

PROVENANCE: Godefroy Collection, sold in Paris (1791, for 700 francs); Saint-Martin Collection, sold in Paris (1805 or 1808, for 3,200 francs), then framed '*avec bordure en or à huit pans*'; probably Baron Roger Collection, sold in Paris (17 April 1844); Prince Anatole Demidoff (1812–1870), Paris, by 1852 (on Fossin's box); his nephew, Prince Paul Demidoff (1839–85), Palace of San Donato sale (15 March –10 April 1880, lot 638); James Jackson Jarves, the American art critic; by family tradition, Cornelius Vanderbilt II; Countess Laszlo Széchényi, *née* Gladys Moore Vanderbilt; Mrs A. Talbot Peterson, *née* Countess Széchényi; Sotheby's, Geneva (17 May 1984, lot 297), through S.J. Phillips, London.

LITERATURE: Maze-Sencier, 1885, p. 491; Thieme-Becker, 1909–1951, IV (1910), p. 345; Clouzot, 1924, p. 34; Clouzot, 1925, p. 42 fn. 1; Schneeberger, 1958, p. 128; Schidlof, 1964, I, p. 96; Bénézit, 1976, II, p. 174; Dorival, 1976, II, p. 187, no. 409; *Art at Auction*, 1983–84, p. 216; Truman, 1991, pp. 158–160, no. 52; exhibition catalogue, London, 1994, p. 77.

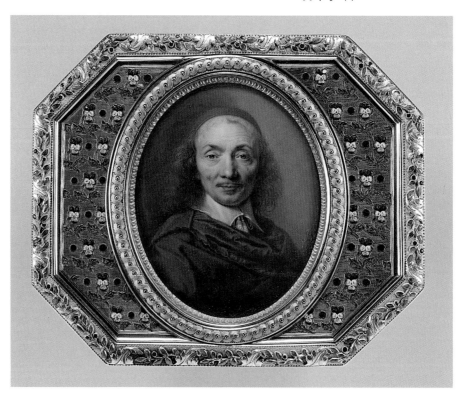

EXHIBITIONS: Los Angeles/Richmond/New York 1986–87, no. 74; Los Angeles/ Memphis 1991–92; Paris, 1998, no. 53.

DESCRIPTION: The sitter bust-length, full face, with dark skull-cap, lawn collar with tassels, and dark silk-lined cloak.

COMMENTARY: Antoine Vitré (1595–1674) acquired the presses of Jacques Duclou in 1616. He was the first printer in Paris to publish a psalter in both Latin and Arabic script. Cardinal Richelieu sponsored Vitré and received from him a polyglot Bible. In 1630, Vitré was appointed printer in oriental languages to the king and later made director of the royal presses. The present enamel was either copied after the now lost oil painting by Philippe de Champaigne or its engraving by Jean Morin after Champaigne, which Dorival (1976) dates to c. 1655 because of the sitter's age of sixty as noted on the print. This date contradicts the date on the miniature. Several explanations are possible: the age date on Morin's print is erroneous or rather approximate; or, if the date of 1651 on the enamel is correct, Bordier's enamel was painted after the oil painting, which may have been painted in 1651 or before; or the last digit on Bordier's enamel, now concealed under the mount, may have been misread in the earlier sale catalogues as 1651 and is indeed a date after 1655. Since it is impossible to unmount the enamel, the question of the correct date will remain unanswered. If the date of 1651 is indeed correct, it is possible to locate the present enamel at Blois where Bordier stayed after his marriage in the same year. Because of the flourishing goldsmiths' and enamellers' workshops at Blois, Bordier would have availed himself of all the technical means to create the present enamel.

Between its sale in the San Donato auction in 1880 and its reappearance on the art market in 1984, this masterwork had become almost legendary. During those mysterious hundred years, authoritative miniature experts such as Clouzot, Schneeberger and Schidlof, none of whom ever saw the present enamel, included it in their articles on Bordier so that the Vitré enamel soon epitomised the finest of Bordier's art. Its justified reputation and superb artistic quality makes it undoubtedly the most important French enamel in the Gilbert Collection, if not in any British public collection.

CONTINENTAL SCHOOL

19 *Field Marshals Prince de Condé and Vicomte de Turenne*

Europe, possibly France, early nineteenth century
Enamels, 4.6 × 3.4 cm (1 $^{13}/_{16}$ × 1 $^{5}/_{16}$ in), ovals
Mounted facing each other on the lid of a rectangular gold snuffbox by John Northam, London, 1817–18
1996.372 (GB1)

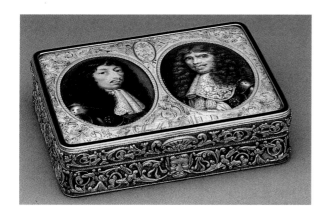

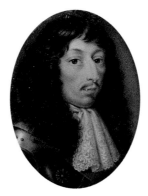 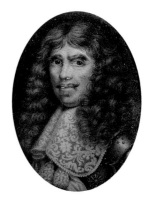

PROVENANCE: Bushell Collection, sold at Parke Bernet Galleries, New York (25–26 January 1963, lot 227); Christie's, London (26 May 1964, lot 64); the Earl of Sefton, Christie's, London (13 November 1973, lot 176); Garrard & Co., London.

EXHIBITIONS: London 1975; Los Angeles/Richmond/New York 1986–87, no. 16.

LITERATURE: Habsburg-Lothringen, 1983, pp. 67–8, no. 31 (identification of sitters inversed); Truman, 1991, pp. 335–7, no. 118 (identification of sitters inversed).

DESCRIPTION: The Prince de Condé, with curly long dark hair, facing right in gold-bordered armour, white lace cravat and blue sash of the Royal French Order of the Holy Ghost; the Vicomte de Turenne, with curly long fair wig, embroidered white lace lawn collar, gold-bordered armour.

COMMENTARY: Louis II, Prince de Condé and Duc d'Enghien (1621–86), known as 'Le Grand Condé', was one of the greatest generals of the seventeenth century. During the Fronde wars he fought on the side of the Fronde, backed by the Duchesse de Montpensier, 'La Grande Mademoiselle', but was pardoned after their defeat by the young King Louis XIV. During the battles of Freiburg im Breisgau (1644) and Nördlingen (1645), he joined forces with the troops of the Vicomte de Turenne.

Henri de la Tour d'Auvergne, Vicomte de Turenne (1611–75), a grandson of William I, Prince of Orange, was sent to the Netherlands at the age of thirteen in order to serve in the army under his uncle, Prince Maurice of Nassau. He subsequently commanded the Imperial forces during the Thirty Years' War. During the Fronde he was opposed to Mazarin's faction, but following his defeat at Rethel by the royal army in 1650, he reverted to the king's cause and later was to command Louis XIV's forces during the king's campaigns in the Low Countries. Turenne conquered Alsace in 1675 and it was during this campaign that he was killed near Sasbach.

Both enamels are copied after engravings by Robert Nanteuil, that of Condé dated 1662 and that of Turenne dated 1665. Habsburg-Lothringen (1983) attributed both enamels to Louis Goullon,

but this attribution cannot be substantiated by comparison with Goullon's other works illustrated in Colding (1991, nos. 80–88) which are all painted in watercolour on parchment and not in enamel.

According to Truman (1991, p. 337), both enamels are taken after Jean Petitot but this appears to be erroneous too. The technique of the two enamels is characteristic of the early nineteenth century, a period when Petitot's works was particularly sought after. It is nevertheless impossible to attribute them to a specific artist. They are probably of French origin.

CONTINENTAL SCHOOL

20 *The King of Rome as a Baby*

Europe, probably France, nineteenth century
Enamel, 3.8 × 3.1 cm (1 1/2 × 1 1/4 in) oval
Mid-nineteenth century gold brooch mount, with crown surmount and base.
1996.815 (MIN49A)

PROVENANCE: Kugel, Paris (September 1994).

EXHIBITION: Portland, 1994–95.

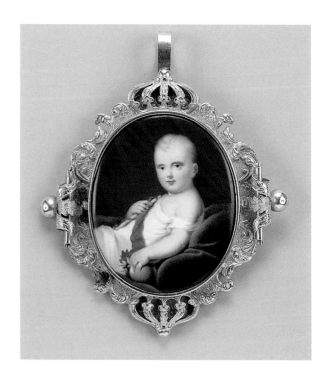

DESCRIPTION: The sitter as an infant, in a white frock with the red sash and cross of the Imperial French Order of the Legion of Honour, holding a gold sceptre and orb, resting on a green velvet cushion, red drapery background.

COMMENTARY: François Joseph Charles Bonaparte, only legitimate son of Emperor Napoleon I of France (with his second wife Archduchess Marie Louise of Austria), was born in Paris in 1811. He was styled King of Rome at birth. During the final stages of the downfall of the Empire in 1814–15, when Napoleon abdicated for the first time, his son was proclaimed Emperor Napoleon II, but, since he had left with his mother, Empress Marie Louise, for Vienna, this was only titular. Excluded from eventual succession to his mother's Italian domains by the Treaty of Paris in 1817, he received the title of Duke of Reichstadt in 1818 from his grandfather, Emperor Francis I of Austria, as compensation. He died of tuberculosis in 1832 at the age of twenty-one at Schönbrunn Castle.

This miniature is a copy after the large-scale oil portrait by Baron François Gérard exhibited at the Paris Salon in 1812, now in the Musée National du Château de Fontainebleau. A copy of Gérard's painting was presented to Napoleon I on the eve of the Battle of Moscow in 1812. The painting proved to be extremely popular and was engraved by A. Desnoyers. Numerous copies in miniature and enamel exist, including an ivory miniature in the Royal Collection (Walker, 1992, p. 432, no. 968) and a fine slightly reduced enamel by Abraham Constantin, signed and dated 1812, with a smaller signed version, sold at Sotheby's, London (25 June 1979, lots 36 and 37).

JEAN-FRANÇOIS FAVRE (1751–1807)

Jean-François Favre, born and brought up in Geneva, was taught drawing by Jacques Saint-Ours and enamelling by Marc Théodore Bourrit. In 1772, Favre left for Paris and entered the studio of the Swiss enameller Charles-Louis Loehr, where he met his compatriot Jaques Thouron. In 1775, Favre and Thouron went into partnership and opened a studio specialising in the enamelling of snuffboxes and jewellery. Soon both artists became well known for their superb enamel portraits, although Favre differed from Thouron in also executing miniatures on ivory and paper. At some point, Favre was obliged to return to Geneva, purportedly for health reasons. His work was continued by his pupils Jean-Rodolphe Gautier and particularly Elizabeth Terroux. Most of Favre's works date from the early 1780s, and only two of his enamels dated after 1790 are recorded. Works by his hand are rare and the only public collections owning portraits by Favre are in the Louvre, the Musée de l'Horlogerie, Geneva and the Société des Arts, Geneva.

21 *Jean-Joseph Mounier*

Jean-François Favre
Paris or Geneva, 1789
Signed and dated, horizontally, mid-right: *Favre / pinxit / 1789*.
Enamel on copper, 5 × 4.2 cm (2 × 1⁵⁄₈ in), oval
Gilt-metal frame with ribbon-twist border
1996.807 (MIN41)

PROVENANCE: Mr Ben-Simon, Paris (in 1923); D.S. Lavender, London (October 1982).

LITERATURE: Clouzot, 1923, p. 58; Clouzot 1924, p. 230; Clouzot 1925, p. 140 (praised as 'superbe'); Hofstetter, 1999, p. 66, illus. p. 67, fig. 83.

EXHIBITION: Paris, 1923, no. 52 (lent by Mr Ben-Simon, Paris).

DESCRIPTION: The sitter is shown bust-length, facing left, wearing a powdered wig, a dark grey

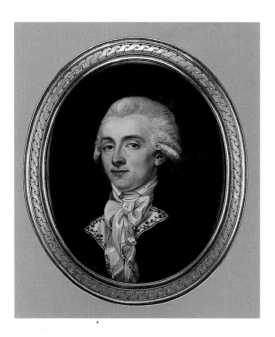

coat, yellow waistcoat with multi-colour embroidered borders, and a knotted white muslin cravat with jabot.

COMMENTARY: Jean-Joseph Mounier (1758–1806), a barrister at the Parlement de Grenoble, was elected as a representative of the Third Estate of the Province of Dauphiné at the States General during the French Revolution of 1789, the year the present miniature was painted. Mounier was responsible for articles I–III of the Declaration of Human Rights. Although Mounier favoured a constitutional monarchy, he was so disappointed by Louis XVI's weakness that he resigned as a deputy in October 1789. He left France for Savoy in 1790 and did not return to Paris from exile until 1801.

The identification of the sitter is supplied by a twentieth-century label glued on the reverse. Nevertheless, the catalogue of the miniatures the 1889 London exhibition (p. 27, case VIII, no. 11, lent by Jeffery Whitehead) listed an enamel miniature by Favre depicting Jean-Pierre Blanchard (1753–1809), the first marine aeronaut, signed and dated in an almost identical way 'Favre pinxt. 1789'. Considering the rarity of Favre's enamels and the recent date of the label, it is possible that both enamels are identical. If the present miniature indeed depicts Mounier, it is almost impossible to locate where it may have been painted. The date of Favre's return to Geneva is unknown, so Mounier

may have sat for Favre either in Paris before his departure or in Geneva on his way to Piedmont.

This expressive portrait is typical of Favre's works. Technically less accomplished than Thouron's enamels, its colourfulness and broad brushstrokes are strongly reminiscent of those of his associate. Favre's main technical characteristics, the thick, almost three-dimensional white heightening of the powdered wig noticed by Schneeberger (1958, p. 169, describing a Favre in the Geneva Museum), is also clearly visible in the present portrait.

FRENCH SCHOOL

22 *The Four Seasons*

Blois or Paris, c. 1630/40
Enamel on gold, 4.8 × 4.2 cm (1⁷⁄₈ × 1⁵⁄₈ in), oval
Two-sided enamelled gold hinged locket pendant, decorated on the lid, reverse and interior of lid, and with the interior of the base in blue opaque enamel
1996.801 (MIN36)

PROVENANCE: D.S. Lavender, London (October 1982).

DESCRIPTION: On the lid, a woman, in gold cape and russet dress with exposed breasts holding bunches of grapes and vine leaves, personifying Autumn, in front of bearded man, personifying Winter, in gold helmet and purple cape, with house and trees in background; on the reverse, two half-dressed female figures, one, with a garland of flowers in her hair, holding a bouquet, personifying Spring, the other, with ears of corn in her hair and holding a sickle, personifying Summer; on the interior of the lid, two peasant figures in a landscape with a lamb.

COMMENTARY: Although it has been fashionable to attribute all early French seventeenth-century enamelled watchcases and lockets to the Blois workshops, Dr Hans Boeckh from Geneva has pointed out that they may just as well have been produced in the workshops of the Paris goldsmiths and enamellers of the Louis XIII period. The present example, with its orangey-brownish colouring and

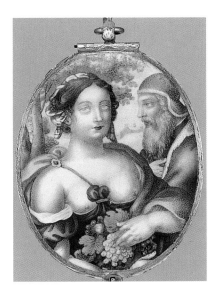

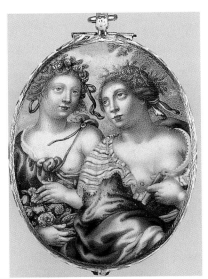

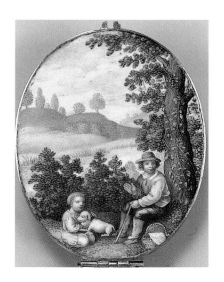

figures reminiscent of Vouet is a work characteristic of this early type of enamelling.

23 *A Young Lady in a Blue Dress*

Probably Paris or Geneva, second quarter of the nineteenth century
Enamel, 3 × 2.6 cm (1⁷/₈ × 1 in), oval
Signed by Johann Christian Neuber, c. 1775/80.
Later mounted on the cover of an oval Saxon gold and hardstone snuffbox
1996.433 (GB81)

PROVENANCE: Viscount Bearsted, M.C. (in 1938); with S.J. Phillips, London (1976).

LITERATURE: Norton/Norton, 1938, pp. 108–9, pl. 40; González-Palacios, 1977, no. 22; González-Palacios, Roettgen, 1982, no. 22; Habsburg-Lothringen, 1983, pp. 81–2, no. 39; Truman, 1991, pp. 229–31, no. 78; Massinelli, 2000, p. 149, no. 58.

EXHIBITIONS: London, 1968, no. 23; London, 1975; Los Angeles, 1977; Atlanta, 1977; San Antonio, 1978; Richmond, 1978; Seattle, 1979; Los Angeles/Richmond/New York 1986–87, no. 35; San Francisco, 1996.

DESCRIPTION: The sitter facing left in low-cut blue dress, with white underslip adorned with pearls and jewelled clasps, pearls in curled long hair and around neck.

COMMENTARY: Many errors have been made in attempting to establish both the date of the miniature and the identity of the sitter. Although it has previously been believed that it belonged to the Louis XIV period, it dates manifestly from the second quarter of the nineteenth century, a period when the production of enamels in the style of Petitot for commercial purposes became very popular in France and in Geneva.

The almost invisible brushstrokes and smooth technique, made possible by the technical advances in enamelling in the nineteenth century, and the sweet features of the sitter confirm this late date. The identification of the sitter by Norton/(Norton

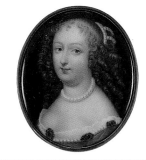

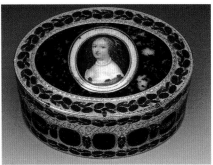

around a red heart centred by a skull and cross bones
1996.783 (MIN18)

PROVENANCE: Countess Charlotte Sophie Bentinck, daughter and heiress of Count Anton II von Aldenburg and Princess Wilhelmine von Hesse-Homburg, married in 1633 to William, 1st Count Bentinck of Rhoon and Pendrecht in the Netherlands and Terrington St Clements in Norfolk; their eldest son, Christian Frederick Anton, Count Bentinck, husband of Marie Catharine van Tuyll van Serooskerken; by descent to Timothy Bentinck; the sale of his family miniatures, Sotheby's, London (30 June 1980, lot 218, as German School, c. 1680); S.J. Phillips, London (1980).

DESCRIPTION: The sitter three-quarters to the right, with long brown wig, armour with red bow cravat.

(1938, pp. 108–9, pl. 40) as Queen Henrietta Maria (1609–69), consort of Charles I, has to be rejected because of a clash between the period of the fashion displayed in the miniature, corresponding to c. 1660, and the age of Henrietta Maria at that date. There is furthermore a total lack of resemblance with other accepted contemporary portraits of her. Truman (1991, p. 229, 230) erroneously identified the sitter as Charlotte Aglaé, Mademoiselle de Valois (1700–61), without indicating his sources. Over sixty years separate the fashion of the clothes in the miniature from the earliest possible date in the life of Mademoiselle de Valois. Again, the features bear no resemblance to those seen in accepted portraits of her. It has not been possible to find the original portrait after which this enamel is copied.

COMMENTARY: Considering the naive, rather stiff representation of the sitter, this miniature may have been painted by a German artist during the third quarter of the seventeenth century. The coronet on the reverse identifies the sitter as a German prince, which is confirmed by the provenance which is the same as for cat. no. 1. The sitter may be a member of the Hesse family, although the close relations of Landgrave Charles (see cat. no. 1) can be excluded because of the lack of resemblance to their published portraits.

GERMAN SCHOOL

24 *A Nobleman with Red Bow*

Germany, c. 1660
Enamel, 2.7 × 2.2 cm (1 1/16 × 7/8 in), oval
Gold and black enamel rim frame, with clasp reverse showing heraldic back with black spiral torsade around, the reverse enamel with the coronet of a German Prince and motto *Les morts y sont vivants*

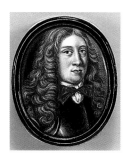

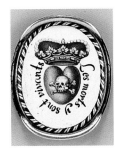

HORACE HONE (1754–1825)

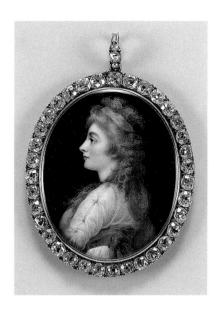

Horace Hone was born in London, the second son of miniaturist Nathaniel Hone, who was also his teacher. He entered the Royal Academy Schools in 1770, exhibited at the Royal Academy in 1772–1822 and was elected ARA in 1779. He went to Dublin, where he practised from 1782 to 1804, when he returned to London after the union of England and Ireland. In 1795 he became miniature painter to the Prince of Wales. He painted in both watercolour on ivory and enamel as well as doing engravings. In 1778 he exhibited in a frame nine portraits in miniature; those set for bracelets in enamel are at the Royal Academy. How much of a role mental illness played in his output is unclear although he continued to exhibit at the Royal Academy until 1822.

His work can be seen in major museums, including the V&A and the Royal Collection.

25 *Georgiana, Duchess of Devonshire*

Horace Hone, after Angelica Kauffman or Jean Guérin
London, 1812
Inscription on counter enamel *Georgiana / Duchess of Devonshire / Born June 9. 1757 / Horace Hone ARA / Pintx. 1812 / London.*
Enamel on copper, 4.3 × 3.6 cm (1^{11}/$_{16}$ × 1^7/$_{16}$ in), oval
Oval gold-rim frame with border of diamonds
1998.23 (MIN61)

PROVENANCE: Sotheby's, London (9 June 1994, lot 4); S.J. Phillips, London (June 1996).

EXHIBITION: Portland 1996–97.

DESCRIPTION: The Duchess is shown bust-length, facing in profile to the left, with golden hair and blue and white dress.

COMMENTARY: Painting this after Georgiana's death, Hone used a Guérin miniature (now in the Wallace Collection) or a subsequent engraving of 'the Two Duchesses' as the source. Like Hurter with the earlier miniature of the same subject (see cat. no. 29), Hone extracted the image of Georgiana from a more elaborate composition – this representation of her with her close friend Lady Elizabeth Foster, later the Second Duchess of Devonshire, holding a basket. Guérin recorded painting them at Passy, Paris, on 12 November 1791, in his journal. A version is cited as 'formerly in the collection of Miss Clifton' which 'identifies the sitters in Lady Elizabeth Foster's own hand' on the reverse' (Reynolds, 1980, cat. no. 137, pp. 168–9). Hone, in isolating the Duchess, creates a striking portrait of her at the height of her beauty. In the Burlington exhibition, 1889, there was a miniature of Lady Elizabeth Foster by Hone, signed by the Duke of Devonshire (London, 1889, p. 128, case XL).

JEAN-PIERRE (1655–1723) AND/OR AMI HUAUT (1657–1724)

Jean-Pierre Huaut and/or Ami (also Amy) Huaut (also spelt Huaud or Huault), born in Geneva, were the two younger sons and pupils of Pierre I Huaut and the younger brothers of Pierre II Huaut (see cat. no. 27). The two younger brothers set up in partnership in 1682, which lasted for six years, but they remained together throughout their careers. When their elder brother returned from Berlin, they were sent as replacements and became painters to the Brandenburg court, executing enamelled watch-cases, enamel portraits and allegories, as well as watercolour miniatures on parchment and ivory. They left Berlin to return to Geneva in 1700, two years after the death of their elder brother Pierre II Huaut. Their output was considerable and their works are much more common than those of their father or elder brother. Whereas Jean-Pierre signed pieces on his own, mainly as *Huaut le puîné* or *Huaut le puisné*, no piece signed by Ami alone is recorded.

26 *Jupiter and Antiope*

Jean-Pierre Huaut and/or Ami Huaut
Geneva, c. 1700/15
Signed on the counter enamel *Huaut p*
Enamel, 4.5 × 6.5 cm (1³/₄ × 2⁹/₁₆ in), rectangular
Rectangular French early nineteenth-century *rever-bère* frame with glazed back to show signature
1996.798 (MIN33)

PROVENANCE: S.J. Phillips, London (6 October 1982).

DESCRIPTION: Jupiter, as a satyr, unveiling the naked Antiope who lies asleep on a blue drape with Cupid and two doves in a landscape.

COMMENTARY: Antiope, a nymph or, according to some, the wife of a king of Thebes, was surprised by Jupiter in the form of a satyr while she was asleep and was ravished by him (Ovid, *Metamorphoses* 6:110–111). As in the present case, this myth was frequently used for the portrayal of the female nude. This plaque may originally have been intended as a cover for a *nécessaire*, a casket or a box. After their return from Berlin, the Huaud Brothers started the mass-production of colourful enamel plaques depicting mythological or erotic scenes and the present plaque is a characteristic example of their output. Its short signature is relatively rare; when working together, the brothers signed '*fratres Huauts pinxerunt*' or '*les deux frères Huaut*' with numerous longer variants. The possibility that the present piece is by the hand of Ami Huaut on his own cannot be excluded.

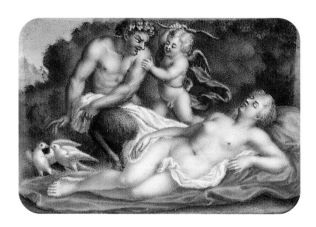

PIERRE II HUAUT (1647–98)

Pierre II Huaut or Huaud or Huault was the eldest of the three sons of the Geneva enameller Pierre I Huaut. In 1685, he left Geneva for Berlin, returning to his home town one year later. He was appointed miniature painter to Elector Frederick III of

Brandenburg (later Frederick I, first King of Prussia) on 19 September 1691. Pierre II Huaud died seven years later. It has been generally accepted that his talent was superior to that of both his father and his two younger brothers Jean-Pierre and Ami

Huaut (see cat. no.26). He painted miniatures both in watercolour and body colour on vellum, portraits and scenes in enamel and decorated numerous enamelled watchcases with mythological and religious scenes. Enamels by his hand are to be found in the Louvre and the Musée du Petit-Palais, Paris, the Schweizerisches Landesmuseum, Zurich, the Musée de l'Horlogerie, Geneva, the Museum for Applied Arts, Frankfurt, and in the Hermitage, St Petersburg.

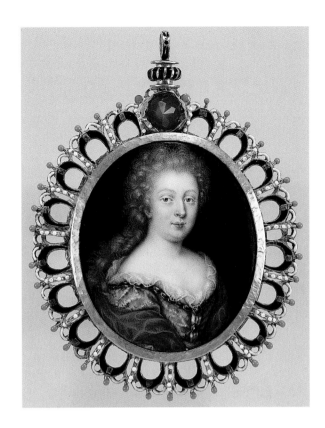

27 *A Lady with a Blue Cloak*

Pierre II Huaut
Geneva, 1688
The counter enamel signed, located and dated *petrus Huaud. major–natus / pinxit Geneuæ / 1688*
 Enamel on gold, 4.1 × 3.6 cm (1⅝ × 1⁷⁄₁₆ in), oval
Contemporary, but not necessarily original oval gold frame with arched openwork border, enamelled in black, blue and white
1996.810 (MIN44)

PROVENANCE: According to an early handwritten notice with photograph in the 'Pierre II Huaut' file (folder 87) of the Witt Library, London: 'S. Richards Collection, Nottingham. H.I. Collection, no. 889. Frame Collection, Boulton, sold 12 December 1911, lot 77. Henry Walters Collection, Baltimore, sold 6 March 1913.' Substantiated provenance: Mrs Henry Walters, New York; the sale of her estate, Parke-Bernet Galleries, New York (30 November to 4 December 1943, lot 791, erroneously as by Johann Peter Huault); Sotheby's, New York (24 June 1987, lot 250).

DESCRIPTION: The sitter bust-length turned towards the right, with long curling greyish fair hair, wearing a grey and yellow dress and blue cloak.

COMMENTARY: According to a note in the Witt Library, the miniature was thought to represent Louise Henriette of Orange-Nassau, the first wife of the 'Great Elector' Frederick William of Brandenburg. This identification must be disregarded in view of the complete lack of resemblance and the dates of this princess (1627–67)

in contrast to the date of the miniature.

Another version of this portrait, identically signed, located and dated, was formerly in the Ströhlin-Bordier Collection, Geneva. It is in now in the Musée de l'Horlogerie, Geneva (illustrated in Schneeberger, 1958, p. 107, fig. 24, and in Schidlof, 1964, III, pl. 298, no. 587, and in Gauthey, 1975, p. 13, no. 6).

The existence of two versions may suggest that the sitter is either a person of social importance or a friend or relative of Pierre II Huaud. It might be assumed that the sitter is Swiss, because of the address *Genevae* (Latin for 'in Geneva'), but this is not conclusive. Indeed, all the four Huauds copied extensively after other paintings and the sitter may well be a foreign princess who had commissioned Pierre II Huaud to execute a copy in enamel of a vellum miniature, a small oil portrait or even a print. The signature on the present enamel is char-acter-istic of Pierre II Huaud. He always used the words '*major natus*' or '*l'aisné* or '*l'ainé* to distinguish his works from those of his two younger brothers who had to sign '*Les frères Huaud*' or, for Jean-Pierre alone, '*Huaud le puisné* or '*Huaud le puîné*. Indeed, the present miniature shows Pierre II Huaud at his best. Painted during Huaud's 'sabbatical' from service at the Elector's court at Berlin, it displays the whole colour range of his palette, with a beautiful, natural rendering of the sitter's curly hair and opulent clothing.

CARL RUDOLPH HURTER (1768–91?)

Carl Rudolph (Charles Ralph) Hurter was born in Berne when his father, Johann Heinrich Hurter, was there in 1768. He accompanied him to London and entered the Royal Academy in 1781, aged thirteen. The following year, he won a silver medal for portrait drawing at the Society of Arts. His first enamel is now in the Museum zu Allerheiligen, Schaffhausen, Switzerland. It is of George, Prince of Wales, after a 1781 painting by Gainsborough, which was exhibited at the Royal Academy in 1782 and engraved by John Raphael Smith in 1783. It is inscribed '*Goerge* [sic] *Prince of Wales Painted by his first/attemp before/he was 15 years/ of age 1783*' (Hofstetter, 1999, p. 51, fig 66). During this latter period exemplified by the following miniature, his work shows the increased influence of English miniaturists – such as the use of the skys a background.

After a trip with his father to Karlsruhe in 1786, he returned, exhibiting at the Royal Academy from 1787 to 1789, and worked until at least 1791. The date of 1791 is the last found on miniatures by Carl Hurter, but his death date is unknown. If the miniatures in the Burlington 1889 exhibition described as by '*JFC Hurter*' are by C.R. Hurter, then he profited greatly from his father's patronage by the Earl of Dartrey. However, it seems more likely that the script of his father's, initials '*JH*' has been misread.

28 *A Man*

Carl Ralph (Charles Rudolph) Hurter
England, 1791
Signed and dated on counter enamel *C. Hurter pinx*, *1791.*

Enamel on copper, 4.0 × 3.1 cm (1⁹/₁₆ × 1¹/⁴ in), oval Oval two-colour gold pendant and open reverse and with foliate scrolls on matte ground
1996.793 (MIN28)

PROVENANCE: Victor and Paula Zuckerkandl, Berlin, sale, Wawra, Vienna (7–8 May 1928, no. 82); D.S. Lavender, London (1981).

LITERATURE: Schidlof, 1964 (vol. I, p. 387); Hofstetter, 1999, p. 62, fig. 67, illus.

DESCRIPTION: The man is shown with powdered hair and a blue jacket, with slightly golden sky as background

COMMENTARY: Schidlof (*Supra*) describes this miniature as 'typical'.

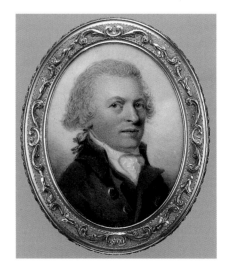

JOHANN HEINRICH HURTER (1734–99)

Johann Heinrich Hurter was born in Schaffhausen. He started his career in Geneva and Berne as an enamel painter, miniaturist and pastellist. From 1768 to 1770 he was working in Berne, according to Foskett, then, at Liotard's suggestion, went to Versailles, where he met with little success, and thence to the Hague in 1772, where he was a member of the painters guild. He settled in London around 1777. Lord Dartrey (Thomas Dawson, 1725–1803) was Hurter's major patron. The family, to this day, own the largest number of Hurter miniatures, although three of his masterpieces, a self-portrait of 1780 and portraits of Lord and Lady Dartrey, are now in the Museum zu Allerheiligen, Schaffenhausen (Hofstetter, 1999, pp. 60–3, 80, illus. no. 68, 69).

Hurter exhibited at the Royal Academy from 1779–81 and was reputedly appointed a court painter, although no documents confirm this. He did however do a number of enamel portraits of George IV, Queen Charlotte and some of their children (see Walker, 1992, p. 121–4.) In 1785 he was back in Schaffhausen and travelled to London and the Continent frequently until his death in 1789. In about 1780, he founded a mathematical and scientific instrument factory in London which he announced in a pamphlet (Schnetzler, 1981, p. 100). He then divided his time between England and the Continent, although in 1787 he received a large commission from Catherine the Great for fifteen enamels with ormolu frames. He was enobled in 1789 in Dusseldorf by the Elector Charles Theodore, becoming *Reichsfreiherr*. He executed both original enamels and copies of existing portraits.

His works are represented in major museums, including the Metropolitan and the Royal Collection.

29 *Georgiana Spencer, Duchess of Devonshire*

Johann Heinrich Hurter, after Angelica Kauffman (1741–1807)
England, 1779
Signed *HHurter* (conjoined) and dated on front, lower right, signed and dated on counter enamel
Enamel on copper, 5.5 × 4.6 cm (2³⁄₁₆ × 1¹³⁄₁₆ in), oval

Frame with paper on reverse in original pressed gilt-metal frame with husk and ribbon decoration (Hurter frame); collection tag 'Spencer Collection, no. E17'; paper on reverse reads, *Georgiana Duchess of Devonshire / Eldest daughter to John Earl Spencer* 1996.778 (MIN13)

PROVENANCE: Christie's, Geneva (13 May 1980, lot 253).

EXHIBITION: South Kensington, 1865, no. 953 (p. 78, wallcase J 953, 'Georgiana Duchess of Devonshire, Eldest daughter of John Earl Spencer, signed and dated 'H. Hurter, ft 1779' enamel H. Hurter) lent by Earl Spencer'.

DESCRIPTION: The sitter is three-quarters right, wearing a mauve ribbon in her blonde hair and a light yellow dress.

COMMENTARY: Apparently painted five years later, the Duchess is shown as she appeared the year of

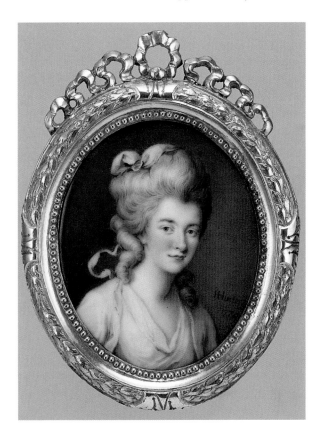

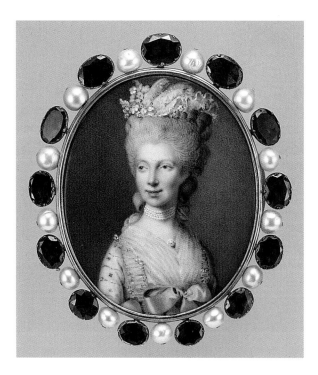

30 Queen Charlotte

Johann Heinrich Hurter, after Gainsborough
England, 1781
Signed and inscribed on counter enamel, *Charlotte Queen / of Great Britain / from the original picture / by Gainsborough / J.H. Hurter pinxit 1781*
Enamel on copper, 5.5 × 4.6 cm (2³/₁₆ × 1¹³/₁₆ in), oval
Gold rim frame with foil-backed rubies and pearls lead-soldered on to frame
1996.799 (MIN34)

PROVENANCE: S.J. Phillips, London (2 October, 1982).

DESCRIPTION: The sitter is shown bust-length, with high-piled white wig and a white dress and hat.

COMMENTARY: Queen Charlotte (1774–1818) was the youngest daughter of Prince Charles, and niece of the reigning Duke Adolphus Frederick III of Mecklenburg-Strelitz. Consort of George III, whom she married in 1761, two weeks before their coronation. Charlotte produced fifteen children, all but two of whom survived infancy.

An almost identical miniature with darker background, of 1782, was sold at Christie's, London (14 October 1998, lot 24, ex. collection David-Weill, no. 4070); Clore Collection sale (17 March 1986, lot 194); another version was sold at Sotheby's (7 May, 1956, lot 40). Another was with Wartski (London, 1971, no. 85, illus.). A smaller rendition, probably by Hurter, is in the Royal Collection (Walker, 1992, p. 124, no. 242 illus.). Hurter's miniature of George III after Gainsborough, painted in 1781, is also in the Royal Collection (Walker 1992, no. 236, p. 121, illus.). The Burlington Fair Arts Club exhibition of 1889 also exhibited a Queen Charlotte enamel, 'after Gainsborough by JFC Hurter lent by the Earl of Dartrey', Hurter's great patron (London, 1889, p. 9, case III, no. 18). Although the catalogue uses the correct 'J.H. Hurter' as the artist of another enamel three items later, the former is obviously by J.H. Hurter too. The 'F.C.' may come from a misreading of a script 'H'. An enamel of George III signed and dated on the reverse *J H Hurter p:1781* was exhibited in Edinburgh in 1965 (collection Earl of Beauchamp).

her marriage to the 5th Duke of Devonshire in 1774.

Two slightly different versions of this miniature exist. They are taken from a full-scale group portrait in the Spencer Collection at Althorp, entitled 'John Lord Althorp with his sisters', 1774, by Angelica Kauffman (Roworth, 1992, p. 107 fig 90, p. 211 list of illustrations). It depicts John, afterwards 2nd Lord Spencer, Georgiana, Duchess of Devonshire and her sister Harriet, Countess of Bessborough, from which Hurter has extracted the head and the shoulders. The other version has the head slightly higher and more at an angle, and has a slightly more *décolleté* dress nearer the bottom edge of the enamel. This version, also signed and dated 1775, is in the Museum Briner und Kern, Winterthur, Switzerland, inventory no. BXVI, and was sold at Sotheby's, Monaco (25 June 1976, lot 384). Another example, signed and dated on the counter enamel, *J Hurter, 1780*, was exhibited in Edinburgh, 1965 cat. no. 396, from the collection of the Earl Beauchamp. The husk and ribbon frames on both versions are extremely similar (the other version has a flat hook). This would suggest that Hurter either made the frames or at least supplied them with the miniatures. Other miniatures by Hurter in the Earl of Dartrey's Collection share these frames.

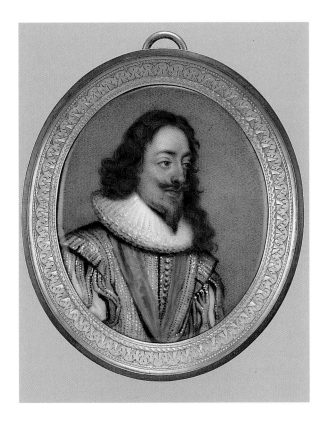

31 *Charles I*

Johann Heinrich Hurter, after Daniel Van Mytens
and Anthony Van Dyck (Royal Collection)
England, 1786
Signed, inscribed and dated on counter enamel
*Charles I. ier Roy. / d Angleterre / peint d'aprés le Tabl:
original / du Chev: van Dyck. au Palais / de Kinsington*
[sic] *par / J.H. Hurter / 1786*
Enamel on copper, 5.8 × 4.9 cm (2⁵/₁₆ × 1¹⁵/₁₆ in),
oval
In oval ormolu frame; inscriptions
1996.820 (MIN52)

PROVENANCE: Au Vieux Paris (3 November 1994).

EXHIBITION: Portland, 1994–95.

LITERATURE: Schidlof, 1964, p. 400.

DESCRIPTION: Charles I bust-length with wavy
auburn hair, moustache, and small beard, white ruff,
grey jacket with blue sash, blue background.

COMMENTARY: Charles I reigned from 1625 to 1649,
when he was beheaded. During his reign, he was
the patron of many Continental artists, including
Anthony van Dyck and Jean Petitot. The painting in
the Royal Collection on which this is based is now
attributed to Daniel van Mytens with additions by
Van Dyck (exhibition catalogue, London, 1999, pp.
14–15, fig. 15, 1630–32). A similar smaller miniature
in the Royal Collection attributed to Hurter
(Walker, 1992, no. 241, p. 123–4, illus.) is based on
Van Dyck's double portrait of Charles I and
Henrietta Maria, in the Archbishop's Palace at
Kremsier (Millar, 1963, fig. 14), also known through
several engravings. In the Burlington 1889 exhibition (p. 10, case II, no. 38), there was an enamel of
Charles I from the collection of the Earl of Dartrey
stated to be 'after C. Jansen by JFC Hurter' (both
'JH' and 'JFC' appear with Hurter's name in this
catalogue, but both seem to refer to the same
person, as the 'JFC' may be a misreading of 'JH'
conjoined script). A pair of enamels by Hurter of
Charles I and Henrietta Maria, signed and dated
1783, after paintings in the Royal Collection were
sold at Sotheby's, London (25 November 1952, lot
100, from the Dudley Collection). In that version
the King is shown in armour.

CARL CHRISTIAN KANZ (1758–AFTER 1818)

Born in Plauen, Carl Christian Kanz arrived in Paris
from Germany in the late 1770s and became a pupil
at the Académie Royale of Paris in 1778. He exhibited at the Paris Salon in 1808. Whereas his portraits of male sitters are extremely rare, over 90 per
cent of his ivory and enamel miniatures depict
scantily dressed young ladies. This prolific artist
specialised in what he called '*têtes d'étude*' or '*têtes
d'expression*' – concentrating not so much on the
heads but on the voluptuous bosoms of his models.

It may be assumed that these technically highly accomplished pictures were erotic fantasies rather than portraits of 'real' people. Even Tsar Alexander I of Russia is said to have acquired two of Kanz's works. Enamels by Kanz can be found in the Louvre, the Musée des Arts Décoratifs, Bordeaux and the Metropolitan.

cape, white muslin dress, grey-brown background.

COMMENTARY: A larger enamel by Kanz depicting another woman with similar hair style was in the David-Weill and Sir Charles Clore Collections, part II, sold at Sotheby's, London (10 November 1986, lot 124). This enamel is a characteristic, although rather restrained, specimen of Kanz's artistic output during the last years of the eighteenth century, mixing the sweetness of Greuze's expression with a classical imitation of Jacques-Louis David's style.

33 *A Young Lady with Bare Bosom*

Carl Christian Kanz
Paris, c. 1800/05
Signed, lower right *Kanz*.
Enamel on copper, 11.7 × 9.7 cm (4⅝ × 3¹³/₁₆ in), oval
Engine-turned gold-rim frame
1996.791 (MIN26)

PROVENANCE: D.S. Lavender, London (October 1980).

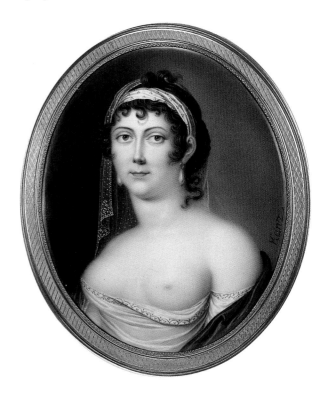

32 *A Young Lady with Purple Drape*

Carl Christian Kanz
Paris, c. 1790/95
Signed, lower right *Kanz*.
Enamel on copper, 6.8 × 5.6 cm (2¹¹/₁₆ × 2³/₁₆ in), oval
Rectangular cast ormolu frame, with *guilloché* border and concave corners
1996.816 (MIN49B)

PROVENANCE: Kugel, Paris (September 1994).

EXHIBITIONS: Portland, 1994–95.

DESCRIPTION: The sitter with blue and white stones in long brown hair, purple and jewelled tie to rose

DESCRIPTION: The sitter half-length, with gold-figured white scarf and veil in dark curling hair, turning slightly to the left, wearing a gold-bordered white dress, revealing her bosom, and plum-coloured shawl.

COMMENTARY: This impressive piece is one of Kanz's largest enamels and must have been a technical *tour de force*. It is also a relatively late work, only post-dated by a similar circular enamel in the Musée des Arts Décoratifs, Bordeaux. Whereas Kanz's *têtes d'expression* of the late nineteenth century display a certain charm, his enamels from the Empire period often have a cold and impersonal quality, despite their technical accomplishment.

J.M. KHAETSCHER (KAETSCHER)

No biographical details about J. M. Khaetscher are known. His signature is sometimes found on the counter enamels of portraits mainly depicting members of the family of Elector John William of Palatinate during the late seventeenth to the early eighteenth centuries. The collection of family miniatures of the Palatine Electors, now kept by the Bayerisches Nationalmuseum, Munich, includes several works by this talented enameller.

34 *An Elector with Red Bow*

J.M. Khaetscher
Germany, probably Düsseldorf, c. 1690–95
Enamel on gold, 3.1 × 2.5 cm (1 1/4 × 1 in), oval
Original contemporary silver-gilt and rose-diamond studded frame, pendant from a rose-diamond-studded Electoral crown with loop, traces of red enamel on the Palatinate crown
1996.803 (MIN38)

PROVENANCE: Sotheby's, Geneva (11 November 1981, lot 203, unillustrated, erroneously as by the Huaud brothers, c. 1660); D.S. Lavender, London (October 1982).

DESCRIPTION: Sitter in armour, wearing white lace jabot with red ribbons on either side of long curly blond wig.

COMMENTARY: A variant, also unidentified, showing the same sitter wearing a blue bow, is illustrated in Schaffers-Bodenhausen/Tiethoff-Spliethoff (1993,

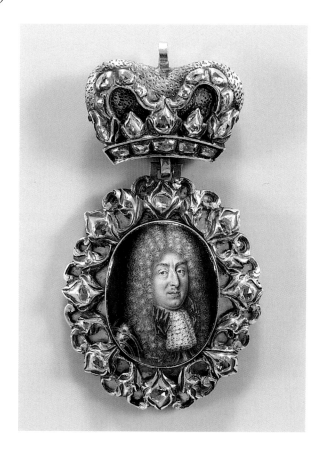

p. 422, no. 589). It is attributed to Khaetscher c. 1680, and an old identification as Rüdiger Starhemberg has been rejected.

Schaffers-Bodenhausen Tiethoff-Spliethoff mention as a 'companion piece' a portrait of Elector John William of Palatinate, also by Khaetscher.

Three facts may give hints as to the identification of the sitter:

1. The sitter must be an Elector because of the original jewelled silver-gilt frame with the enamelled Elector's hat. Very few of these original pendants have survived; a similar one, depicting Palatine Elector John William, was sold at Hôtel Drouot, Paris (10/11 November 1985, lot 100).

2. The fact that the variant of our miniature is to represent a 'companion piece' to that of Palatinate Elector John William may suggest that the sitter is related to John William, possibly his father and predecessor Philip William – a potential identification rejected by Karen Schaffers-Bodenhausen of the Iconografisch Bureau, The Hague.

3. The artist, Khaetscher, was extensively employed by Elector John William of Palatinate, so the sitter may well represent a family member (again possibly John William's father Philip William).

The present miniature, like the variant in the collections of the House of Orange-Nassau, distinctly shows Khaetscher's traits: the curly blond wig, a fine brushstroke and a yellowish look.

Jean-Etienne Liotard (1702–89)

Born in Geneva the son of a French Protestant jeweller, Liotard studied first with enameller Daniel Gardelle in Geneva. Liotard's first known enamel is a watchcase cited by Schneeberger (1958, p. 146). He also produced a plaque of Diana and Endymion between 1720 and 1723 (Boeckh, 1989, p. 120–1) which was more typical of the Geneva style of enamel snuffbox panels than his later work would suggest. From 1725, he worked under J.B. Massé in Paris. Starting in 1735, he travelled extensively in Italy, where he met Sir William Ponsonby (later Lord Bessborough) and travelled with him to Constantinople, where he stayed five years. There he adopted the Turkish fashion, which he used in some of his portraits. He went to Vienna in 1743, and between 1745 and 1747 was in Venice, Darmstadt, Lyons and Geneva, before spending five years in Paris. He was in England several times between 1753 and 1774 and exhibited at the Royal Academy in 1773–4. He had important patrons, including the Princess of Wales, as he was one of the best miniaturists of his era. He painted miniatures on ivory and in enamel and did portraits in pastel and oil and drawings. It was the pastels which were exhibited at the Royal Academy. The individuality of the subjects is made more vivid by the striking colouration of his enamels, which, unlike many of the pastels, have not faded. An enamel of George III, on gold, dated 1754, is in the Orange-Nassau Collection (Schaffers-Bodenhausen/Tiethoff-Spliethoff, 1993, p. 207, no. 193).

His works are represented in major museums, including the Musée de l'Horlogerie, Geneva, and the Royal Collection.

35 *John, First Earl Spencer*

Jean Etienne Liotard
London, England, c. 1755
No signature on face
Enamel on copper, 4.4 × 3.3 cm (1³/₄ × 1⁵/₁₆ in), oval
Mounted in carved ivory snuffbox with gold

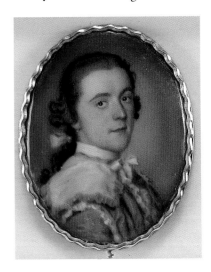

mounts, London c. 1750; no. X567 in Spencer
inventory (Strong Room)
1996.485 (GB137)

PROVENANCE: Spencer family collection, S.J.
Phillips, London (2 November 1988).

LITERATURE: Truman, 1991, cat. 4, pp. 38–39;
Connoisseur, January 1937, XCIX, 425, p. 33.

DESCRIPTION: Shown three-quarters to the right,
wearing blue and white jacket, brown hair in bow-
tied tail and *en queue*, grey background.

COMMENTARY: The subject married Georgiana
Poyntz in 1755 and was created in 1761 Baron
Spencer of Althorp, and Viscount Spencer and
advanced to the Viscountcy of Althorp and Earldom
of Spencer in 1765. They had three children, one of
whom, Georgiana (see cat. nos. 29, 25), the elder
daughter, married William 5th Duke of Devonshire.
This miniature and one by Liotard of Georgiana,
Countess Spencer, were illustrated as nos. VI and V

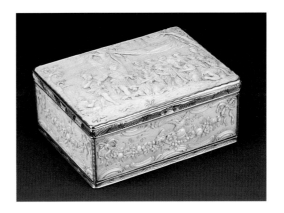

in *Connoisseur* in 1937, when they were listed as
being in the Spencer Collection, Althorp. The same
miniatures are in the Witt photo archive (B58/542),
are also listed as being in the collection of Lord
Spencer, Althorp. They were not part of the published *List of Pictures at Althorp, Northamptonshire* of
1831, but only a few enamels were listed, and as this
one was on a box it might not have been considered
with the other pictures. The one of Georgiana
Poyntz, signed and dated 1754, is now in Geneva,
at the Musée de l'Horlogerie, (inv. no. AD3721).

CIRCLE OF JEAN-ABRAHAM LISSIGNOL (1749–1819)

Jean-Abraham Lissignol was born in Geneva. He
was a pupil of Jean-Marc Roux, and painted in
watercolour on both ivory miniatures and enamels.
He is best known for his very finely painted enamel
plaques decorating gold snuffboxes, depicting
mythological or historical scenes. The fine quality
of the present enamel is quite close to his works,
although, by the early nineteenth century, many
other Geneva enamellers had reached this degree of
technical accomplishment.

36 *Nessus and Deianeira*

Circle of Jean-Abraham Lissignor (1749–1819)
Geneva, c. 1800
Enamel on copper, 5.1 × 4.4 cm (2 × 1³/₄ in),
rectangular
Rectangular gold frame, originally to be fitted into a
box top, later mounted as a brooch

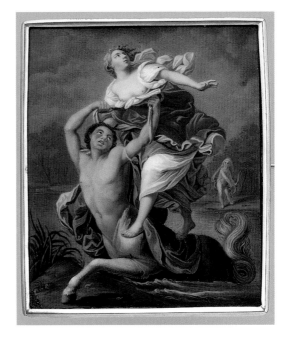

1996.812 (MIN46)

PROVENANCE: Christie's, New York (27 April 1992, lot 59).

DESCRIPTION: The triumphant Centaur Nessus carrying Deianeira, the wife of Hercules, with Hercules in the background on the other bank of the river.

COMMENTARY: This is after Guido Reni's large oil on canvas painting in the Louvre, painted in about 1621 for Ferdinando Gonzaga, Duke of Mantua, later in the collections of Charles I of England and Louis XIV of France (Brejon de Lavergnée Thiébaut, 1981, II, p. 226, inv. 537 and also Pepper, 1988, p. 246, no. 67, colour pl. VII). Ovid's *Metamorphoses* (9:101–133) relates how, on a journey, Hercules and his wife Deianeira came to a river where the Centaur Nessus was the ferryman. While carrying Deianeira across the waterway, Nessus tried to ravish her. Hercules drew his bow and slew Nessus. The Centaur, knowing that his blood was now poisoned with the Hydra's gall from Hercules' arrow, cunningly told Deianeira with his dying words to collect it, as it would one day serve as a love potion. Later, jealous Deianeira sent a messenger to Hercules with the poisoned gift which finally killed her husband.

Guido Reni's painting was very popular with enamellers. An almost identical enamel version, but with canted corners and mounted on a gold box, was in the collection of Baron von Steengracht, Moyland Castle, part I sold A. Creutzer/M. Lempertz, Aachen (Aix-la-Chapelle) (17 September 1919, lot 225). We are indebted to Dr Peter Wegmann, Oskar Reinhardt Foundation, Winterthur, for his help in the cataloguing of the present miniature.

JAMES/GIUSEPPE MACPHERSON (1726–C. 1780)

James MacPherson is almost certainly the same artist as the one recorded as Giuseppe, born in 1726 in Florence, according to *Supplemento agl' (Serie dei Trecento) Elogi e in Pittura, Scultura e Archittettura* (see Fleming, 1959). According to this anonymous source, MacPherson was born in Florence on 19 March 1726 and studied painting under Pompeo Batoni. He also painted large group portraits, one of which included the painter Johann Zoffany and himself, now in the Uffizi. Many of these were commissioned by 'gran personaggi Inglesi', as his patrons were described in 1776. The author also called MacPherson a skilled copyist and mentioned the copies of the Uffizi self-portraits done by MacPherson. In April 1754, Giuseppe Baretti wrote that he had had his portrait 'done in enamel by a young gentleman called MacPherson, a Florentine by birth, but of Scotch extraction, who was in Italy three or four years ago'. Later, in 1754, Baretti mentions MacPherson as 'being still in London'[1] and possibly in Vienna.[2]

He returned to Florence in the 1760s. There he was commissioned by George, 3rd Earl Cowper (1738–89), one of the leading connoisseurs of the era, who had settled in Florence in the early 1760s, to copy the series of self-portraits in the Uffizi. By 1767 Cowper was able to lend sixty of these to an exhibition organised by the Florentine Academy at SS Annunziata. Ultimately, this series grew to 224 miniatures which Cowper presented to King George III, the first starting in 1773, the second probably when Cowper returned to England in 1786. MacPherson also painted a full-scale group portrait which included Zoffany and himself. That MacPherson was held in high esteem in Florence is made clear by the Director of the Uffizi, Boncivenni Pelli, who describes him as one of the most skilled *professore* in Florence on MacPherson's application to Grand Duke Pietro Leopoldo to paint a copy of Corregio's *Madonna* and Guercino's *Sibyl in the Tribuna* (Webster, 1972, p. 1446). The next year, Pelli helped to persuade MacPherson to overcome his modesty and submit his own self-portrait. When he did, he executed a large miniature, 23.8 × 18.2 cm (9³/₈ × 7³/₁₆ in) in watercolour on vellum, in which he chose to depict himself in a suit pointing to a miniature and showing his mortar for grinding up colours, a glass of water and a scraper with a pencil. Both his physical appearance and the presence of these attributes allow us to identify a previously unidentified enamel miniature, also undoubtedly a self-portrait of MacPherson, illus. p. 10 now in the Hamburger, Kunsthalle which was illustrated in Geismeier Burock, 1986, p. 15. (We are grateful to Rachel Layton of the Gilbert Collection for making this indentification.) In the latter miniature, MacPherson is shown with the miniature and materials, but also with the kiln in the background, rather then the painting of *St Joseph with Christ* and the statue head at his feet. Webster quotes extensively from the account of Lockhart Gordon visiting Florence in 1799 and purchasing some enamels and numerous drawings from MacPherson's daughter, impoverished by a bad marriage. As two miniatures in the Gilbert Collection were purchased by Mr Lavender in Scotland, it is possible that these enamels are among those purchased from MacPherson's daughter by Lockhart Gordon in Florence in 1799 and brought back with him. MacPherson's works are also in the Royal Collection, the National Gallery of Ireland, Dublin and in the Hofburg, Vienna.

[1] Webster, 1972, p. 1446.
[2] Keil, 1999, p. 266 (There are eight miniatures in the House of Habsburg collection by MacPherson).

37 *A Man at His Easel*

James/Giuseppe MacPherson
Probably Florence, c. 1760
Signature on counter enamel *Macpherson pinx=757*
Enamel on copper, 6.5 × 5.2 cm (2$^9/_{16}$ × 2$^1/_{16}$ in), oval
Oval gold rim frame, probably original, set in c. 1890, jewelled and pearl set filigree surround
1996.792 (MIN27)

PROVENANCE: D.S. Lavender, London (October, 1981).

DESCRIPTION: The artist is shown half-length turned toward the right in a brown cloak, with blue lapels and cuffs, powdered wig *en queue*. The painting, apparently of a bull or cow and a rustic figure holding a gun or a staff in landscape is oval.

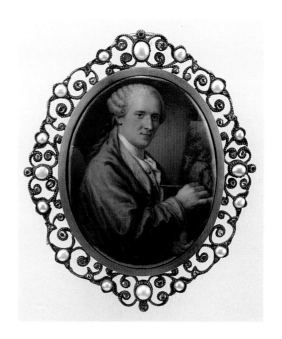

COMMENTARY: This would appear to be a portrait of an artist contemporary with MacPherson. There is a vague resemblance to the copy of a self-portrait of Charles Joseph Natoire (1700–77) in the series of artists' self-portraits now in the Royal Collection (no. 630), although in the latter the artist is somewhat rounder of face and more humbly dressed. The same is true of the difference between MacPherson's self-portrait in the Uffizi and the one in the Royal Collection. This is a very well-depicted portrait which is more than just the head-and-shoulders image typical of those in the group commissioned from MacPherson by George 3rd Earl Cowper (1738–89), after the collection of full-scale self-portraits in the Uffizi.

38 *An Elderly Man*

James/Giuseppe MacPherson
England, c. 1770
Signed on front *Macpherson pinx* on right edge
Enamel on copper, 4.5 × 3.5 cm (1$^3/_4$ × 1$^3/_8$ in), oval
Original oval pendant gold rim frame (formerly hinged now fixed); now set in a French rectangular ormolu frame of c. 1800–10 (misc. no. 182), with laurel borders; with the number (possibly an inventory number) '2768' on counter enamel
1996.795 (MIN30)

PROVENANCE: D.S. Lavender, London (October, 1981).

DESCRIPTION: The man is shown head and neck length with white hair and a beard, a blue shirt and a red jacket.

COMMENTARY: This is possibly a peasant figure inspired by the enthusiasm for the rustic. As he appears to be wearing an overcoat, it is unlikely that he is a saint or prophet, although some of Guido Reni's saints especially Joseph, have a similar shirt. No source painting from which this might be a quotation has yet come to light.

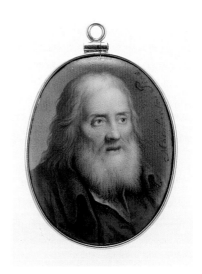

GAETANO MANINI (FL. C. 1752–C. 1780/90)

Gaetano Manini is said to have been a pupil of D. Creti at the Bologna Academy in about 1728. He arrived in England in the late 1750s and painted allegories and enamel miniatures. He exhibited at the Free Society of Arts from 1761 to 1772. Numerous enamels depicting Frederick Prince of Wales by Manini have survived. Manini is said to have worked also in Ireland. Enamels by his hand are to be found in the Ashmolean Museum, Oxford, the V&A, the National Gallery of Ireland, Dublin, and the Museum Briner and Kern, Winterthur.

39 *An Enigmatic Scene*

Gaetano Manini
Probably Milan, Bologna or London, 1752
Signed with initials and dated, lower right *G.MF / 1752*
Enamel on copper, 6.5 cm (2⁹/₁₆ in) diameter, circular
Gold rim frame with glazed reverse, with label inscribed *FRANCOISE LECINSKA* [sic] / *SOREL-LA DI MARIA / LECINSKA REGINA / DI FRAN-CIA*'
1999.63 (MIN73)

PROVENANCE: Bossi & Son, Genoa/Nice; private collection, Switzerland; Christie's, London (21 October 1997, lot 13, to D.S. Lavender Antiques, London).

DESCRIPTION: A bare-bosomed young woman in white silk dress with gold border, seated full-length

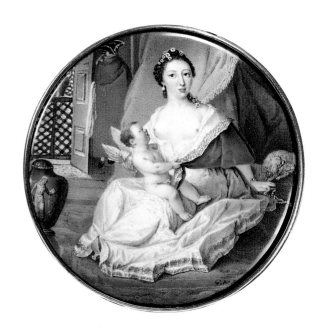

in an interior, holding a rosary in her left hand and in her right hand the right wing of a nude putto seated on her lap, the putto with adult face preparing to be breast-fed and clasping the woman's blue stole; a trelliswork fence, an open door, a mysterious male figure with tricorne hat, draped in brown cloak, light green curtain, with a dog cleaning itself in the right-hand background.

COMMENTARY: An old label written in Italian on the reverse identifies the sitter as Françoise Leszczynska, sister of Queen Maria Leszczynska, wife of Louis XV of France. The Queen had only one sister, Anna Leszczynska (1699–1717), favourite daughter of King Stanislas Leszczynski of Poland, later Duke of Lorraine. The discrepancy in the Christian names and the dates exclude this identification, apart from the fact that a king's daughter would probably not be depicted in such an indecorous way. The highly enigmatic scene may either depict an opera/theatre scene or be the result of a special commission with a symbol-loaded message to the recipient of the piece. In quality, this miniature stands out from Manini's slightly naïve and stiff portraits. The full-length representation of the seated woman with her folded silk dress and left slipper, the embroidered carpet and the naturalistically depicted dog supply an occasion to display the whole range of the artist's craftsmanship.

JEAN ADAM MATHIEU (C. 1698–1753)

Jean Adam Mathieu, born in Stralsund, Pomerania, was a pupil of his compatriot Charles Boit. A goldsmith, porcelain painter, enameller and large-scale oil painter, he was undoubtedly one of the most fashionable enamellers of the second quarter of the eighteenth century in France. His clientele included Queen Maria Leszczynska of France and her father King Stanislas Leszczynski of Poland, the Duke and Duchess of Orléans, the Prince de Condé and the Marquise de Pompadour. In 1745, he was in charge of the painting department at the Vincennes porcelain factory. Two months before his death, on 18 April 1753, he was appointed '*peintre orfèvre du roi en émail*'. Enamels by his hand are in the V&A, the Louvre and the Museum Briner und Kern, Winterthur.

40 *Louis XV, Wearing Armour*

Jean Adam Mathieu
Paris, c. 1740/50
Signed on the counter enamel *JMathieu. p:*
Enamel, 4.8 × 3.8 cm (1⅞ × 1½ in), oval
Gold frame set with rose-cut diamonds and gold

flower heads
1996.800 (MIN35)

PROVENANCE: S.J. Phillips, London (6 October 1982).

DESCRIPTION: The sitter is shown bust-length in a white tie wig, purple velvet cloak embroidered with gold *fleurs de lys* over armour and gold sun-form

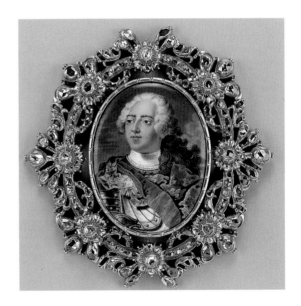

clasp, decorated with the blue sash of the Royal French Order of the Holy Ghost; cloudy sky background.

COMMENTARY: Louis XV (1710–74) succeeded his great-grandfather Louis XIV as King of France in 1715 at the age of five. Until his adulthood in 1725 the Duc d'Orléans acted as regent. In 1725 Louis XV was married to Maria Leszczynska, daughter of the former King of Poland and had numerous children including a son who died before his father. Most of his political enterprises failed, but in his private life he devoted himself to pleasure and had a series of mistresses including the notorious Marquise de Pompadour and the ill-fated Comtesse Du Barry.

Four other similar enamels of King Louis XV by Mathieu are known: one, measuring 5 × 4.3 cm (2 × $1^{11}/_{16}$ in), in an unopened frame, is in the

Foundation Historic Collections of the House of Orange-Nassau, The Hague (Schaffers-Bodenhausen/Tiethoff-Spliethoff 1993, p. 225, no. 225), a large one, signed almost identically on the reverse, is in a French private collection, one in the V&A, and another small enamel, unsigned, is at the time of writing with Galerie Kugel, Paris. An enamel depicting Louis XV in coronation robes, formerly in the Whitehead Collection, is illustrated in the exhibition catalogues, London 1889, pl. XXXII, no. 38 and Geneva, 1956, no. 292.

The present enamel is a very characteristic specimen of Mathieu's work and shows his visible stipple and dot technique. Its stylised, wooden and affected quality is counterbalanced by the beauty of the colours and the almost three-dimensional modelling of the features and clothing. For a miniature of the same subject, see cat. no. 86.

CIRCLE OF MARTIN VAN MEYTENS (1695–1770)

Martin van Meytens theYounger was a large-scale oil painter, miniaturist and enameller. Born in Stockholm, he went to London in 1712 to study portrait painting, particularly with Anthony Van Dyck. Three years later, he went to Paris where he was taught enamelling by his compatriot Charles Boit. Meytens was sponsored by the *Régent* and painted the portraits of his benefactor, of Louis XV and of Tsar Peter the Great who tried, in vain, to hire him for his court at St Petersburg. Meytens travelled extensively to Dresden, Vienna, Italy and to his home town of Stockholm. He turned down the Swedish king's offer of work at his court and preferred to return to Vienna where he became director of the Imperial Academy in 1759. Probably owing to the rarity of his miniatures and enamels, Meytens is better known nowadays for his oil portraits. Signed enamel miniatures by his hand are to be found in the National Gallery of Ireland, Dublin, in the Nationalmuseum, Stockholm, and in the Gemäldegalerie, Berlin.

41 *A Gentleman in buff-coloured Cloak*

Circle of Martin van Meytens (1675–1770)
Possibly England, France or Germany, c. 1720
Enamel on copper, 4.5 × 3.7 cm ($1^3/_4$ × $1^7/_{16}$ in), oval
Later gilt-metal frame
1996.817 (MIN49C)

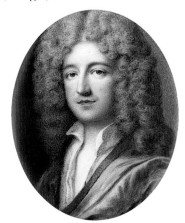

PROVENANCE: Phillips, London (17 July 1989, lot 320, unframed, as French School, c. 1720); private collection, Paris; Hôtel Drouot, Paris (24 June 1992, lot 130, framed, erroneously attributed to Charles Boit, c. 1710; to Kugel, Paris). Kugel, Paris (September 1994).

EXHIBITION: Portland, 1995.

DESCRIPTION: The sitter facing right in buff-coloured cloak, open white shirt and powdered full-bottomed wig.

COMMENTARY: Despite its apparent English look, this enamel is painted in a Continental technique with a soft, 'woolly' brush stroke unknown to Zincke and his English contemporaries. Comparison with the pieces in the Nationalmuseum, Stockholm, can justify the attribution to Meytens.

DENIS BROWNELL MURPHY (C. 1745–1842)

Denis Brownell Murphy was born in Dublin. He exhibited at the Dublin Society of Artists in 1765 and 1768. He left Ireland to study and work in England, returning in 1792 but moving back to England in 1798, when he worked in Lancaster and Scotland. He finally settled in London in 1803, according to Foskett, (1987, p. 604), although this date seems in doubt in the light of the Edinburgh 1804 inscriptions on the present miniatures. In 1810, he was appointed Painter in Ordinary to Princess Charlotte. His portrait of her is in the Dutch Royal Collection. In the same year, the Prince Regent commissioned him to copy Lely's *Windsor Beauties*, which were in the Royal Collection in 1812 (but was subsequently deaccessioned, reappearing at Christie's in 1949).

From 1800 to 1827, Murphy exhibited both copies of full-scale works and some original portraits in at the Royal Academy and British Institute. Interestingly, in 1809 he is recorded as exhibiting, along with thirty other miniatures of contemporary figures, no. 631, *The Earl of Moira*, who is represented in the Gilbert Collection twice with enamels by other artists – Henry Spicer after Hoppner (see cat. no. 56) and Henry Bone (see cat. no. 9). He did not restrict his enamels to portraits. In 1811, a year in which Henry Bone did not exhibit at the Royal Academy, Murphy had no. 388 'Enamel, from a picture by Carlo Dolci'. His work is in major museums including the National Portrait Gallery.

42 A *Mary Queen of Scots*
  B *James I*
  C *Charles I*
  D *Charles II*
  E *James II*
  F *The Old Pretender, James Francis Edward Stuart*
  G *The Young Pretender, Charles Edward Stuart 'Bonnie Prince Charlie*

Denis Brownell Murphy, after various paintings
Scotland, 1804

Seven enamel on copper, rectangular

A 7.9 × 6.1 cm (3^1/$_8$ × 2^3/$_8$ in)
B 7.9 × 6.1 cm (3^1/$_8$ × 2^3/$_8$ in)
C 7.9 × 6.2 cm (3^1/$_8$ × 2^7/$_{16}$ in)
D 7.9 × 6.2 cm (3^1/$_8$ × 2^7/$_{16}$ in)
E 7.7 × 6.1 cm (3 × 2^3/$_8$ in)
F 7.9 × 6.2 cm (3^1/$_8$ × 2 /16 in)
G 7.9 × 6.2 cm (3^1/$_8$ × 2^7/$_{16}$ in)

Original papier-mâché frame with ormolu mounts, the first five with crowns.

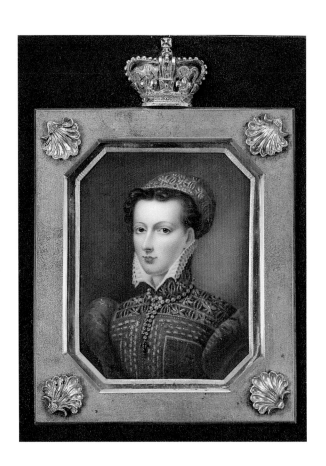
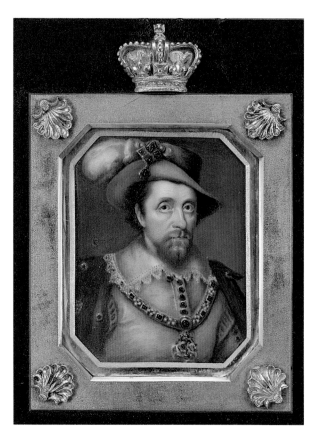
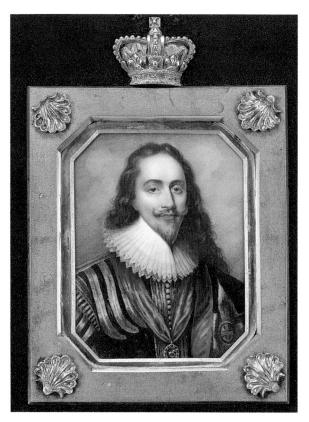
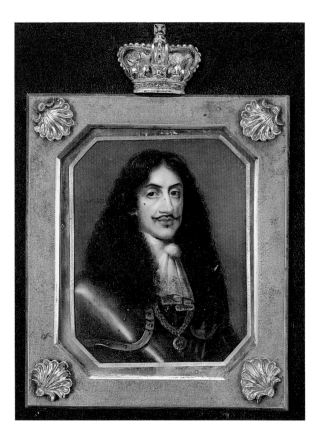

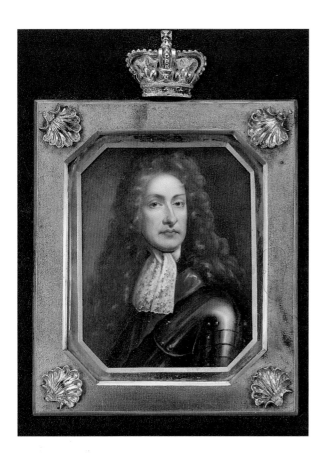

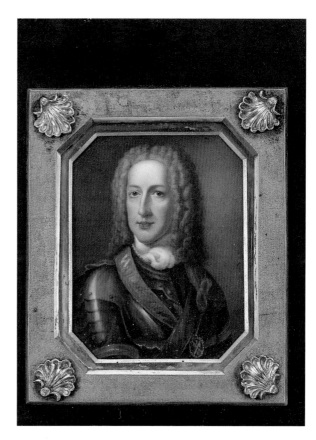

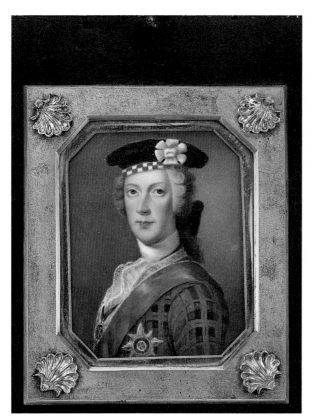

A Missing original backing paper
B Inscribed on backing paper, *James 1st of England /
and* 6th *of Scotland / from* the *original at /* Hamilton
Palace by */ Cornelius Jansen – / Painted in Enamel by /
DB Murphy / Edinbr 1804*
C Inscribed on backing paper, *Charles I / from* the
original by van Dyke
D *Charles 2nd &c& / from a fine picture in the posses-
sion of Mr. Anderson – / done in Enamel by / DB
Murphy*
E *James 2nd &c / from an excellent original / in
Holyrood Palace by / Sir Godfrey Kneller – / painted in
Enamel by / DB Murphy / Edinb 1804*
F Remains of backing paper with signature *DB
Murphy and Chev St* [faint] *George*
G No original backing paper
1996.760-766 (MIN3A–G)

PROVENANCE: Johnson, Walker & Tolhurst, London
(1979).

DESCRIPTION:
A The sitter wearing a red embroidered dress with high ruff and gold cap, a cross at her neck
B in grey with a plume in his hat wearing the Order of Saint George and the Dragon
C in grey striped doublet, with white lace collar, wearing the blue sash and Star of the Order of the Garter
D after Pieter Nason, wearing armour and a white lace cravat
E after Sir Godfrey Kneller, wearing armour, with white lace cravat and blue sash
F after Luti, Chevalier de St. George wearing armour, blue sash and red banding
G in Stuart tartan with blue velvet tam, with white bow, blue sash and Star and Order of the Garter.

COMMENTARY: Although not of the brilliance of Henry Bone's work, these miniatures are of good quality, displaying a similar enthusiasm for historicism. In this group, the subjects have been chosen as a would-be line of succession of monarchs for the Scots starting with James I (James VI of Scotland) down to Charles Edward Stuart 'Bonnie Prince Charlie'. Based on paintings in Scottish collections and executed in Edinburgh, these miniatures enlarge our knowledge of this artist. They compliment the general theme of the collection which shows as a strong an interest in important subjects as in the enamel artists themselves.

WILLIAM PREWETT/PREWITT (ACTIVE 1730–50?)

According to Bénézit William Prewett/Prewitt was born in Suffolk. If this is so, it makes him, if not the earliest, certainly one of the earliest English-born portrait enamellers. Two signed and dated miniatures of 1735 and 1736, on a double portrait, are in the V&A. Another of Horace Walpole of 1735 is in the collection of the Duke of Buccleuch (Foskett, 1972, vol. II, pl. 279, no. 695) but most of his work is unsigned. Although a pupil of Zincke's, Prewett's works are often softer in style. Other examples are in the collection of the Duke of Buccleuch, formerly in the Holzscheider Collection, Meilen, Zurich and in the National Gallery of Ireland, Dublin, and in the Ashmolean Museum, Oxford.

43 *George II*

Attributed to William Prewett
England, mid-18th century
Unsigned on face
Enamel on copper, 4.7 × 3.8 cm (1⁷/₈ × 1¹/₂ in), oval
In gold case, later inscribed, *by Zinke*
1996.825 (MIN56)

PROVENANCE: Henry Nyburg, Esq., Sotheby's London (13 December 1976, lot 19); Frederick Joachim (1904–1994) Christie's, London (8 March 1995, lot 10, through S.J. Phillips).

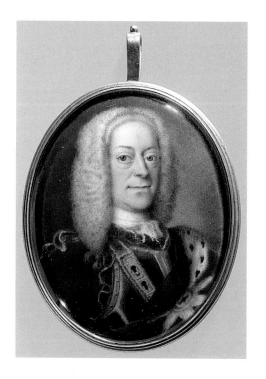

DESCRIPTION: Shown bust-length, wearing red cape with ermine trim, Order of the Garter, blue sash, armour and green bodice, shoulder-length powdered wig, grey-brown background.

COMMENTARY: There are a few, slightly varying miniatures of this type which have been alternately ascribed to William Prewett and Noah or Abraham Seaman. None to date has emerged with a signature. The example attributed to Prewett in the Royal Collection,[1] one in a private collection illustrated in Foskett,[2] (attributed to Abraham or Noah Seaman) and a third sold Sotheby's (16 December 1975, as perhaps by Seaman) have the face in the same direction but the body direction reversed. All have differences in the cape ornament. A fourth, of similar pose in red jacket with blue ribbon, is in the Habsburg Collection.[3] The Sotheby's 1996 catalogue gave the work to Prewett and cited as the source a painting in the Royal Collection acquired by George IV (when Prince Regent) in 1810, probably painted in Hanover c. 1740/50, artist unknown. That painting is now at Windsor Castle.[4]

Similar portraits possibly based on the one at Windsor, exist by Reynolds in the Diocese of York,[5] Franz Lippoldt and Gottfried Boy. In addition, a wash drawing, also artist unknown, where the King is wearing armour with the Ribbon of the Garter, was sold at Christie's, London (9 February 1960, lot 27a). Another miniature from a private collection, of George II in armour, was exhibited at D.S. Lavender, London (1993, no. 73). Attributed in the catalogue to Zincke, this work could possibly be by the same artist as the Gilbert miniature. Thus at least one of the miniatures may have been painted *ad vivum* or alternatively painted with the Windsor painting as the source, varying the costume.

[1] Walker, 1992, p. 9.
[2] Foskett, 1979, vol. II, pl. 10.
[3] Keil, Robert, 1999, p. 197.
[4] Millar, 1963, cat. 620, pl. 190
[5] Kerslake, 1977, no. 258.

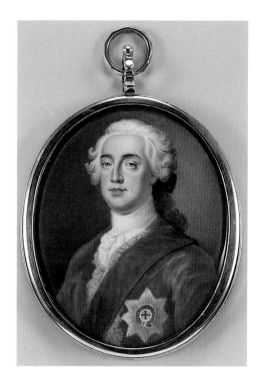

44 *A Gentleman*

Manner of William Prewett
England, c. 1750
No signature on face
Enamel on copper, 5.4 × 4.5 cm (2 1/8 × 1 7/8 in), oval
Silver-gilt oval pendant; paper label on back of frame *HICK / SON*;
1996.780 (MINI5)

PROVENANCE: S.H.V. Hickson, Sotheby's, London (29 March 1965); Sotheby's, London (30 June 1980, lot 5, through S.J. Phillips).

DESCRIPTION: The sitter wearing a powdered tye-wig and a brown velvet jacket ornamented with golden lace over a white lace jabot, having the blue Sash and Star of the Order of the Garter.

COMMENTARY: A full-scale portrait of this subject, indentified as the 2nd Duke of Portland, was listed as being in the collection of Madame D. Coppe, Brussels in 1960 (National Portrait Gallery Heinz archive). It differs in the attire, but it too has the Sash and Order of the Garter. Also in the archive is a photograph of this or an almost identical miniature also described as being William Bentinck, 2nd Duke of Portland. However, the Thomas Hudson portrait of the 2nd Duke of Portland (Witt Archive, as Portland Collection) shows an apparently different subject, as do some Zincke enamels of him when younger, with known family provenance in a private collection.

As the Duke was made Knight of the Garter in 1741, it is tempting to connect him to this subject. However, without firm documentation for the Brussels portrait, this seems unlikely.

By the time this was painted, Zincke's eyesight was fading [1] and his studio produced much of the work. It is possible that this commission was picked up by Prewett as a known artist who had worked in Zincke's studio.

A virtually indentical miniature signed *N. Seaman* in the counter enamel exists in the David-Weill Collection at the Louvre (DW no. 4036). It is listed (as unidentified English Lord) in the collection catalogue.[2]

1. As early as 1725, Zincke complained to the father of the future Duchess about his eyesight (see Goulding, 1916, p. 54).
2. Paris, 1956–7, no. 299, pp. 139–40, illus. National Portrait Gallery Heinz archive.

PAUL PRIEUR (C. 1620–84)

Paul Prieur, son of a Huguenot goldsmith from Paris, active in Geneva, was apprenticed to a Geneva goldsmith between 1635 and 1638. He is said to have travelled to Paris around 1640 and learned enamelling there, possibly with the Toutins. From 1655, he is recorded at the Danish court, painting enamel portraits for Frederick III and later Christian V. He was the first miniature painter to use the enamelling technique in Denmark and worked for the court until 1681. Although a talented and prolific artist, his work was rather uneven in quality, as remarked by Gauthey (1975, p. 26). Signed enamels by his hand are mainly in Danish museums such as Rosenborg Castle and Frederikborg Castle, but some are also in the V&A, the Musée Cognac-Jay, Paris, the Musée de l'Horlogerie, Geneva, the Gemäldegalerie, Berlin, the Kunstgewerbemuseum, Hamburg, and in the Städtisches Museum, Flensburg.

45 *A Gentleman in Slashed Black Doublet*

Attributed to Paul Prieur
Possibly Paris, c. 1645–50
Enamel on gold, 3.4 × 3.1 cm (1⁵/₁₆ × 1¹/₄ in), oval
Later gold frame
1996.773 (MIN8)

PROVENANCE: Dr Adolf List Collection, Magdeburg; sold to Hans W. Lange, Berlin (28–30 March 1939, lot 511, unframed, as attributed to Jean Petitot); Galerie Dr phil. Hans Rudolph, Hamburg, Hotel Atlantic (28–29 September 1950, lot 180, unframed, as by Jean Petitot, c. 1650); Günther Muthmann Collection, Wuppertal, part I sold at Sotheby's, Zurich (17 May 1979, lot 35, unframed, as by Jean Petitot Senior, c. 1645)

DESCRIPTION: The sitter wearing a white lawn collar, white shirt with slashed black doublet, centre-parted long curly brown hair and slight moustache.

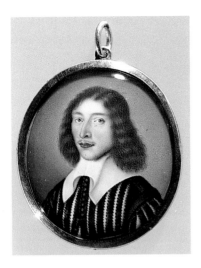

attributed, had reached the height of his talent and had already executed his masterworks, such as the famous *Duchess of Richmond* of 1643 in the Nationalmuseum, Stockholm, or the two enamels of *Rachel de Ruvigny* of 1641 and 1642, at Sherborne Castle and Chatsworth respectively. Comparison with these masterworks of enamel painting exclude any attempt of attribution to Petitot. The stiff representation and hesitant brushstroke with sometimes harsh colours, particularly in the lips, would suggest that this is the work of a youthful artist. Paul Prieur is said to have learnt the enamelling technique in Paris after his apprenticeship as a goldsmith in Geneva between 1632 and 1638. The present work shows the finely stippled, blue background which is characteristic of all his later works and substantiates considerably the attribution of this work to Paul Prieur. Katherine Coombs has tended to endorse the attribution to Prieur.

COMMENTARY: Dr Aileen Ribeiro dates the costume of the sitter at mid- to late 1640. By this time, Petitot, to whom this miniature has previously been

---

CHRISTIAN RICHTER (STOCKHOLM 1678-1732 LONDON)

The son of a goldsmith who was the assessor to the Goldsmiths Corporation, Richter apprenticed as a goldsmith from 1695-98 in Stockholm. There, according to Vertue, he also studied the art of engraving in steel for coins and medals under Arvid Karlsteen (1647-1718) and miniature painting with Elias Brenner (1647-1717), who worked in enamels.

After visiting Berlin and Dresden Richter arrived in London in 1702. It is unclear whether he knew Dahl and Hyssing beforehand, but the former fellow-Swede did much to promote him upon his arrival. Richter soon was painting many of the figures of the court.

Vertue says that

> wars and national misfortune drove him to Dresden, the King of Poland's residence where Karlsteen was the 'Princes Medallist' but there likewise the great disbursements made on the warrs and other expences. hindred his progress that way of art after having modelld in Wax the portraits of K. Augustus who sat to him.& also the King of Prusia. waited near two years in expectation of being imploy'd by that Court had

his final answer. therefore he was neccessitated to imploy himself otherways. took to painting in Water Colours. gained knowledge.& practice joynd with it. he intirely persud it. but not finding imployment enough there, he came to England (1702) was recommended to Mr Dahl. his countryman who encouragied him & promoted him all he cou'd. by which means he became an excellent Master coppying from several of our best painters, Vandyke Lilly Kneller Dahl.& others, & drawing from life in a very just & good manner really better than any other of his contemporaries. by his continual labour. his Eyes seem to dimn'd. his nose fall'n by some accident in y Gardens of Venus made him look't on with suspicious Eye, & did much prevent his public apperance & at the same time in the reaping such advantages by his Art Sutable to his merit his face being no Agreable prospect for fine Ladys to see those scarrs were rather a motive of compassion than to inspire their graces & charms. such as always they expect shoud be represented by y Painter-after a tedious indispotion & illness he dyd Nov. 1732. in St. James Parish Westminister (and was buried in that Parish Church yard).[2]

While Vertue generally refers to Richter as a 'limner' and none of the known signed works by him are enamels, it is very possible he learned something about enamelling in Sweden. More significantly, a later comment by Vertue indicates that he took it up later in England in response to its popularity.

Mr. Christian Rechter limner born in Stockholm. first learnt silversmith of his father being of that profession-his Manner of Painting very tender & Curious. his tincts had a great variety his pencil regular and neat. his lines of drawing very just & toucht with freedom. certainly his manner was peculiar to himself-having much immitated Mr. Dahls works he followed him closely. its plain from his beginning in limning, as he was first initiated according to the rudiments of graving. his lines was sure & his colouring proceeded from light to strenghtning- (Richter 1719 his name thus to a limning)[col.2] contrary to those that begin from oil colours of any strong operations. he finding laterly that Enamelling was much encouraged & liked by Persons of fortune & Nobility he therefore set about the practice of it wherein tho' a begginner he succeeded so well that in time he might have arrivd to great perfection'.

It would not be suprising that his disfigurement might have inspired him to do enamels a less receptive medium to *ad vivum* work. His work is in the V&A, the National Portrait Gallery, the Wallace Collection and the Welbeck Abbey Collection.

1 Vertue III, v 18 BM 18, 1725, Walpole XXII, p.24–25
2 Ditto.
3 Vertue III v 62 BM 40, 1732 Walpole XXII p. 63–64 . The entry contiunues 'he dyd in Brewer Street near Golden Square the second week of Nov 1732 he had been many years in a bad state of health from an ill Curd Veneral distemper. Which had fallen his nose & scarryfyd his face which much depres'd his fortune & disperited his undertakings he seldom therefore appeard in public and never in any companies of Artists. tho' this blemish in his Countenance apperd. he was Naturally a well meaning modest man- he came into England about 1702–3 and lived to the age of 50- he has living several brothers ingenious artists. one at Vienna a Medalist another a Venice a painter. of Views very Free & Masterly as some of his work here appear to be – that have bought a Venice.'

46 *Oliver Cromwell*

Attributed to Christian Richter, after Samuel Cooper (1609–72)
England, c. 1720
Enamel on copper, 4.1 × 3.6 cm (1⁵/₈ × 1⁷/₁₆ in), oval
Gold frame with a pierced border set with table-cut diamonds; the counter enamel with initials *O* as a sun face, *C* as a moon face and *P*, the last below a crown, and above a broken oak tree, surrounded by laurel, on a white ground
1996.826 (MIN57)

PROVENANCE: J.H. Fitz-Henry Collection,

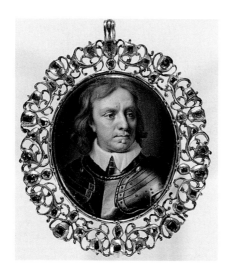

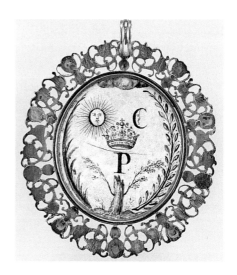

Paris/London; Fitz-Henry Collection sale, Hôtel Drouot, Paris (18–21 February 1914, lot 304, the miniature described as seventeenth century, the frame as eighteenth century, then within its shagreen case); David-Weill (1871–1952), Neuilly-sur-Seine, no. 4041; Sir Charles Clore (1905–79), London; Clore Collection sale, part II, Sotheby's, London (10 November 1986, lot 59, to Andreas Thies); Paris, Louvre des Antiquaires, Galérie Andreas Thies 'Les Arts de la Chevalerie'; Christie's, London (8 March 1995, lot 122), through S.J. Phillips.

LITERATURE: Gillet, Jeannerat, Clouzot, 1957, p. 382, no. 256.

EXHIBITIONS: Brussels, 1912. cat. no. 1373, case VIII, no. 54 (on a velvet panel, together with five other enamels lent by J.H. Fitz-Henry, Paris); London, 1961, no. 256 (as by Charles Boit); Portland, 1994–95.

DESCRIPTION: Cromwell facing right in armour and a lawn collar, brown background.

COMMENTARY: Oliver Cromwell (1599–1658), Lord Protector of England, was descended from the sister of Thomas Cromwell, chief minister of Henry VIII. Her son acted as agent to Thomas Cromwell and took his surname. Representing first Huntingdon in the Parliament of 1628–29 then Cambridge in the Short Parliament of 1640 and the Long Parliament that followed it, he was active in the House of Commons and was a vehement supporter of Puritanism. At the outbreak of the Civil War in 1642, he helped to raise armed forces against King Charles I and, with his formidable 'Ironsides' regiment, won the important Battle of Naseby in 1645.

His effective and forceful leadership both on the field of battle and in Parliament led to the eventual success of the Parliamentary forces and the execution of Charles I in 1649. The Commonwealth was then established. As army commander, Cromwell ruthlessly conquered Ireland and then turned his attention to the Scottish army of Charles II which he defeated at Dunbar in 1650 and at Worcester in 1651, effectively bringing the Civil War to an end.

Cromwell became the 'Lord Protector' of England. During the 1650s he ended the wars against the Dutch States-General and Portugal, concluded treaties with Sweden and Denmark and made an alliance with France against Spain. However, he failed in his attempt to form a league of Protestant powers in Europe. He died in 1658 and was buried in Westminster Abbey, but in 1661 his body was disinterred and hung on the gallows.

The strength of character that is shown in his face made him a subject of interest for many – apparently regardless of political point of view. The fact that the Royal Collection contains miniatures of him is an indication of this.

This is one of the most interesting and difficult miniatures in the collection to attribute. It is a very fine enamel copy after Samuel Cooper whose previous attributions include to Charles Boit (Gillet, Jeannerat, Clouzot, 1957), an English follower of Petitot, and Christian Richter (Sotheby's sale). The technique does not reveal the use of a delicate brush stroke like Boit's, although it is tempting to compare this miniature with the one in the Orange-Nassau Collection (Schaffers-Bodenhausen/Tiethoff-Spliethoff, 1993, p. 383, no 511) given to Boit, which purports to be lot 71 from Strawberry Hill. The effect and brushstroke technique are quite similar to copies by Richter based on the official miniature by Cooper after Cooper's own unfinished sketch in the collection of the Duke of Buccleuch of c. 1653,[1] especially the one in the Wallace Collection (Reynolds 1980, no 42). From the inscription on the Richter copy *sum possessor / CRichter* [the C and R in monogram] */ 1708*, it would appear that Richter himself owned a version by Cooper. For another miniature of Cromwell attributed to Richter after Copper on vellum, see D.S Lavender (1993, no. 30 illus.). The attribution to Richter thus would seem a good one. The problem is that no signed enamels by Richter exist. However, an enamel of a Gentleman, stated to be the Duc d'Orleans was catalogued as by Christian Richter when it was sold at Sotheby's, London (2 February, 1969, lot 140), having previously been in the T. Whitcombe Greene Collection, sold at Sotheby's, London (7 July, 1932, lot 84 illus.). Vertue does indicate that Richter took up enamelling late in his career (see p. 95). Thus, it would seem reasonable to assume that Richter was trained in this art. However, without a signed accepted work in this medium, there must remain some doubt. The potential Scandinavian connection should not, however, be ignored, and it may be that this miniature was painted there. Signac probably copied the works of Alexander Cooper (see Cavalli-Bjorkman, 1981, p. 33). Several full-length paintings based on or by Robert Walker exist. One waist-only painting is in Gripsholm Castle in Sweden, which also has a miniature version. Another, with the golden chains and Latin verses to Queen Christina, ascribed to Milton, is in the collection of the Duke of Grafton. Thus, although this is clearly based on

the vivid depiction by Samuel Cooper rather than Walker, there is a reasonable basis for a Swedish connection. However, without any specific Swedish-owned Samuel Cooper of Cromwell as a source and with the overall symbolic content of the counter enamel being more appropriate for an English patron, it seems more likely that Richter would have painted this in England.

[1] D.Piper, 1954, pp. 31, 38–39 (D. Piper 'Contemporary Portraits of Oliver Cromwell', *Walpole Society Journal*, Vol. XXXIV, 1952–1954, Glasgow, plate VII.

JEAN ANDRÉ ROUQUET (1701–58)

Jean André Rouquet was born to French Huguenot refugees in Geneva. In the mid-1720s he went to London where he stayed for about thirty years, until he went to Paris. From his time in London, his works show the influence of Boit and Zincke. In Paris, he is first recorded exhibiting enamels at the Salon in 1753 and again in 1755 and 1757. Louis XV, by *brevet* of 21 July 1754, gave Rouquet a studio in the Louvre previously occupied by Jean Mathieu (see *Nouvelles Archives* 1873, p. 92, no. 214) and commissioned him to paint his portrait as well as that of Madame du Pompadour. Rouquet published *L'etat des arts en Angleterre* (On the Present State of the Arts in England) in 1755, a guide to fashions in portrait painting in England. Rouquet was also a friend of William Hogarth so the attribution to him of an enamel portrait based on an early self-portrait of Hogarth in the National Portrait Gallery seems reasonable. Rouquet was elected a member of the Académie Royale in Paris on 23 December 1754, by order of the King, despite being a Protestant.[1] He died in an insane asylum in 1758. His works are in the V&A, the National Gallery of Ireland, Dublin, and the Fitzwilliam Museum.

[1] See NAAP, 1884, p. 255.

47 *A Gentleman*

Attributed to Jean André Rouquet
England, c. 1750
Enamel on copper, 4.1 × 3.3 cm (1⅝ × 1⁵/₁₆ in), oval
Enamel and gilt-metal frame with pierced ribbon-twist surround and pierced ribbon-tie surmount
1996.779 (MIN 14)

PROVENANCE: Fischer Galleries, Lucerne (23 June 1960, as by Jean Mathieu, cat. no. 827); Ernst

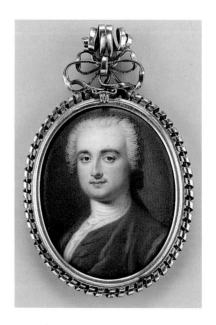

Holzscheiter Collection; Sotheby's, London (1 May 1980, lot 31)

DESCRIPTION: The gentleman wearing a powdered tye-wig and brown velvet jacket over a white stock.

COMMENTARY: From the costume of this unknown gentleman, it would appear that this miniature was painted in 1750 while Rouquet was in England. It has the soft brushwork and the fairly small, slightly beady eyes, both characteristics of Rouquet. There is a signed miniature by Rouquet of William Pitt in the V&A.

ABRAHAM SEAMAN / SEEMAN (FL. 1724–C. 1753)

Little is known about Seaman's life, but he appears to be a close relative, probably the brother, of Noah Seaman, as a miniature in the Dutch Royal Collection is signed 'NS' in script on the front and 'Abraham' on the reverse (Schaffers-Bodenhausen/Tiethoff-Spliethoff, 1993, p. 384, no. 515). In turn, he may have been the son of, or related to, a Danzig portrait painter whose sons Enoch and Isaac also painted miniatures in London. The dates in which he flourished are extended to at least 1736 by the signature on the miniature in the Gilbert Collection. Another miniature of a gentleman signed and dated 1733 was sold at Sotheby's London (21 March 1978, lot 47). A miniature of a gentleman, looking very much like an *ad vivum* Zincke of c. 1735 was signed on the reverse *AB Seaman* (sold at Sotheby's, London (9 July 1986, lot 104). As miniatures by both Noah and Abraham Seaman are in English and Dutch private collections, they may well have painted in both countries. However, it appears that Abraham Seaman was still in England at a later date, if, as seems likely, he is the same person who was in Birmingham in the early 1750s. Judging from an advertisement placed in Aris's *Birmingham Gazette* in 1751 (see essay), 'Abraham Seeman' was a Birmingham painter and maker of enamels and a vendor of enamelling colours.

48 Frances Lady Carteret, later Countess Granville and Lady Thynne

Abraham Seaman
England, 1736
Signed, dated and inscribed on counter enamel *R.t Hon.ble Francis Lady Carteret 1713 A. Seaman 1736*

Enamel on copper, 6.2 × 5.2 cm (2⁷/16 × 2¹/16 in), oval
Oval gilt-metal frame, engraved on reverse of frame
Frances Worseley Countess of Granville by A. Seeman
1996.772 (MIN7)

PROVENANCE: Collection of the Earls Spencer (H545, E.6, 6th frame); S.J. Phillips (1979)

LITERATURE: Althorp, 1831, p. 31; London, 1889, p. 93, no. 54.

EXHIBITIONS: London 1889, case XXXII, no. 54, as by 'A Leeman' *[sic]*.

DESCRIPTION: The sitter shown waist-length, wearing a gold dress with pearl-entwined bodice, rose-coloured shawl, posies in her fair which cascades below her shoulders, green-gold background.

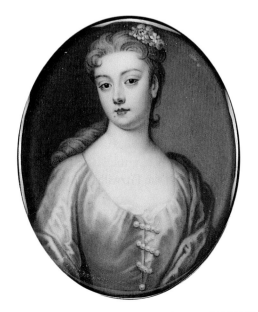

COMMENTARY: Frances, Lady Carteret, was the wife of John, 1st Earl Granville (1690–1763). The Burlington Fine Arts Exhibition catalogue (London, 1889, p. 94, no. 65) illustrates a miniature of him by C.F. Zincke, case XXXII plate XXX . The miniatures of both husband and wife, the latter presumably this miniature, were both lent by Earl Spencer to that exhibition. From the date of 1736 we can assume that Daphne Foskett's dates (Foskett, 1987, p. 641) of 1724–31 for when Seaman flourished can be expanded. The signature on the counter enamel makes this useful for chronicling the various styles of Abraham Seaman. It also shows, from the two dates of 1713 and 1736, that Seaman was copying an earlier depiction of Lady Carteret. The strong influence of Zincke shown in this miniature could result from something other than his great popularity. It could indicate that Seaman was working in Zincke's studio, or that he was working from an earlier work by Zincke, or that both this and numerous Zinckes were copies after works by the same artist, such as Kneller.

NOAH SEAMAN/SEEMAN (FL.1724–C.1741?)

Like Abraham Seaman, who was probably his brother, Noah Seaman seems to have painted in the Netherlands as well as in England. Enamel miniatures exist in the Dutch private collections as well as two in the Dutch Royal Collection. One of the latter (no. 515) is signed 'NS' on the front and 'Abraham Seaman Pinx 1724' on the reverse suggesting some form for collaboration.

Other signed miniatures by Noah Seaman exist in the V&A, and two in the David-Weill Collection at the Louvre. One is of George Frederick Handel signed and dated '1741', the other is of the Duke of Portland signed 'NS', but which must date to 1741 or later when the Duke received the Garter. Other examples have been on the market including one signed and dated '1723' sold at Sotheby's London 28 April 1981 illus., the earliest dated example available.

49 *General Hatton* (?)

Attributed to Noah Seaman
England, c. 1730
Enamel on copper, 5.2 × 4.4 cm ($2\frac{1}{16}$ × $1\frac{3}{4}$ in), oval
Contemporary gold pendant rim frame; inscribed
on case *General Hatton / Compt / Grandfather to Lady Muncarte*
1996.806 (MIN40)

PROVENANCE: D.S. Lavender, London (1982, October).

DESCRIPTION: The sitter is wearing a white wig and blue jacket over armour.

COMMENTARY: No portrait of General Hatton has been located, but the inscription is probably reliable, as it appears to date to the late eighteenth century. The blocky quality of the subject's face is consistent with signed examples of Noah Seaman's work. This has a more linear and less stippled effect than most of Zincke's followers.

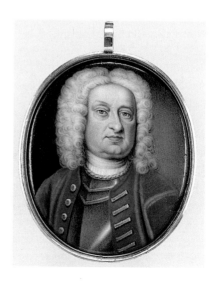

NICOLAS SORET (1759–1830)

Nicolas Soret, born in Geneva, was apprenticed as
a watchmaker before embarking on a career as an
enameller. After the political turmoil in Geneva in
1782, Soret was forced to quit his home town in
1783 and emigrated to Ireland where he joined
the newly founded Swiss colony 'New Geneva'
at Waterford. The failure of this enterprise
encouraged him to return to Geneva in 1785. He
subsequently travelled to Russia and became court
miniature painter to Catherine the Great and Tsar
Paul I from 1792 to 1799. Whereas his enamel portraits from his Irish period are quite coarse, his fine
portraits painted in St Petersburg are to be counted
among the most beautiful Swiss enamel miniatures.
No enamel miniatures dated after his return to
Geneva in 1799 are recorded. Works by his hand are
in the Louvre, the Musée de l'Horlogerie, Geneva,
and in the Hermitage, St Petersburg.

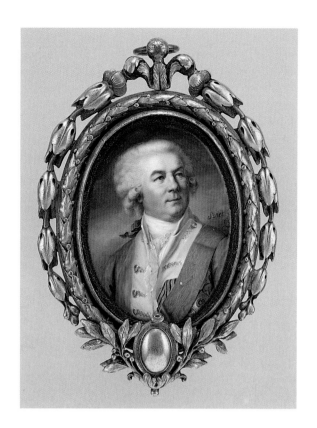

50 *Count Peter Vassilievich Zavadovsky in a Green Uniform*

Nicolas Soret
St Petersburg, 1793
Signed and dated, mid-right *Soret px / 1793*
Enamel on copper, 6.5 × 4.9 cm (2⁹⁄₁₆ × 1¹⁵⁄₁₆ in), oval
Later ormolu frame with husk surround and inner
velvet mount
1996.808 (MIN42)

PROVENANCE: D.S. Lavender, London (October
1982).

LITERATURE: Hofstetter 1999, p. 70, illustrated
p. 71, fig. 94.

DESCRIPTION: The Count is shown bust-length
turned to the right in a green uniform with silver-
braided yellow lapels, decorated with the striped
ribbon of the Imperial Russian Order of St George
and the red sash and breast star of the Imperial
Russian Order of St Alexander Nevsky. The lower
border of the breast star of another order are partly
visible under the sash (possibly the Imperial Russian

Order of St Andrew the First Called), white jabot,
powdered short wig, stormy dark sky background.

COMMENTARY: Count Peter Vassilievich Zavadovsky
(1739–1812) started his career in the service of the
Chancellery of Count Rumiantsev who, together
with Bezborodko, recommended the young man to
the Catherine the Great. The Tsarina could not
resist Zavadovsky's charm and good looks and he
immediately became her favourite. In 1777,
Potemkin's jealousy succeeded in breaking up the
relationship; Zavadovsky nevertheless stayed at
the Court of St Petersburg. As a protégé of
Bezborodko, he obtained important appointments
in the administration, becoming Senator and member of the Council of the Empire. Towards the end
of Empress Catherine's reign, he was appointed
Director of the Bank of Nobility and of the State
Credit Bank. The Tsarina showered him with gifts
including immense estates in Tshernigov and
Mohilev, but in spite of all these consolations he
could never forget the great love of his life. After all
these years, the Tsarina's numerous affairs still filled
his heart with jealousy. After his accession, Tsar Paul

immediately repealed his mother's ex-lover's title of Count of the Russian Empire and his decoration of the Order of St Andrew. In 1800, he was exiled to live on his estate in Lalichi where Catherine II had built a splendid palace for her lover. On the day of his accession, Tsar Alexander I called Zavadovsky back to Court and made him President of the Legislative Commission. In 1802, he was appointed Prime Minister of Public Instruction, after which he became President of the legislative department of the Imperial Council. Despite his marriage (in 1787) to Countess Vera Nicolaievna Apraksine, with whom he had two surviving sons and a daughter, he was a notorious womaniser. He died in 1812.

The identity of the sitter can be established by comparison with a variant of the present miniature, possibly on ivory, formerly in the collection of Grand Duke Nicholas Mikhailovich (illustrated in Nicholas Mikhailovich 1906, II, fasc. 2, no. 52, and in Polovtsoff 1939, opp. p. 139). The major difference from the present enamel is the Cross of the Order of St George which is visibly placed on the sash of the Order of St Alexander Nevsky. Another miniature of Zavadovsky is illustrated in Mikhailova, Smirnov 1974, I, pl. 53, no. 61 and again in Karev 1989, p. 179, fig. 86. The present enamel is possibly one of the finest pieces in the Gilbert Collection as far as technical skill and 'invisible' brushstrokes are concerned. It may be considered as a part of the 'series' of Russian statesmen painted by Soret in the 1790s.

GERVASE SPENCER (C. 1715–63)

According to Edwards, 'Jarvis Spencer was originally a gentleman's servant who when shown a portrait miniature of one of the family with whom he lived . . . he could copy it. He was "indulged with permission" and the result gave a perfect satisfaction acquiring the encouragement and patronage of those he served, and, by their interest, became a fashionable painter of the day'.[1] Vertue records his having been a footman to a 'Dr. W' in 1740, a year for which dated works are recorded. He exhibited at the Society of Artists in 1761–62 and (as 'Gervas Spencer') was one of twenty-four portrait miniature artist listed in Mortimers *Universal Director* of 1763 and painted both ivory and enamel miniatures, some of the latter on gold. It is unclear from whom he learned the art of enamelling. His style in enamel is quite different from Zincke's, being less stippled. He often signed his miniatures 'GS' or 'S' on the face, often in red on gold, occasionally in full on the reverse. He specialised in young ladies and usually his miniatures are small. Examples of his work are in the V&A and the Ashomolean Museum, Oxford.

[1] E. Edwards, , 1818, p. 18.

51 *A Young Girl*

Gervase Spencer
England, 1752
Signed and dated on the counter enamel *G. Spencer pinxt 1752.*
Enamel on copper, 4.5 × 3.5 cm (1¾ × 1⅜ in), oval
Metal rim frame
1996.781 (MIN16)

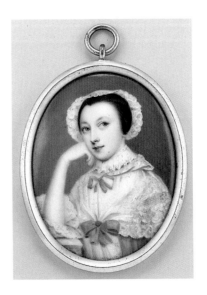

PROVENANCE: Wartski, London (1979).

EXHIBITION: London, 1979, no. 153.

DESCRIPTION: A girl resting her head upon her hand, in pink and white lace dress and cape with pink ribbons, white bonnet.

COMMENTARY: While the date on the counter enamel is somewhat darker than 'G. Spencer pinxt', it would appear that this is the correct date for the miniature.

52 *George Spencer, 4th Duke of Marlborough*

Gervase Spencer
England, 1756
Signed and dated with initials, *G. S./ 1756* in red, lower right
Enamel on copper, 3.0 × 2.6 cm (1³/₁₆ × 1¹/₁₆ in), oval
Original oval gold-fronted and gilt-metal rim set into a later rectangular tortoiseshell and gold frame; paper label on reverse *George Spencer / Duke of Marlborough / from / Rev Hawkins Collection*
1996.786 (MIN21)

PROVENANCE: Ex. collection Reverend Hawkins (collection no. 22, but this miniature does not appear in the Reverend Hawkins Collection Dispersal sale of 1904); D.S. Lavender, London (1980).

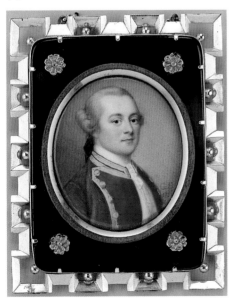

DESCRIPTION: The sitter is shown bust-length, with powdered hair in a pigtail, and a red and blue uniform.

COMMENTARY: George Spencer, 4th Duke of Marlborough (1739–1817), eldest son of Charles, 3rd Duke, was named Lord Lieutenant of Oxfordshire in 1760 through the influence of Lord Harcourt, after turning away from his father's leader, Henry Fox. He was bearer of the Sceptre and Cross at George III's coronation, being appointed Lord Chamberlain and sworn in as a member of the Privy Council the next year, holding the office of Lord Privy Seal in the Grenville ministry from 1763 to 1765. In 1768, he was appointed to the Order of the Garter, which had only been instituted in 1771. He married Lady Caroline Russell (d. 1811), only daughter of John, 4th Duke of Bedford, in 1762. They had three sons and five daughters. A full scale portrait of the same subject but not in the same pose, by Romney, is at Blenheim.

53 *A Gentleman stated to be Thomas Tilson, Father of Lady Deane*

Gervase Spencer
England, c. 1740
Signed *GS* in red on lower right
Enamel on copper, 5.8 × 3.8 cm (2⁵/₁₆ × 1¹/₂ in), oval
In paste-set silver-rim frame with agate backs;

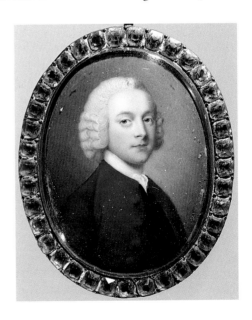

engraved on silver-rim frame *Thomas Tilson Father of Lady Deane*.
1996.804 (MIN39A)

PROVENANCE: Lord Muskerry; Christie's, London (24 November 1981, lot 53); D.S. Lavender, London (1 October 1982).

DESCRIPTION: The subject has a powdered wig and a blue jacket.

COMMENTARY: This miniature and the one by Zincke, of a Lady stated to be Mrs Tilson, mother of Charlotte Tilson, Lady Deane, were sold with another Zincke stated to be Charlotte Lady Deane as three successive lots all with the same Lord Muskerry provenance at Christie's (see provenance).

Dr Aileen Ribero believes that Mrs Tilson's costume would indicate a date of around 1720, whereas the man's costume dates to c. 1735–45. The daughter, also by Zincke, looks very like her mother and is described as 'having a contemporary gold frame with reeded border, the reverse inscribed Charleton Tilson, Dublin by Mr Zinzts 1732'. Charleton, second daughter of Thomas Tilson of Dublin, married the Rt Hon. Sir Robert Deane on 24 August 1738. Thus the c. 1720 date would be appropriate for the age of the mother of a young woman married in 1738. Possibly Zincke might have painted it based on an earlier painting at the time he painted the daughter in 1732. Spencer's earliest miniatures date from c. 1740, thus putting the identity of this subject somewhat in doubt. It would seem more reasonable that this would have been the young lady's husband either in 1738 at the time of their marriage or soon thereafter. There is a slight variation in the pastes, frames and inscriptions of the two, so they are not an exact pair. The inscriptions, while different, are not new. It would make sense if the daughter (whose miniature had no pastes) had had the miniatures of her husband and her mother framed alike. Another example of later pairing of two miniatures with paste frames are two miniatures in the Metropolitan (see Reynolds, Baetjer, 1996, p. 127, nos. 118, 119) of Richard Abell and a lady possibly Mrs Vanderbank by Zincke with matching paste frames of c. 1770– 80. These, however, are by the same artist and are the same size.

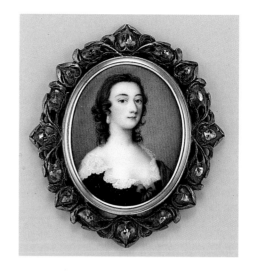

54 *A Lady*

Gervase Spencer
England, 1747
Signed and dated on the counter enamel *G. Spencer fecit / AD 1747*
Enamel on copper, 3.9 × 3.1 cm (1⁹/₁₆ × 1¹/₄ in), oval
Original gold-rim frame with open reverse with silver and diamond pierced border
1996.797 (MIN32)

PROVENANCE: The same or a replica (?), Sotheby's, London (16 December 1974, lot 29); D.S. Lavender, London (October 1981).

DESCRIPTION: The sitter is shown bust-length with brown curling hair and a black dress, with blue bow and dark red shawl, against a grey-green background.

COMMENTARY: This is very typical of Spencer's enamel miniatures of this period, stylistically using an almost fuzzy, small-dot technique. The costume and jewellery may well be from his studio as they show up in various other miniatures of this period. An example, but on ivory, is in the Yale Center for British Art (B 1974. 2. 105).

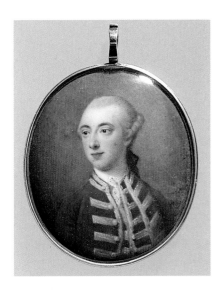

55 *A Gentleman stated to be Sir William Morden (?)*

Gervase Spencer
England, 1755

Signed and dated *GS 1755* (?) on lower right (the signature and date appear to be *GS 1755* in red, the last number being illegible).
Enamel on copper, 4.6 × 4.0 cm (1 7/8 × 1 9/16 in), oval
Original oval gold pendant case, unopened
1996.796 (MIN31)

PROVENANCE: D.S. Lavender, London (October 1981).

DESCRIPTION: The sitter is shown bust-length turned slightly left with powdered hair *en queue* and a wearing a red and white uniform with white braid against a grey-green background.

COMMENTARY: This miniature was acquired as being of Sir William Morden, but, to date, no other image of him has surfaced.

HENRY SPICER (1743–1804)

Henry Spicer was born in Reepham, Norfolk. A pupil of Gervase Spencer, he exhibited at the Society of Artists from 1765–83 and at the Royal Academy from 1774–1804. He was appointed Painter in Enamel to H.R.H. The Prince of Wales in 1789 and painted his portrait as well as that of the Princess of Wales and of Sir Joshua Reynolds. Spicer taught William Russell Birch, who also first exhibited at the Society of Artists from Spicer's house in 1775. In addition to Birch, Spicer presumably was the teacher of his two daughters Miss J. and Miss M. A. Spicer, who both painted enamel miniatures and exhibited at the Royal Academy, the first in 1801 and 1802, the second in 1799–1803, listed at their father's address. Among his friends were George Stubbs and Ozias Humphry, the latter whose portrait he also painted. After a long illness, Spicer died leaving his wife in straightened circumstances and Humphry lodged with her.

    His work is in the Holburne Museum, Bath, and the Fitzwilliam Museum, Cambridge.

56 *Francis Rawdon-Hastings,
      2nd Earl of Moira*

Henry Spicer, after John Hoppner (c. 1758–1810)
England, c. 1802
Unsigned on front
Enamel on copper, 20.9 × 16.6 cm (8 1/4 × 6 9/16 in), rectangular
Rectangular ormolu-mounted papier-mâché and wood frame, husk border surmounted by Earl's coronet; inscription on backing paper reads, (?) *Rt Honble* (?) */ Earl of Moira / born the 7th December 1756 / (?) painted (?) by Spicer / Enamel painter to / HRH the Prince of Wales* (faint)
1996.777 (MIN12)

PROVENANCE: Christie's, London, (19 March 1980, lot 49).

EXHIBITION: Royal Academy, 1802, no. 537.

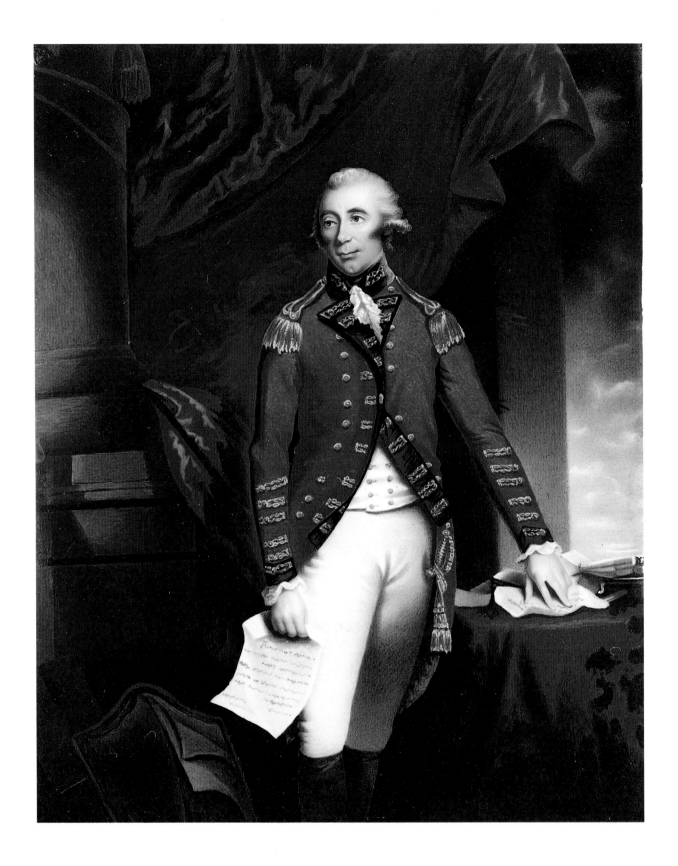

DESCRIPTION: The Earl is shown full length, holding a document, in scarlet uniform with blue facings and gold epaulets, beside a table with further papers and documents, a pillar to left, crimson curtain background.

COMMENTARY: The original painting by Hoppner is in Buckingham Palace. An enamel, by Spicer, presumably this one, is listed in the Royal Academy catalogue, 1802, no. 537, as 'Earl Moira'. Francis Rawdon-Hastings (1754–1826), 1st Marquis of Hastings and 2nd Earl of Moira, soldier and statesman, was the son and heir of John, Earl of Moira and Elizabeth, Baroness Botreaux, Hungerford, Moleyns, Hastings of Hastings and Hastings of Hungerford. He succeeded his father in 1793 and his mother in 1808. He married Flora, Countess of Loudon, daughter of James (Mure-Campbell), 5th Earl of Loudon, in 1804. He was educated at Harrow and University College, Oxford.

After distinguishing himself at Bunker Hill in 1775 and fighting in the battles of Brooklyn and White Plains in 1776, he became adjutant-general to the forces in America in 1778, defeating Greene at Hobkirk's Hill in 1781.

In 1783, on the voyage home from America, he was captured by the French. The same year he was created Baron Rawdon. He joined the opposition in 1789 and was intimate with and an active supporter of the Prince of Wales from 1810 to 1811. He assumed the Irish title of Earl of Moira in 1793. He was MP for Randalstown, 1780–3. He commanded an expedition to Brittany in 1793 and the reinforcements for the Duke of York in Flanders in 1794. He spoke against the Irish Union in 1799. Promoted to General in 1803, he was appointed commander-in-chief of Scotland in 1803. He was Colonel of the 105th Foot from 1781 to 1783 and the 27th Foot from 1804 to 1826. He was appointed master of the ordinance in 1806–7 and then became ADC to George III.

From 1813 to 1822 he was Governor-General of Bengal, being created Marquis of Hastings in 1817. He extirpated the Pindaris, and, by defeating the Marathas, established British supremacy in Central India between 1817 and 1818. Governor-General of Fort William from 1813 to 1823, he secured the cession of Singapore in 1819 and opened relations with Siam in 1822. In 1824 he was appointed Governor of Malta. In recognition of his public services, he received £60,000 from the East India Company. He died at sea on board HMS *Revenge* in Baia Bay off Naples and was buried in Malta. A statue of him was erected at Dalhousie Institute, Calcutta.

John Hoppner was one of the better known followers of Reynolds. After being accepted as a student at the Royal Academy in 1775, he became Portrait Painter to the Prince of Wales in 1793 and was elected a member of the Royal Academy in 1795.

FRANCIS SYKES (1746–85)

Some confusion exists about whether there is more than one artist named Sykes who did miniatures. Foskett records a Frans Sykes who registered his will in The Hague in 1743 and was a miniaturist (Foskett, 1985, p. 659). An enamel miniature of Princess Caroline, signed 'F Sykes Pinx 1759', is in the Hesse Collection. The *Public Advertiser* refers to 'the ingenious Mr Sykes' as the painter of miniatures in a ring set with brilliants presented by Queen Charlotte to George III on his birthday in 1764 or 1769 (Foskett, 1987, p. 659 and Walker, 1999, p. 567). An artist named Sykes exhibited at the Society of Artist from 1761–74. Mortimer's *Universal Director of 1763* listed twenty-four miniature artists in London, one of which was 'Francis Sykes' (Reynolds, 1988, p. 115).

57 John Stuart, 3rd Earl of Bute

Attributed to Francis Sykes, after Allan Ramsay
England, c. 1760–63
Unsigned on front
Enamel on copper, 4.8 × 3.8 cm (1⁷/₈ × 1¹/₂ in), oval
Original oval hinged frame, in sharkskin case with
glass cover
1996.811 (MIN45)

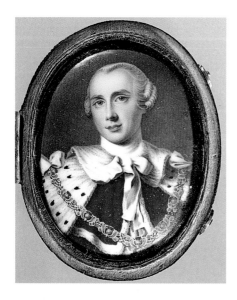

PROVENANCE: D.S. Lavender (1987).

DESCRIPTION: The sitter is shown bust-length in
ceremonial robes, a red coat and ermine cape.

COMMENTARY: Bute was a Scottish favourite, first of
Frederick Prince of Wales, by whom he was
appointed a Lord of the Bedchamber in 1750, and,
after the latter's death in 1751, of the future George
III. Upon the accession of George III, he became a
Privy Councillor, Groom of the Stole, and First
Gentleman of the Bedchamber. A Knight of the
Thistle and of the Garter, he was appointed Lord of
the Treasury in 1762 after he concluded the peace
treaty called the Treaty of Paris. From 1761 to 1763,
he was Prime Minister to George III, after which he
fell from influence.

A full-length original by Ramsay painted by
order of the Prince of Wales, later George III, given

to His Majesty in 1763 by Lord Mountstuart, is in
Bute House, Edinburgh [property of] the National
Trust for Scotland). It was exhibited and illustrated
in *Allan Ramsay*, Scottish National Portrait Gallery,
Edinburgh, 1992; National Portrait Gallery,
London 1992–3, cat. no. 60.

A miniature by Gervase Spencer, of 1757, stated
to be of the same subject, wearing the Ribbon of the
Thistle, is in the Waldgrave Collection, Chewton
(National Portrait Gallery, 1987, no. 27 on R.
Walker list). A miniature of Bute by Samuel Shelley,
signed and dated 1781 on the reverse, was sold at
Sotheby's, London [Silver/Miniature sale] (28 April
1988, lot 88).

The attribution to Francis Sykes is made on the
basis of an enamel of the Earl of Bute inscribed and
dated on the reverse *Painted by F. Sykes 1760 / 3ʳᵈ
Earl Bute* seen by Walker in 1967 when it belonged
to Paul Coutts Ltd, Edinburgh. This miniature was
mounted on the inside of the lid of a snuffbox.

Similar miniatures exist of George III as Prince
of Wales, also after the Ramsay in the Bute
Collection, apparently by the same hand. One,
attributed to Jeremiah Meyer, is in the Royal
Collection (see Walker, 1992, p. 127, no. 249). A
second in profile is attributed to Sykes (Walker,
1992, pp. 156–7, no. 312). A third is mounted on a
rectangular enamel and gold presentation snuffbox
by George Moser. This box was presented to John
3rd Earl of Bute by either George III or Augusta,
Dowager Princess of Wales, and descended in the
Bute family until it was sold in a sale of works of art
from the Bute Collection, Christie's, London (3 July
1996, lot 60). A fourth was in the Woollett
Collection and was sold at Sotheby's (10 November
1969, lot 25). A somewhat stylised profile of George
III in the Royal Collection is attributed to Sykes
based on its apparent similarity to another in the
Shelley-Rolls Collection, signed and dated 'F. Sykes
1764', sold at Christie's, London (13 February 1962,
lot 28, no illus.), also in its original shagreen case,
and to its similarity to the one of Bute owned by
Paul Coutts.

NICOLAS CLAUDE VASSAL (FL.SECOND HALF EIGHTEENTH CENTURY)

The French enameller Nicolas Claude Vassal was admitted to the Académie de St-Luc of Paris in 1766, where he exhibited in 1774 and 1779. His exhibits included his self-portrait and a portrait of Louis XV. Most of his enamels are signed and dated on the counter enamel. Works by his hand are rare but can be found in the Louvre.

58 *A Young Lady in a White Gown*

Nicolas Claude Vassal
Paris, c. 1775/80
Enamel, 3.5 × 2.7 cm (1³/₈ × 1¹/₁₆ in), oval
Mounted later (?) on the cover of an octagonal
Saxon gold and hardstone snuffbox by Johann
Christian Neuber, Dresden, c. 1780
1996.483 (GB135)

PROVENANCE: Garrard & Co., London (1987).

LITERATURE: Holzhausen, 1935, fig. 20; Truman, 1991, pp. 232–3, no. 79; *World of Interiors*, December 1996, pp. 104–5; Massinelli 2000, p. 150, no. 59.

EXHIBITIONS: Los Angeles/Memphis, 1991–92.

DESCRIPTION: The sitter is full face, bust-length, in lace-bordered white gown with white underdress and pink bow, high-piled powdered hair falling in a curl on to her shoulders, seated on a red-upholstered gilt-wood chair.

COMMENTARY: Although contemporary with the snuffbox, it is likely that the miniature was mounted on the box at a later date, probably replacing the portrait of a member of the notoriously unattractive family of Elector Frederick Augustus III of Saxony (see cat. no. 89), a common 'upgrading' procedure for Neuber boxes. This enamel is characteristic of Vassal's work, with its slightly fuzzy aspect, obtained by the use of rather thick dotting, and the pinkish carnation. The pleasant but rather impersonal expression of the model is to be seen on many of his works and makes the identification of most of his sitters virtually impossible.

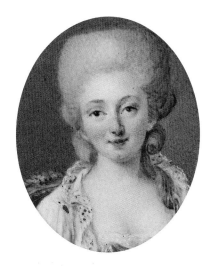

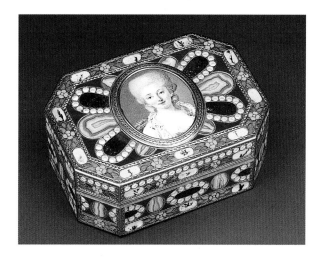

Jean-Baptiste Weyler (1747–91)

Jean-Baptiste Weyler was born in Strasburg, where he first studied under the Haldenwangers and Redlob, before moving to Paris, where he was a pupil of J.M. Vien from 1763. He painted miniatures on ivory and enamel as well as pastels. He became a member of the Académie Royale de Peinture on 2 October 1779, despite his Protestant religion, an obstacle which required the personal intervention of the Comte d'Angiviller to remove. Weyler exhibited at the Salon from 1775 until his early death in 1791. Leo R. Schidlof (1964, II, p. 898) considered him to be the best French enamel painter of his time.

59 *Charles-Claude de La Billarderie, Comte d'Angiviller*

Jean-Baptiste Weyler
Paris, c. 1779
Enamel, 9.1 × 7.2 cm (3⁵/₈ × 2¹³/₁₆ in), oval
Oval ormolu frame with laurel leaves and wreath

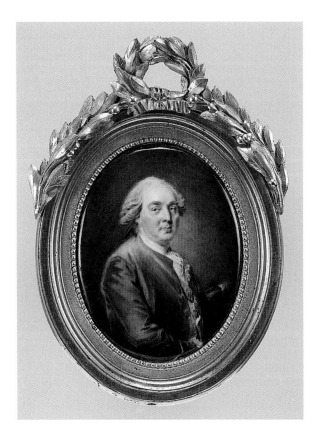

surmount, paper label on back of miniature inscribed, '*Marquis* [sic] / *d'Angivilliers*' 1996.790 (MIN25)

PROVENANCE: S.J. Phillips, London (October 1981).

DESCRIPTION: The sitter is depicted three-quarters to right wearing a purple jacket and the green neck sash of the Royal French Order of Saints Maurice and Lazare, powdered hair *en queue*, a tricorn hat under his left arm.

COMMENTARY: The numerous titles of Charles-Claude de Flahaut de La Billarderie, Comte d'Angiviller (1730–1809) included Director-General of Buildings, Gardens and Factories to the Crown, protector of the Academy of Sciences and Field Marshall of the Army of the King. For the artistic world of his time, his influence was crucial as he was also *Conseiller du Roy* and *Directeur Général des Arts*. As such, he recommended to Louis XVI's Minister, the Comte de Vergennes, those artists who would receive the royal commissions. Thus it is not surprising that he was painted by the most celebrated artists of his time such as Jean-Baptiste Greuze and Joseph-Siffrein Duplessis. Naturally, he was also one of the favourite sitters of Weyler, who owed him at least two major favours. Weyler's acceptance at the Royal Academy, although a Protestant, was the result of d'Angiviller's protection, as was an important royal command which Weyler was to receive in 1785.

At least three variants of Weyler's miniature of d'Angiviller are known, both on ivory and in enamel. Two of them are in the Louvre: Weyler's highly important, slightly larger *Morceau de Réception*, at the Académie Royale in 1779, was acquired by the Louvre for 3,000 gold francs in 1853 (illustrated in Schidlof, 1911, pl. III) and a smaller bust-length enamel version was part of the Doistau Donation in 1922 (Demonts, Terrasse, 1922, pp. 82–3, no. 145, illustrated in Lespinasse, 1929, pl. XXIV, fig. 80). A large ivory version is in a Swiss private collection, formerly in the David-Weill/Sir Charles Clore Collections (illustrated in G. Henriot, 'La Collection David-Weill', *L'Amour de l'Art*, 1925, pl.

XXXII, no. 15, and in Gillet, Jeannerat, Clouzot, 1957, p. 324). From an artistic point of view, the present version is certainly the most sketchy one; it exemplifies the translation of the free and broad brush stroke of the pastellist and watercolour miniaturist into the art of the enameller.

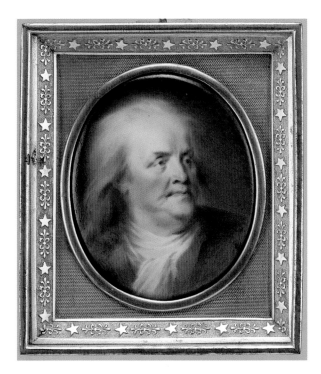

60 *Benjamin Franklin in a Mauve Jacket*

Jean Baptiste Weyler
Paris, c. 1785/90
Enamel on copper, 5.5 × 4.5 cm (2³/₁₆ × 1³/₄ in), oval
Slightly later rectangular Empire ormolu frame with star border
1996.822 (MIN54A)

PROVENANCE: 'Au Vieux Paris' (Michel Turysk), Paris (3 November 1994).

EXHIBITION: Portland, 1995.

DESCRIPTION: The sitter is depicted facing right, with swept flowing grey hair, mauve jacket with gold trim, grey-green background.

COMMENTARY: Benjamin Franklin (1706–90) was sent as a deputy of Pennsylvania to France in order to seek her assistance in the struggle against Britain. Paris received him with enthusiasm and, in 1783, he signed the peace treaty which recognised the independence of the United States of America. Franklin was a popular model for many other artists including the painter Joseph-Siffrein Duplessis, the sculptor Houdon and the miniaturist François Dumont.

In 1785, the Comte d'Angiviller approved a project submitted by Jean-Baptiste Weyler consisting of the creation of a '*panthéon iconographique*'. This pantheon was meant to display the portraits of famous men both of French and foreign origin, painted in the enamel technique in order to ensure them in a place in posterity. Among the celebrities selected as 'sitters' for this enterprise were field marshals Turenne and Catinat, Henry IV of France, Tsar Peter the Great, Admiral de Ruyter and also Benjamin Franklin. These portraits were copied after earlier portraits which had been borrowed from collectors and first copied by Weyler in pastel and subsequently as enamel miniatures. In the supplement to the Paris 1789 Salon, Weyler encouraged owners of historical portraits to lend them to him and to have them preserved for posterity as enamels. Benjamin Franklin was certainly the most popular celebrity of the pantheon. At least five enamel versions and two ivory versions are recorded, all unsigned and of oval shape, with heights ranging from 2 cm (¹³/₁₆ in) to 9 cm (3⁹/₁₆ in): a large ivory version, 8.2 × 6.5 cm (3¹/₄ × 2⁹/₁₆ in), is in the Louvre (Jean-Richard 1994, p. 339, no. 636), and a slightly smaller version, 7 cm (2³/₄ in) high, was sold at Christie's, Geneva (14 November 1989, lot 230). The smallest enamel version, 2 cm (¹³/₁₆ in) high, was in the D. David-Weill/Sir Charles Clore Collections, sold at Sotheby's, London (10 November 1986, lot 197, also illustrated in Gillet/Jeannerat/Clouzot, 1957, no. 381). The present version is the second smallest one. A slightly larger enamel version, 6.4 × 5.4 cm (2¹/₂ × 2¹/₈ in), is in the Nationalmuseum, Stockholm (inv. NM Khv 601/1895, illustrated in Hofstetter 1994, p. 70, fig. 29). A large enamel version is in the Louvre (inv. 35727) and two other large ones were sold at auction at Christie's, London (8 June 1971, lot 49, 8.8 cm (3⁷/₁₆ in) high) and at

Christie's, Geneva (15 May 1990, lot 251, 9 cm (3⁹/₁₆ in) high).

Considering this unusually high number of versions, it may be assumed that Weyler produced these enamels in a semi-industrial way in order to satisfy the demand of his contemporary collectors. This can be substantiated by the fact that Weyler's sponsor, the Comte d'Angiviller, owned an enamel version. On d'Angiviller's emigration during the French Revolution, this enamel had to be left behind, was seized by the Revolutionaries and is now in the Louvre (Furcy-Renaud, 1913, p. 251).

Although this miniature and its variants could have been painted *ad vivum*, it is, in the light of Weyler's appeals for 'originals' to be copied by him, more probable that he copied a pastel or oil portrait. The flowing hair and impressive features of his 'sitter' gave Weyler the opportunity to display the 'genius' of his light, soft and free brushstroke which contrasted favourably with the dry stipple technique used by most of his French contemporaries.

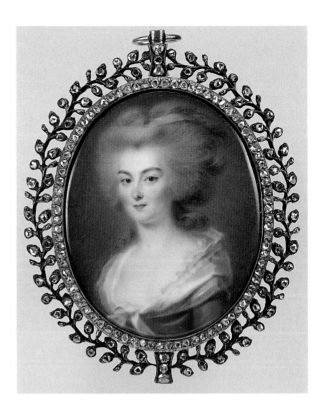

61 *A Young Lady in a Blue Dress*

Jean Baptiste Weyler
Paris, c. 1785/90
Enamel on copper, 6 × 4.9 cm (2³/₈ × 1¹⁵/₁₆ in), oval
Oval rose-cut diamond studded silver frame with pierced vine border of possibly later date
1996.823 (MIN54B)

PROVENANCE: 'Au Vieux Paris' (Michel Turysk), Paris (3 November 1994).

EXHIBITION: Portland, 1995.

DESCRIPTION: The sitter is shown bust-length with powdered high-piled hair dressed '*à la conseilleur*', with blue ribbon and matching dress with white gauze *fichu* and bow, against a greyish background.

COMMENTARY: Within Weyler's *oeuvre*, the present enamel stands out because of its fine, powdery technique and its apparent *ad vivum* likeness. The harmony of colours and perfect mastering of the enamel technique, in addition to the ravishing charm of the sitter, show that Weyler's strength was much more in the representation of 'real' portraits than in the mass-production of multiples for commercial purposes which was the reason for his contemporary popularity.

CHRISTIAN FRIEDRICH ZINCKE (1683/4–1767)

Christian Friedrich Zincke was the son of a Dresden goldsmith. He was apprenticed to his father and he also studied painting. He arrived in England in 1706, at Charles Boit's request to assist him in his studio. In Dresden Zincke appears to have studied with Boit and worked in his studio until Boit left for France in 1714. By this time, Zincke seems to have inherited a good many of Boit's fashionable clients. He painted enamels after Lely, Kneller etc., as well as from life. He was appointed Cabinet Painter to Frederick Prince of Wales in 1732. He lived in England for the rest of his life and was the most

successful enamel painter of his era, having
numerous royal and other important clients. By the
1740s, his deteriorating eyesight reduced his output,
but he did teach Jeremiah Meyer, and William
Prewett. Although his early miniatures are very
much like Boit's in style, Zincke adopted his own
stipple technique of tiny red dots, sometimes
described as 'measles', which mixed visually with the
white ground for the flesh tones. His work is in
major museums, including the V&A, the Ashmolean
Museum, Oxford, and the Metropolitan.

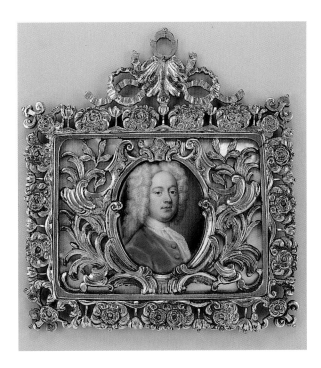

62 A *William, 7th Baron Brooke*
B *Lady Mary Brooke*

Christian Friedrich Zincke
England, c. 1716
Enamel on copper, oval
A 3.8 × 3.1 cm (1¹/₂ × 1¹/₄ in)
B 4.0 × 3.5 cm (1⁹/₁₆ × 1³/₈ in)
Rococo rectangular openwork ormolu and mother-
of-pearl frame, probably mid-1700s; inscribed on
the frame's bone plaque backing the miniature – A
William Lord Brooke, B *Mary Lady Brooke*
1996.770–771 (MIN6A and 6B)

PROVENANCE: Christie's, London (28 June 1978, lot
66); S.J. Phillips Ltd, London (1979).

DESCRIPTION: Three-quarter facing each other, he
(6A) on blue jacket with white jabot, powdered long
wig; she (6B) in green dress with white *fichu*, light
brown hair cascading over her shoulders.

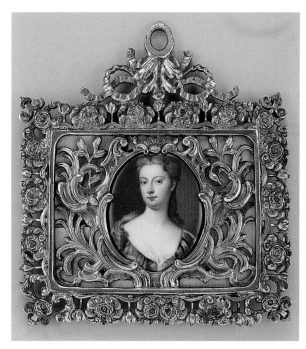

COMMENTARY: William Greville (c. 1694–1727), 7th
Baron Brooke, succeeded to the barontcy in 1711
and married Mary Thynne (c. 1702–1720) in 1716.
The subjects' identities are confirmed by a pair of
portraits attributed to Michael Dahl in Warwick
Castle in a 1954 photograph (National Portrait
Gallery, from Witt Library, neg. B54/241).

    A marriage was a frequent reason for commis-
sioning a pair of miniatures of husband and wife.
The costume and style are appropriate for this date,
although they could also be seen in miniatures as
much as ten years later. Lady Mary Brooke's suggested birth date of 1702 may be a little late if they
married in 1716, but, if it is not, her depicted age
appears to be more than fourteen. These 'keepsake'
size miniatures would have been more likely to have
been mounted originally in small pendant frames,
especially if they were commissioned at the time of
their marriage. Putting them into a double frame
made them into a cabinet piece to be hung on the
wall rather than contemplated in private.

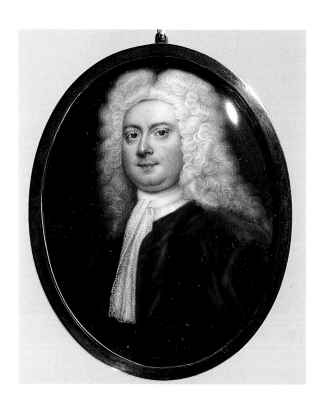

He entered Magdalene College, Cambridge in
1700 and, after gaining his MB in 1705 and MD in
1710, was elected Fellow of the Royal College of
Surgeons in 1725. In 1726, he was admitted as a
Fellow of the Royal College of Physicians.

Hollings' classical scholarship was renowned. In
1734 he published the Harveian oration for that
year entitled '*Status Humanae Naturae expositus in
Oratione coram Medicis Londinensibus habita.*'

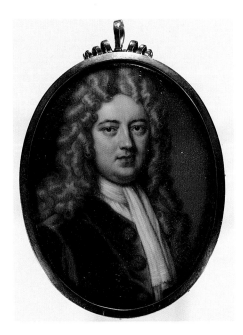

63 *A Gentleman probably Dr. John Hollings, M.D.*

Christian Friedrich Zincke
England, c. 1725
Enamel on copper, 7.1 × 5.6 cm (2 $^{13}/_{16}$ × 2 $^{3}/_{16}$ in),
oval
Oval gold pendant frame
1996.784 (MIN19)

PROVENANCE: Mrs Katharine Paull, *née*
Champernowne; Sotheby's, London (10 December
1979, lot 86); S.J. Phillips, London (1980).

DESCRIPTION: The sitter is three-quarters to the left
wearing a bright purple jacket and waistcoat with
white lace jabot, white wig, against an olive green
background.

COMMENTARY: No documentation or corroborating
portrait has yet come to light for the identification
of the sitter. Dr John Hollings, MD (c. 1685–1782),
was Physician in Ordinary to George I. He also held
the appointment of Physician General to the army.

64 *A Gentleman formerly called John Churchill, First Duke of Marlborough*

Christian Friedrich Zincke
England, c. 1715
Signed with monogram *CFZ*
Enamel on copper, 7.2 × 5.5 cm (2 $^{13}/_{16}$ × 2 $^{3}/_{16}$ in),
oval
Gold-rim frame with glazed fruit and reverse and
scroll on top; paper sticker '13 (W.W.–A)',
presumably for W.W. Aston; later ink inscription
on counter enamel *John Churchill / Duke of /
Marlborough / C F Zinke*
1998.24 (MIN62)

PROVENANCE: W.W. Aston, S.J. Phillips (June 1996).

1) 'John, 1st Duke of Marlborough 1650–1722,
plate XXIX enamel CF Zincke signed "C.F.Z" in
monogram' lent by W.W. Aston; Portland, 1996–97.

DESCRIPTION: The sitter is shown bust-length facing
right, with a long light brown wig, white cravat and
dark mauve coat.

COMMENTARY: Close inspection of this miniature
reveals a somewhat different appearance from the
Duke depicted in catalogue number 65, which is
clearly a correct identification. Many variations of
physical appearance do occur especially in enamel.
However, the deliberate inclusion of a mole on the
cheek of this subject, and the presence of one on the
lip on the other side of the face of the other who is
clearly the Duke of Marlborough, suggest two
different subjects.

   With similar or matching wigs and similarly
attired, out of robes or uniform, the Earl of Oxford,
the Duke of Marlborough, and Joseph Addison,
among others, can all look somewhat alike in the
hands of the same artist. By contrast, Sarah
Churchill (see cat. nos. 66, 67 and 68), descended
from the Spencer family, looks almost like three
different women, with different poses and dress,
despite being all by Zincke. Thus, diversity
of appearance should be allowed. However,
specific identifying physical characteristics,
such as a mole, should be taken into account and
lead to the conclusion that this is not the Duke of
Marlborough. Unfortunately the identification of
the subject remains obscure. It does, however, have
a resemblance to Admiral George Churchill, as seen
in a miniature by Charles Boit (with a dark wig) in
the Duke of Buccleuch's collection (Kennedy, 1917,
pl. LXVI).

65 *John, Duke of Marlborough*

Christian Friedrich Zincke
England, c. 1710
Unsigned on front
Enamel on copper, 8.4 × 5.3 cm (3⁵/₁₆ × 2¹/₁₆ in),
oval
Back of frame is engraved, *John Duke of
Marlborough*; has Althorp tag E-8
1999.55 (MIN71B)

PROVENANCE: Spencer Family, Althorp; S.J. Phillips,
London (August 1997).

EXHIBITIONS: London, 1865, no. 969, London,
1889, p. 95 case XXXII, 76 and 78 are both of this
subject by this artist lent by Earl Spencer
(illustrated).

DESCRIPTION: The sitter is shown facing forward
wearing a white lace neck cloth, blue cape and chain
of the Order of the Garter.

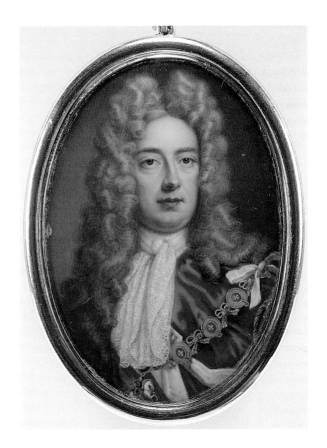

COMMENTARY: The 1865 exhibition catalogue, p. 80 wallcase J, reads as follows: '969 John Duke of Marlborough in his robes as a Knight of the Garter. Enamel CF Zincke'. This is undoubtedly the miniature in enamel listed in the 1831 Althorp inventory, no. 456, as 'John Duke of Marlborough, in an oval / Zinck. (Artist)'. Another miniature of John, Duke of Marlborough, in a similar pose, but wearing armour also by Zincke is in the Edward B. Greene Collection in the Cleveland Museum of Art.[1]

[1] H. A. Kennedy, London, 1917.

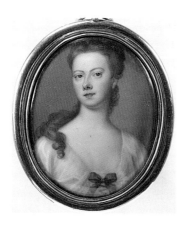

66 *Sarah, Duchess of Marlborough*

Christian Friedrich Zincke
England, c. 1720
Unsigned on front
Enamel on copper, 4.2 × 3.5 cm (1⅝ × 1⅜ in), oval
Back of gold frame is engraved, *Sarah Duchess / of Marlborough* tag; with Althorp No. E-2
1998.26 (MIN68)

PROVENANCE: Spencer family, Althorp; S.J. Phillips, London, (August 1997).

EXHIBITION: London, 1865, no. 931.

DESCRIPTION: The Duchess is shown facing forward in a white gown with a blue bow at the bodice.

COMMENTARY: Sarah was the daughter of Richard Jennings and was in the household of Mary of Modena, second Duchess of York, as an attendant to the Duchess's stepdaughter, the Princess Anne,

when she met John Churchill. They married in 1678. She became one of the Ladies of the Bedchamber to Princess Anne in 1683. As Mistress of the Robes and Keeper of the Privy Purse and a close friend of Queen Anne, she wielded great influence at court until 1707 when she and the Queen had a sudden falling out. Thereafter she spent more time at Blenheim Palace, remaining one of the most painted women of her day.

This and/or the following two miniatures maybe those on an 1831 inventory of pictures at Althorp listed as 'Miniatures in Enamel 455' where two listing of 'Sarah Duchess of Marlborough' appear without an artist listed (Althorp, 1831, p. 31).

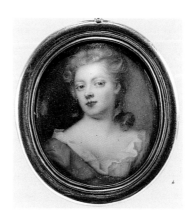

67 *Sarah, Duchess of Marlborough*

Christian Friedrich Zincke
England, c. 1720
Unsigned on front
Enamel on copper, 3.3 × 2.9 cm (1⁵⁄₁₆ × 1⅛ in), oval almost round
Back of frame is engraved, *Sarah Duchess / of Marlborough* (in script); Althorp No E5
1999.52 (MIN69)

PROVENANCE: Spencer Family, Althorp, with family history (from Spencer notebook) 'Probably given by the Duchess to Lady Georgiana Spencer'; S.J. Phillips, London (August 1997).

EXHIBITIONS: Possibly London 1862, which had two miniatures of 'Sarah Jennings Duchess of Marlborough' by Zincke lent by the Earl of

Spencer, exhibition nos. 2655 and 2656, although no mention is made of the Spencer inventory numbers.

DESCRIPTION: The Duchess is shown bust-length, facing forward towards the right.

COMMENTARY: The source for this miniature is Kneller's oval bust-length portrait of 1691 at Althorp. Another miniature of the Duchess, in similar pose, but in a rose-coloured dress, is in the collection of the Duke of Buccleuch (Kennedy, 1917, pl. LIX).

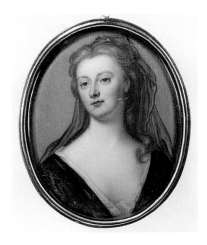

68 Sarah, Duchess of Marlborough

Christian Friedrich Zincke
England, c. 1720
Unsigned on front
Enamel on copper, 4.6 × 3.8 cm (1 13/16 × 1 1/2 in), oval
Back of gold frame is engraved *Sarah Jennings / Duchess of Marlborough / by Zinke*, in block letters, no inventory number tag, but no. H544 in family papers; slightly different style of engraving on reverse from others in the group.
1999.53 (MIN70)

PROVENANCE: Spencer family, Althorp; S.J. Phillips, London (August 1997).

EXHIBITION: London, 1865, no. 929

DESCRIPTION: The Duchess is shown facing forward wearing a black gown and black veil, probably widow's weeds.

COMMENTARY: If indeed these are widow's weeds, this would indicate that the Duchess was painted in 1722 after the death of her husband John, Duke of Marlborough. Another version of this enamel, after a painting by Kneller at Blenheim Palace, mounted on a box, was sold at Phillips, London (9 November 1987, lot 13) and again Hôtel Drouot, Paris (22 February 1988, lot 49).

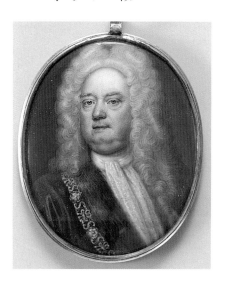

69 Sir George Mertins, Lord Mayor of London

Christian Friedrich Zincke
England, c. 1725
Unsigned on front
Enamel on copper, 4.6 × 3.7 cm (1 13/16 × 1 7/16 in), oval
Oval gold glazed case with pendant loop
1998.25 (MIN65)

PROVENANCE: Sotheby's, London, (24 February 1969, lot 120, as Sir William Gore, Mayor); D.S. Lavender (July 1996).

DESCRIPTION: The sitter has a long white wig, wearing a red fur-collared jacket with his chain of office.

COMMENTARY: A mezzotint of the same subject, labelled 'Rt Hon. Sr. Geo. Mertins. Knt. Lord Mayor', by John Simon after an unknown artist published in 1725 is in the National Portrait Gallery (D3656 Archive Engravings Collection). It is three-quarters in the opposite direction, suggesting that this enamel and the original painting on which the mezzotint is based are posed in the same direction. The subject died on 3 November 1727, aged sixty-three.

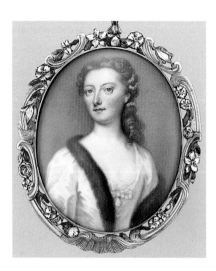

70 *A Lady, possibly Margaret, 2nd Duchess of Portland*

Christian Friedrich Zincke
England, c. 1730
Enamel on copper, 4.6 × 3.8 cm (1 $^{13}/_{16}$ × 1 $^{1}/_{2}$ in), oval
In original gold and enamel frame decorated with scrolls and flowers, with original black shield-shaped sharkskin case with tag on back for BADA, number hard to decipher, possibly 'L 103'
1998.30 (MIN66)

PROVENANCE: D.S. Lavender (1996, July).

EXHIBITION: London, 1932.

LITERATURE: *Art News*, 1930, XXVIII, 15 January 1930, S.J. Phillips advertisement illustration.

DESCRIPTION: The sitter is shown half-length facing the viewer with brown curls and wearing a white dress trimmed with brown fur and with a pearl bow pin on the bodice.

COMMENTARY: This is a good mid-period Zincke, showing a little extra embellishment in the depiction of the fur trim.

While many of Zincke's subjects look very similar and the repetition of clothing has been noted, Margaret (1715–85) (formerly Margaret Cavendish Harley) is known to have sat for Zincke. There is a similarity between this subject and one of the Duchess on a George II portrait box sold at Christie's, London (8 March, 1995, lot 21). This box also included three other miniatures including two of her best friends, Mrs Mary Delany and Mrs Elizabeth Montagu.

A letter from Mrs Donnellan to Elizabeth Robinson says 'I saw the Duchess of Portland yesterday morning at Zincke's where she and Mrs Pendarves (later Mrs Delany) are sitting for their pictures.'

Goulding lists seven miniatures by Zincke of the Duchess alone. She was both beautiful and a widely respected collector and botanist. Her most notable acquisition was the Portland Vase.

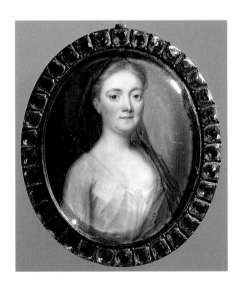

71 *A Lady stated to be Mrs Tilson, Mother of Lady Deane*

Christian Frederick Zincke
England, c. 1730
Unsigned on front
Enamel on copper, 4.5 × 3.7 cm (1 $^{3}/_{4}$ × 1 $^{7}/_{16}$ in), oval

Paste-set silver-rim frame with agate backs;
engraved on silver-rim frame *Mother of Charlot
Tilson Lady Deane*
1996.805 (MIN39B)

PROVENANCE: Lord Muskerry; Christie's, London
(24 November 1981, lot 54); D.S. Lavender,
London (1 October 1982).

DESCRIPTION: The sitter is in a white dress.

COMMENTARY: For a full discussion of this miniature
and the one stated to be of her husband Thomas
Tilson of Dublin, see G. Spencer (see pp. 102–05).

72 *Queen Caroline of Ansbach, Consort of George II*

Christian Friedrich Zincke
England, c. 1732
Unsigned on front
Enamel on copper, 7.6 × 6.0 cm (3 × 2³/₈ in), oval
Pierced scroll, oval gold frame, presumably original
with thick ivory backing
1996.785 (MIN20)

PROVENANCE: Robert. H. Rockliff; Sotheby's,
London (11 November 1947, lot 138); estate of the
late Honourable Lady Shelley-Rolls; Christie's,
London (13 February 1962, lot 62, p. 13 illus. facing
p. 24); Christies, London, (17 December 1968, lot
50); S.J. Phillips, London (1980).

LITERATURE: Kerslake, 1977, vol. I, p. 35, illus. vol.
II, pl. 99.

DESCRIPTION: The sitter is three-quarters to the left
wearing purple dress and ermine-lined purple cape.

COMMENTARY: The subject is Queen Caroline
(1683–1737), consort of George II (r. 1727–60), who
married her husband, then Electoral Prince of
Hanover, in 1705. They arrived in London in 1714
with the accession of her father-in-law to the throne
of England as George I. A close friend of Robert
Walpole, 1st Earl of Orford, she took an active role
in promoting him up until her death.

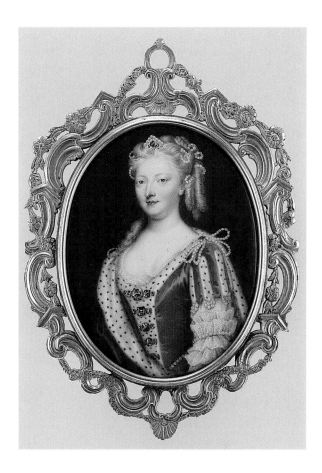

This enamel shows the Queen in the same dress
as in the full-scale painting by Kneller of 1716, in
the Royal Collection (see O. Millar 1963, vol. I, no.
345, pl. 148 illus.). The Kneller was the source for a
miniature by Christian Richter (see Walker, 1992,
no. 16, p. 11–12, ills). This miniature more closely
relates to two in the Royal Collection (see Walker,
1992, no. 37, 38, p. 23, illus.), the latter in the same
dress but head and shoulders, both wearing a tiara,
the Gilbert miniature also with ermine-trimmed
purple robe of state. Walker states that no. 38
'belongs to a group painted *ad vivum* in 1732 when
Vertue says "Mr Zincke often at Court drawing the
pictures of the Royal Family . . . the King and
Queen have sat to him"' (Vertue, *Notebooks*, II, p.
63). The Gilbert miniature also may belong to this
ad vivum group.

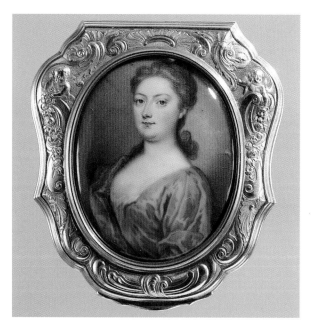

73 A *Lady Selina Dering*
B *Lady Katherine Guilford*

Christian Friedrich Zincke
England, c. 1740
Enamel, oval
A 4.4 × 3.6 cm (1³/₄ × 1⁷/₁₆ in)
B 4.4 × 3.6 cm (1³/₄ × 1⁷/₁₆ in)
Two enamel miniatures, one mounted on lid and the other mounted inside George II gold cartouche-shaped box, c. 1740.
1996.529 (MINI81

PROVENANCE: Through S.J. Phillips, Christie's, London (13 July 1994, lot 39).

LITERATURE: Truman, 1999, cat. no. 35, p. 59.

EXHIBITION: Portland, 1994–95.

DESCRIPTION: A) Lady Selina is shown three-quarters to the left in a blue dress, with light brown shoulder length hair; B) Lady Katherine is shown almost full-face in green dress, with brown hair.

COMMENTARY: A) depicts Selina Dering, daughter of Sir Robert Furnese, Bt, of Waldershard, Kent, and co-heir of the half-brother, Sir Henry Furnese, 3rd and last Bt (died 1735), married, as his first wife, Sir Edward Dering, 6th Bt, MP for New Romney in 1755. She died in 1757.

B) depicts Katherine, daughter of the same by his second marriage and co-heir with above, married first in 1736 Lewis, 2nd Earl of Rockingham (1714–45) and secondly Francis, 1st Earl of Guilford (1704–90), as his third wife. She died in 1766 at her seat in Kent and was buried at Wroxton, Oxfordshire. A portrait of her when Lady Rockingham at Rockingham Castle is recorded in C. Wise, *Rockingham Castle, its Antiquity and History*, 1852.

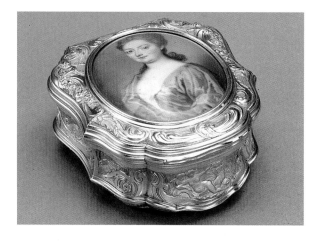

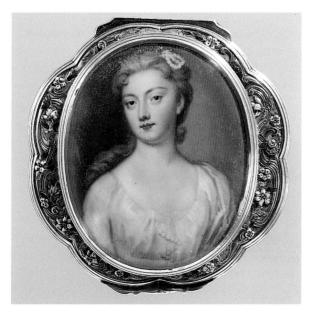

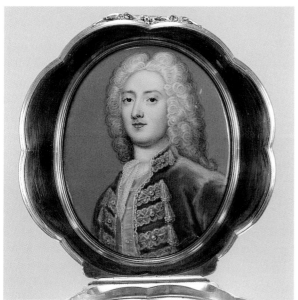

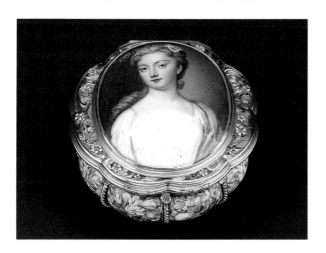

74 A *A Lady*
   B *A Gentleman*

Christian Friedrich Zincke
London, c. 1735
Unsigned on front
Enamel on copper, oval
A 4.4 × 3.7 cm (1³/₄ × 1⁷/₁₆ in)
B 4.4 × 3.7 cm (1³/₄ × 1⁷/₁₆ in)
Two enamel miniatures, one mounted on lid, the
other mounted inside George II gold and enamel
box made from a French gold and enamel watch-
case, signed *RVP* (Robert Vauquer Pinxit), Blois,
c. 1600
1996.444 (GB94)

PROVENANCE: Belarte Ltd, Hapsburg (1984).

LITERATURE: Truman, 1991, no. 96, pp. 284–5.

EXHIBITIONS: Los Angeles/Richmond/New York,
1986–87, no. 43; Los Angeles/Richmond, 1991–92.

DESCRIPTION: A) The lady is shown facing slightly
to the left, in a white dress and pink shawl, with
pearl hair decoration and brooches; B) The gentleman is shown facing slightly to the left, in a powdered wig, brown coat with gold embroidery, white
cravat and pink waistcoat.

COMMENTARY: The subjects, while unidentified, are
clearly of some standing as is apparent from their
attire. Another miniature by Zincke apparently of
the same Gentleman was sold at Sotheby's, Monaco
(25–26 June 1976, lot 385 illus.). While the gentleman would appear to be *ad vivum*, the lady may
well have been painted from an earlier portrait.
The fashion for mounting miniatures in gold boxes
for personal reasons as opposed to presentation
purposes seems to have increased in this period.
Another example also by Zincke, is cat. no. 73.

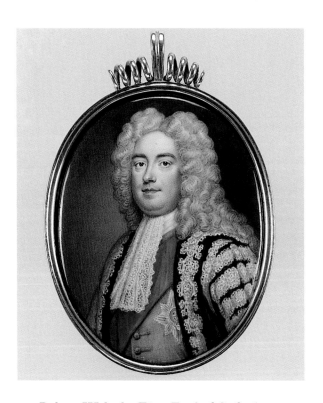

enamel also derives, presumably, from an original portrait by Zincke, painted *ad vivum* in 1743–4 after the battle of Dettingen, in which he wears Garter robes. The original is now on loan to the Manchester Art Gallery. Versions in Treasury robes exist at Chewton House and another sold at Christie's (5 March 1974, lot 65), now in the National Portrait Gallery. Long cites a miniature by Zincke of Sir Robert Walpole as being sold at Knight, Frank and Rutley's on 14 December 1911 (1929, p. 474).

An engraving and etching of Robert Walpole by George Vertue after C.F. Zincke, 1744, is the frontispiece to *Aedes Walpolianae*, 1752. Various full-scale portraits exist.[1] The most similar in aspect is one by van Loo at Lyme Hall, facing the opposite direction.

[1] Keerslake, J., 1977, *Early Georgian Portraits*, NPG, London, no. 602.

75 *Robert Walpole, First Earl of Orford*

Christian Friedrich Zincke
England, c. 1743
Unsigned on front
Enamel on copper, 7.3 × 5.9 cm ($2^7/_8$ × $2^5/_{16}$ in), oval
In contemporary silver frame with scroll ornament at top
1998.22 (MIN60)

PROVENANCE: Sotheby's, London (6 June 1996, lot 30, through S.J. Phillips).

EXHIBITION: Portland, 1996–97.

DESCRIPTION: Robert Walpole is half-length facing left with a full-bottomed grey wig, wearing the Lord Chancellor's Treasury robes and a lace cravat, with the blue sash and star of the Order of the Garter.

COMMENTARY: Robert Walpole was also Chancellor of the Exchequer and Prime Minister (1721–42), having supported the Hanoverian succession. Another similar, smaller enamel by Zincke with a Walpole family provenance is in the Royal Collection (see Walker, 1992, p. 35 no. 68, illus.). While there is some variation in the wig, this

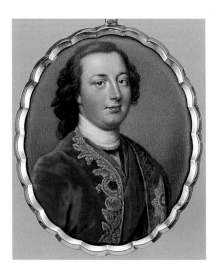

76 *William Augustus, Duke of Cumberland*

Christian Friedrich Zincke
England, c. 1745
Unsigned on front
Enamel on copper, 4.4 × 3.1 cm ($1^3/_4$ × $1^1/_4$ in), oval
Frame with the Duke's initial *W* in gold script upside down in red enamel on the reverse.
1998.29 (MIN64)

PROVENANCE: D.S. Lavender, London (July 1996).

DESCRIPTION: The sitter is shown in a blue velvet coat with gold-braid oak leaf embroidery, emblem of the Hanoverian victory, and an Order of the Garter on his left breast, hair in brown pigtail, grey background.

COMMENTARY: The subject, William Augustus, was the third son of George II and Queen Caroline and was created Duke of Cumberland at the age of five. Unsuccessful in his attempt to get into the Royal Navy, he joined the army in 1742 and became a major general later that year. After the Battle of Dettingen in 1743, he was made a lieutenant general. He was recalled from Flanders in 1745 to quell the Jacobite rebellion led by Prince Charles Edward Stuart, winning the decisive Battle of Culloden in April 1746. After suffering various defeats in the Seven Years' War, he was finally forced to surrender at Kloster-Zeven in 1757 and retired to England, subsequently regaining his popularity with the British public when he tried to restore William Pitt to office.

A very similar miniature appears in the Royal Collection, which, according to Walker, has been there since it was painted, probably soon after the return of William Augustus to London in November 1743, having defeated the French army at Dettingen.[1] Another version in the same pose, but with powdered wig and red jacket, is in the National Portrait Gallery, London, no. 6285.[2]

[1] Walker, 1992, p. 31–2 no. 62.
[2] Walker, 1998, pp. 60–1, no. 44.

77 A Lady, possibly Mary Duchess of Montague

Studio of C.F Zincke
England, c. 1745
Unsigned on front
Enamel on copper, 4.4 × 3.6 cm (1³/₄ × 1⁷/₁₆ in), oval
With gold and enamel closed locket frame, outside enamelled with floral bouquets on a green ground; signature; inscriptions
1996.787 (MIN22)

PROVENANCE: The Earls Spencer; D.S. Lavender, London (1980).

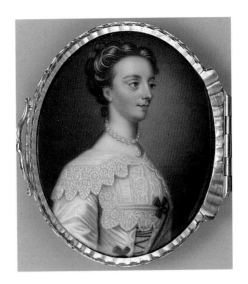

EXHIBITION: London, 1865, no. 925.

DESCRIPTION: The sitter is shown half-length with light brown hair and a light blue dress.

COMMENTARY: Mary, Duchess of Montague, daughter of the Duke of Marlborough, was married in 1705, the same year her father-in-law, Ralph Montague, was elevated to the dukedom. Her husband, John (1688?–1749) became 2nd Duke upon the death of his father in 1709 and the title became extinct with his death in 1749.

There is some question about the identity based on other portraits of Mary Churchill, Duchess of Montague – most notably a Kneller and a Kneller studio portrait where she is seen in profile facing left, both in the collection of the Duke of Buccleuch. While her darker colouring could have been changed by the enameller, the period of the costume has also been updated in the enamel to 1740–45 when the Duchess would have been fifty to fifty-five years old. However, John Faber Jr engraved the Kneller portrait in 1740, so this may have inspired an adaptation. A similar miniature of a Lady stated to be in the Booth family and catalogued as 'Follower of Zincke' is in the Yale Center for British Art (B1974. 2. 113), sold at Sotheby's, London (24 February 1969, lot 116, collection of Mrs Walker Raleigh Gilbert as a Zincke, wearing the same dress without the lace cape.

Miniatures on ivory, paper, porcelain and other materials

BIANCA BONI (FL. EARLY NINETEENTH CENTURY)

Bianca Boni flourished in Florence during the first third of the nineteenth century. A miniature by her hand, dated 1823, is in the V&A.

78 Pope Pius VII

Bianca Boni
Italy, probably Florence or Rome, c. 1820
Signed, lower right *Bianca Boni*
Watercolour and body colour on ivory, 5.3 cm ($2^1/_{16}$ in) diameter, circular
Square heavy ormolu frame surmounted by Papal crown and keys
1996.813 (MIN47)

PROVENANCE: Osterley Park, no. 10.49/2, according to an old label; Sotheby's, London (10 March 1994, lot 41, through S.J. Phillips).

DESCRIPTION: The sitter has dark hair and a white skull cap and is wearing ermine-lined papal robes.

COMMENTARY: Pius VII, Gregorio Luigi Barnaba Chiaramonti (1742–1823), was Pope from 1800 to 1823. He signed a Concordat with Revolutionary France in 1801 and came to Paris in 1804 to crown Napoleon emperor. Nevertheless, when Pius VII refused to join Napoleon's Continental Blockade, his state was occupied by French troops in 1808. After excommunicating the Emperor, Pius was first imprisoned in 1809 in Savona and in 1812 in

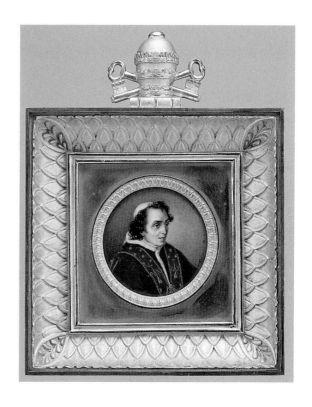

Fontainebleau, where the Pope refused to revoke his excommunication. Pius VII returned to Rome in 1814.

The exceptionally impressive frame may suggest that this miniature was a Papal present.

GIOVANNI DOMENICO BOSSI (1765–1853)

Giovanni Domenico Bossi was born in Trieste, studied in Venice and emigrated to Hamburg, where he worked from 1794 to 1796. In 1795 his wife ran away with his pupil Jannasch and Bossi spent the years 1796–1802 in Sweden, mainly in Stockholm. In 1802, he was recorded in St Petersburg where he later returned and became a court painter. His travels included Paris in 1812, Venice in 1813 and Vienna in 1816, 1822, 1824 and 1826. In about 1840 he settled down in Munich where he died. He developed a special and unique 'sculptural' style and precise technique which only a few of his Swedish pupils could attempt to imitate. Miniatures by Bossi are to be found in the Rijksmuseum, Amsterdam, in the Bayerisches Nationalmuseum, Munich, in the Albertina and the Academy, Vienna, in the Ateneum, Helsinki, in the Nationalmuseum, Stockholm, in the Museum of Fine Arts, Copenhagen, in the Metropolitan and in most of the major Russian museums.

79 *Tsar Alexander I of Russia in Semi-profile*

Giovanni Domenico Bossi
St Petersburg, c. 1802–05
Signed, lower left *Bossi p.*
Watercolour and body colour on ivory, 6.6 × 5 cm (2⁵/₈ × 2 in), oval
Mounted on the cover of a Russian rectangular enamelled gold snuffbox by Otto Samuel Keibel (fl. 1797–1809 in St Petersburg)
1996.535 (GB187)

PROVENANCE: Presented by the sitter to Lord Granville Leveson Gower (1773–1846); thence by descent to the Rt Hon. the Earl Granville, MC, DC; his sale, Sotheby's, Monaco (25 June 19767, lot 541); the British Rail Pension Fund; their sale, Sotheby's, Geneva (15 May 1990, lot 42) with S.J. Phillips, London.

LITERATURE: Solodkoff, 1981, pp. 184–5, pl. 204; Bury, 1982, room 1 (no. 5/M/91); Truman 1999, pp. 87–8, no. 54.

EXHIBITIONS: V&A, London, in 1991 (no. 5/M/91); Portland 1995.

DESCRIPTION: The sitter is bust-length, almost in profile to the left, in the dark green uniform, with gold-figured red collar, of the Peobrajensky Regiment, decorated with the badge of the Order of St John of Jerusalem and the blue sash and breast star of the Imperial Russian Order of St Andrew; he

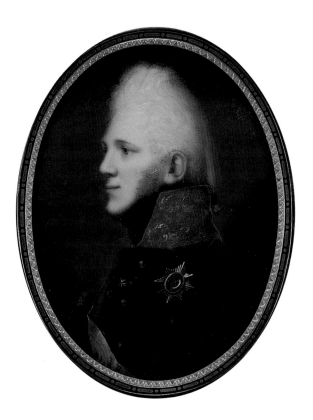

wears a black stock and has powdered upswept hair with pigtail.

COMMENTARY: Tsar Alexander I of Russia (1777–1825), eldest son of Tsar Paul I and his wife Maria Feodorovna, succeeded his father in 1801. Although his reign was overshadowed by many wars and the horrors of Napoleon's invasion of Russia, he was considered an excellent ruler. Bossi executed many portrait miniatures of Tsar Alexander during

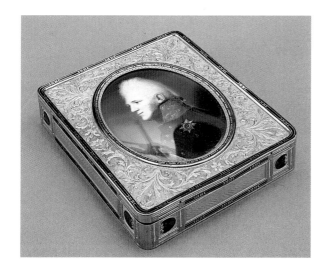

CONTINENTAL SCHOOL

80 *A Young Lady with a Long Pearl Necklace*

Possibly Italy, c. 1880–90
Watercolour and body colour on ivory, 3 × 2.3 cm
(1³/₁₆ × ¹⁵/₁₆ in), oval
Within a diamond border, mounted on an earlier
rectangular Swiss green-enamelled gold snuffbox
1998.34 (GB 210)

PROVENANCE: J.S. Bourdon-Smith, London
(November 1995).

LITERATURE: Truman, 1999, pp.84, no. 52.

EXHIBITION: Portland, 1995.

DESCRIPTION: The sitter is shown bust-length,
facing left in low-cut white dress with jewelled
brooch at corsage, wearing a long pearl necklace.

COMMENTARY: This well-painted miniature is a
typical specimen of the 'revival' of the miniature
during the late nineteenth century, a period when
photography had largely taken over and miniature
painting had become the luxury of an elitist, possibly old-fashioned, upper-class minority. The best
artists of this time came from Russia or from Italy.

the first years of the nineteenth century. The
present portrait appears to be the earliest recorded
one compared to the numerous miniatures by Bossi
dated between 1804 and 1808: for example, one
dated 1804, sold at Christie's, London (24 May
2000), another one dated 1807, sold at Christie's,
Geneva (10 May 1983, lot 235); another one dated
1807, sold at Sotheby's, London (14 December
1995, lot 62) and one dated 1808, sold at Christie's,
Geneva (15 November 1988, lot 308). The present
box was given to Lord Granville Gower either on
the Tsar's coronation in 1801 or during his visit to
St Petersburg as ambassador extraordinary in
1804–05. The unusually high quality of the present
piece contrasts with Bossi's later portraits of the Tsar
which appear rather stiff and show all the signs of a
mass-production.

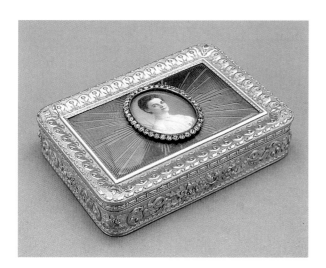

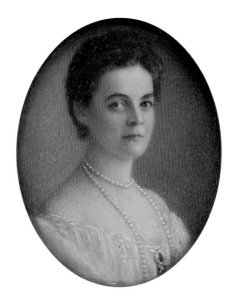

RICHARD COSWAY (1742–1821)

One of the best-known English miniaturists, and the most sought-after of his day, Cosway was the artistically precocious son of a headmaster who collected pictures. At the age of twelve Cosway was sent to London in order to learn how to paint. He started with Thomas Hudson, also from Devon, but soon entered Shipley's drawing school, where he excelled himself from the start. Although he hoped to become a full-scale painter in oils, Cosway's talent lay in miniatures and in drawing.

He entered the Royal Academy in 1769 and exhibited in 1770, being elected ARA in the same year, and RA in 1771. His early miniatures show good draughtmanship and delicacy combined with the more solid use of colours typical of other artists of the period. He increasingly used transparent colours, exploiting the luminosity of the ivory to maximum effect, and by the mid-1780s he was very much in command of the miniature on ivory.

Following his marriage to fellow artist Maria Hadfield, Cosway moved to Pall Mall in 1784 where the couple lived a flamboyant lifestyle. Guests included the Prince of Wales, from whom Cosway obtained a commission for a miniature of Mrs Fitzherbert. This led to Cosway being appointed 'Miniaturist to the Prince of Wales' in 1786.

Graham Reynolds (1988, p. 26) says that Cosway's first known work was an enamel of a gentleman 'signed in full and dated 1753' (when Cosway was eleven and probably not yet in London). There are no records to suggest that he trained in this medium – he worked either on ivory or on paper.

Cosway enjoyed a long period of popularity, but the death of his only child, a daughter, at the age of six in 1794, increased his bouts of strange behaviour and eccentricities. When the Prince of Wales became Prince Regent in 1811, Cosway dropped from favour. His popularity and health continued to decline and in 1821, after two strokes, he died. His works are found in most major collections including the V&A, the Fitzwilliam, Cambridge, the Wallace Collection and the Metropolitan.

81 *A Lady*

Richard Cosway
London, England, c. 1780
Unsigned on front
Watercolour on ivory, 5.7 × 5.0 cm (2¼ × 2 in), oval
Mounted under glass on cover of gold snuffbox by John Pukhaver, London, c. 1780
1996.498 (GB150)

PROVENANCE: Property of a lady, Christie's, London (25 November 1970, lot 153, D.S. Lavender; S.J. Phillips, London (1989).

LITERATURE: Truman, 1991, cat. 109, pp. 316–7.

EXHIBITIONS: Los Angeles/Memphis, 1991–92; San Francisco, 1996.

DESCRIPTION: The sitter is shown bust-length three-quarters to the right, in pink ermine-trimmed cape and white dress, upswept powdered hair, dark background.

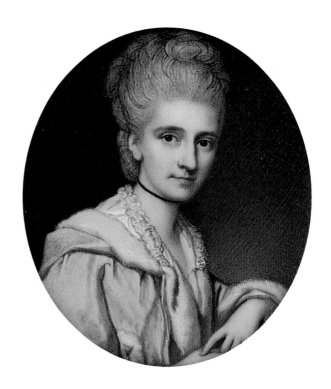

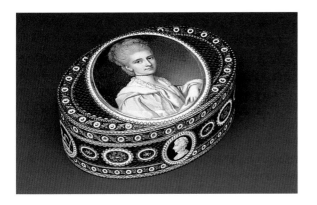

COMMENTARY: This is an excellent example of Cosway's work. It is somewhat unusual for a miniature of this size by him to have a dark background. The particular colouration, ranging from a gold tone through to a dark blue suggests a specific commission for this box, as it relates to the colour of the enamel.

RICHARD CROSSE (1742–1810)

Richard Crosse was born a deaf mute near Cullompton, Devon. He took up miniature painting as a hobby until 1758 when he won a prize from the Society of Artists and went to London. He exhibited at the Society of Artists from 1760–91 (becoming a member in 1763) and the Royal Academy from 1770–96. He was appointed Painter in Enamel to George III. A prolific artist, he painted miniatures on ivory and in enamel as well as some portraits. He kept an account book, published by Basil Long (*Walpole Society Journal*, vol. XVII, 1929, pp. 61–94), which reveals a distinguished clientele. Among other family miniatures, an enamel of one of his brothers was exhibited in Edinburgh, 1965, from the collection of the Hon. Kenneth Thomson of Canada.

His works are also at the V&A, the Fitzwilliam, Cambridge and the Royal Collection.

82 *George III*

Richard Crosse
England, 1793
Unsigned on front
Watercolour on ivory, 7.9 × 6.4 cm (3^{1}/$_8$ × 2^{1}/$_2$ in), oval
Ivory in gold and enamel frame in the form of a bright-cut blue and white Garter with *honi. soit. qui. mal. Y. pense.*, the motto of the Order of the Garter, surmounted by a gold crown with red enamel inset, gold back, together with a gold-link chain with

bright-cut clasp, c. 1790
1996.827 (MIN58)

PROVENANCE: Presented to the first owner Aga Chachick Arakel by the Honourable East India Company on behalf of George III and the British Government, sold at Christie's London (4 February 1964, lot 54); Garrard's, London (8 August 1995).

LITERATURE: FitzRoy, 1979, illus. p. 38.

EXHIBITION: Portland, 1994–95.

DESCRIPTION: The King is shown bust-length facing slightly right, with powdered wig *en queue*, a white cloak with large gold chain, blue background.

COMMENTARY: George William Frederick was the eldest son and second child of Frederick Louis, Prince of Wales, and his wife Augusta of Saxe-Gotha. His father's sudden death in 1751 made him Prince of Wales until his succession in 1760. Two weeks before his coronation, he married Charlotte of Mecklenburg-Strelitz, with whom he had fifteen children. They enjoyed a simple domestic life. George III purchased Buckingham House in 1762 and supported the foundation of the Royal Academy in 1768. He suffered from occasional attacks of porphyria, the second of which was probably precipitated by the loss of the American colonies. In 1810, he suffered a fatal attack and the Prince of Wales was appointed Regent.

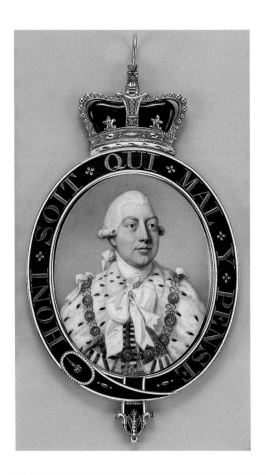

This miniature was presented to the Aga Chachick Arakel by the Honourable East India Company on behalf of George III and the British Government for the Aga's acts of generosity, such as releasing debtors from Calcutta Prison when he heard of the recovery of George III in 1789. The Aga Arakel donated the clocktower and clergy houses to the Church of St Nazareth, Calcutta. His son later suffered misfortune and, appealing to His Majesty's government for help, was granted a pension of 100 rupees a month. The Christie's catalogue states 'Richard Crosse records in his account book that he handed a miniature of the King to Mr. Devaynes, a jeweller, to be framed on June 15th 1793'. The Crosse account book for that date shows payment by Mr Devaynes for a miniature of the King (see Long, 1929, p. 82). At the time of the sale of the miniature at Christie's, it was accompanied by 'a leaflet containing the correspondence relating to the pension and an excerpt from the *Indian Daily News*, July 24, 1806'. This was not included by Garrard's. Although Crosse was Painter in Enamel to George III, this miniature depicts his royal patron in watercolour on ivory and shows his clear mastery of this technique.

FRANÇOIS DUMONT (1751–1831)

François Dumont, born in Lunéville, was apprenticed to the Lorraine court painter Jean Girardet in Nancy. He arrived in Paris in 1768 and almost immediately started to paint for the court, particularly the Countesses of Provence and Artois, wives of the future kings Louis XVIII and Charles X. During the late 1770s, Dumont painted Queen Marie-Antoinette several times and in the late 1780s he became the Queen's favourite miniaturist. In 1788 he was admitted to the Académie Royale de Peinture. During the French Revolution, he was just as successful at adapting his style to the classicist fashion and to a *parvenu* clientele. During the imperial reign he did not receive any official commissions but with the return of the Bourbons in 1814–15 he regained his position at court. His last works were painted in the year of his death. During the sixty years of his artistic career, he produced watercolour miniatures, drawings, oil paintings and even lithographs. His fee book indicates that he executed over 2,400 works. He was undoubtedly one of the most successful and celebrated French miniaturists of his time.

83 *Benjamin Franklin in Grey Coat*

François Dumont
France, probably Paris, c. 1780/1785
Signed, lower right *Dumont / f*
Watercolour and body colour on ivory, 6.7 cm (2⅝ in) diameter, circular
Mounted on the lid of a circular gold-mounted tortoiseshell bonbonniére with marks for Paris, 1786
1998.13 (GB227)

PROVENANCE: Purportedly given by the sitter to the Marquis de Lafayette; Count Joseph de Castelli (d. 1820); by descent to his great nephew, Ascanio Negretti; Julio F. Mendez (gift from Negretti in 1927); Robert Lehmann (gift from Mendez in 1946); thence by descent; Christie's, New York (17–18 January 1992, lot 182); Stanley Paul Sax, Detroit; the sale of his estate, Sotheby's, New York (16–17 January 1998, lot 130).

LITERATURE: Truman, 1999, pp. 20–21, no. 6.

EXHIBITION: Philadelphia, 1990, no. 137.

DESCRIPTION: The sitter waist-length, facing left, with long receding grey hair, in open grey silk coat and waistcoat with white pleated jabot.

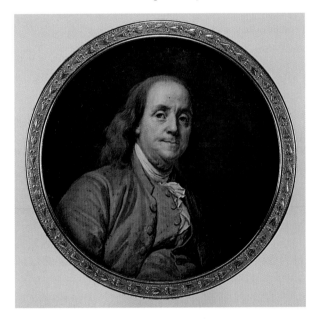

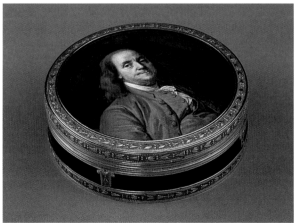

COMMENTARY: This miniature is copied after the rectangular oil painting by Joseph-Siffrein Duplessis (illustrated and discussed in exhibition catalogue Douvres–La Délivrande 1960, pp. 28–9, no. 21). Duplessis painted Franklin several times, and the best-known portrait is that depicting Franklin in a coat with fur collar, now in the Museum of Fine Arts, Boston. The oil painting which most probably served as the model for the present miniature was painted by Duplessis in about 1778 and given to Madame Brillon de Jouy by Franklin himself. The Brillon de Jouy family was one of Dumont's most important clients and it might be that the miniature was copied for Madame Brillon de Jouy by Dumont after the Duplessis painting in her possession. From the technical point of view, the miniature belongs to the years 1780–85, a period in Dumont's career characterised by cold, bluish colours and a fine, almost invisible brushstroke, as can be observed in the present miniature.

For another miniature of Franklin, see cat. no. 60.

ENGLISH SCHOOL

84 *Double-Sided Miniature of a Young Lady*

Probably England, c. 1590–1600
Oil on rock crystal (?), reverse-painted on crystal or glass in one direction (red dress), with back-to-back painting, the other side with crystal or glass laid over the painting (green dress), 4.5 × 3.5 cm (1³/₄ × 1³/₈ in), oval
Pendant brass-rim frame, later engraved *Queen Mary*
1996.802 (MIN37)

PROVENANCE: D.S. Lavender, London (October 1982).

DESCRIPTION: The sitter is wearing a lace ruff and her hair is dressed with jewels; one side (in greater detail) with green and gold dress; the other side in red with green and gold bodice.

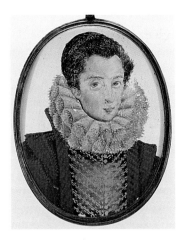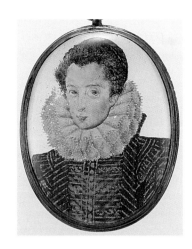

COMMENTARY: As the dates of neither Mary Tudor nor Mary Queen of Scots are right for the miniature, the later inscription must be presumed to be inaccurate. This highly unusual work has the very delicate linear style of the works of the end of the sixteenth and beginning of the seventeenth century like those of Isaac Oliver. The use of oil might suggest a Continental, possibly Dutch, connection. The use of smooth convex crystal in each direction creates a depth and luminosity more associated with enamels and other works in crystal or hardstone than with small paintings. As an object, it comes out of both the limning and the jewellery tradition, suggesting someone with Hilliard's background, although more of Isaac Oliver's style.

A miniature in the Gutman Collection, part IV, sold at Parke Bernet (3 April 1970, lot 74) described as a 'Lady called Mary Countess of Kent, probably Isaac Oliver, c. 1605', is similar in appearance both in its detail and with its use of convex glass, although it has an enamelled border to the simple oval rim of the frame.

Also in the Gutman Collection, part II, sold at Parke Bernet, New York (17 October 1969, lot 71, illus. p. 38), there was a South German enamelled gold and rock crystal oval pendant, late sixteenth century, with the two rock crystal windows held by an enamelled gold frame, within which is a figure of Christ and Mary Magdalene on either side of a tree.

CIRCLE OF JOHANN CHRISTIAN FIEDLER (1697–1765)

A former law student, Johann Christian Fiedler started painting miniatures in 1717. He was born in Pirna. After studying in Paris, he returned to Germany in 1724 and established himself in Darmstadt. In 1725, Grand Duke Ernest Ludwig bestowed on him the title of court painter. Ernest Ludwig's successor Ludwig VIII confirmed this appointment in 1738 and, in 1754, appointed him 'Ober-Cabinett und Hoffmahler' with the rank of a Councillor.

85 *Landgrave Ludwig VIII of Hesse-Darmstadt in Breastplate*

Darmstadt, c. 1750/55
Enamel on porcelain, 5.8 × 7.9 cm (2$^5/_{16}$ × 3$^1/_8$ in), cartouche-shaped
Painted on the inside of the lid of a gold-mounted German rococo porcelain snuffbox
1996.509 (GB160)

PROVENANCE: The Grand Dukes of Hessen-Darmstadt; Christie's, Geneva (14 May 1990, lot 100).

LITERATURE: Beaucamp-Markowsky, 1985, p. 85; Beaucamp-Markowsky, 1988, pp. 36–8; Truman 1991, pp. 260–3, no. 88.

DESCRIPTION: The sitter is shown half-length, almost full-face, in copper-bordered breastplate, ermine-lined red velvet cloak, blue Hessian uniform with embroidered red cuffs, decorated with the blue sash and breast star of the Royal Polish Order of the White Eagle and the jewel of the Bavarian Order of Saint Hubertus.

COMMENTARY: Landgrave Ludwig VIII of Hesse-Darmstadt (1691–1768), was a passionate hunter and also a renowned military leader. He was made a Marshal of the Holy Roman Empire by Empress Maria Theresa. The portrait is taken from a painting by Fiedler, engraved by Johann Martin Bernigeroth. It must have been among the most popular images of the Landgrave, as several versions, in the form of miniatures and box decorations, have survived.

A Kelsterbach porcelain box with identical portrait is illustrated in Beaucamp-Markowsky, 1985, no. 323, and in Le Corbeiller, 1966, no. 516. An oval miniature after the same original is illustrated in Biermann/Brinckmann, 1917, pl. 33, no. 110.

FRENCH SCHOOL

86 *King Louis XV and Queen Maria Leszczynska of France*

Paris, Louis XV c. 1725/1730 and Queen Maria Leszczynska probably at least partially much later
Watercolour and body colour on vellum, rectangular
Louis XV, 7.5 × 5.2 cm (2$^{15}/_{16}$ × 2$^1/_{16}$ in)
Queen Maria Leszczynska, 6.7 × 4.6 cm (2$^5/_8$ × 1$^{13}/_{16}$ in)
Decorating a rectangular gold and tortoiseshell snuffbox with hallmarks Paris, 1728/29, adorned with a dolphin in gold *piqué*; the miniature of the King mounted at the inside of the lid, the miniature of the Queen probably mounted later on the inside of a secret compartment under the tortoiseshell plaque decorating the lid
1996.467 (GB117)

PROVENANCE: Mr Dubosc, Mayor of Etretat; Kugel, Paris; 'Au Vieux Paris' (Michel Turysk), Paris.

LITERATURE: Truman, 1991, pp. 32–5, no. 2.

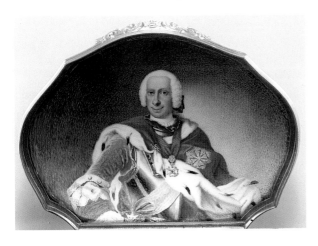

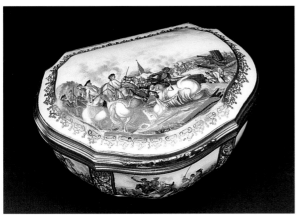

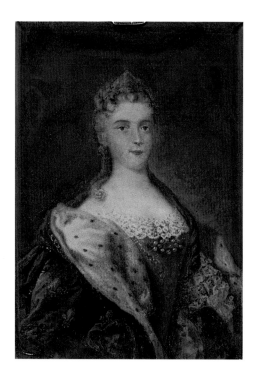
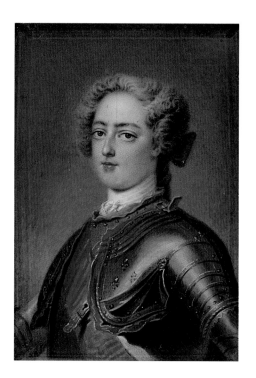

EXHIBITIONS: Geneva, 1953, no. 345; Los Angeles/Memphis 1991–92; San Francisco, 1996.

DESCRIPTION: Louis XV as a young man, bust-length facing left in armour, white stick, wearing the blue sash of the Royal French Order of the Holy Ghost, grey-powdered hair and black wig-bag; the Queen three-quarters length, facing right in embroidered red dress with jewelled corsage and lace border, mauve velvet cloak embroidered with gold fleurs-de-lys and lined with ermine, gold tiara in curled powdered hair.

COMMENTARY: For another miniature of Louis XV, see cat. no. 40. He married Maria Lesczcynska (1703–1768), daughter of King Stanislas Leszczynski of Poland, Duke of Lorraine in 1725. Truman (1991, p. 33) suggests that the present box may have been ordered to commemorate the birth of Louis XV's first male child, the Dauphin. Furthermore, he attributes the miniatures to Jean-Baptiste Massé (1687–1767) or, alternatively, to a mysterious Jean-Baptiste Ducanel. The miniatures are not by Jean-Baptiste Massé, whose loose technique is completely different from the fine, enamel-like brush stroke used for the portrait of Louis XV (see Hofstetter 1994, pp. 58–9). Not a

single miniature by Ducanel (probably misread for Durand) is recorded and the attribution to this artist cannot be substantiated.

The portrait of the King is after Jean-Baptiste van Loo's full-length equestrian state portrait of 1723 (Constans, 1995, pp. 897–8, nos. 5063, 5066, 5067 and 5070). The miniature of the Queen dates either entirely from the nineteenth century or has been retouched to a degree which makes the identification of the original parts almost impossible.

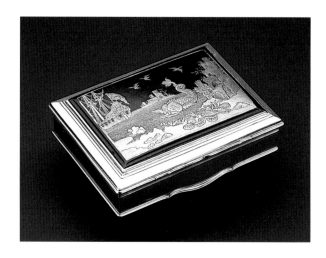

FRENCH SCHOOL

87 *King Louis XVI and Queen Marie-Antoinette of France*

Probably Paris, probably c. 1790
Watercolour and body colour on ivory, each
4.1 × 3.2 cm (1⁵/₈ × 1¹/₄ in), oval
Later (?) mounted on both sides of a rectangular
Saxon gold and hardstone notebook by Johann
Christian Neuber, Dresden, c. 1780
1996.319 (MM218)

PROVENANCE: King Farouk of Egypt; the Palace
Collections of Egypt, sold at Sotheby's, Koubbeh
Palace, Cairo, (18 March 1954, lot 703); Baron de
Redé and Baron Guy de Rothschild, Paris and
Château de Ferrières; sold at Sotheby's, Monaco
(25 May 1975, lot 41).

LITERATURE: Massinelli, 2000, p. 200, no. 86.

EXHIBITIONS: Los Angeles, 1977–79; Israel, 1995.

DESCRIPTION: The King is shown bust-length,
facing right in blue coat and frilled white lace jabot,
wearing the breast star of the Royal French Order
of the Holy Ghost, the red badge with jewel of the
Order of the Golden Fleece and a red sash; the
Queen bust-length, facing right in low-cut pale
blue dress with lace-bordered white muslin fichu,
knotted bandeau in high-piled hair; both with
column background.

COMMENTARY: Louis XVI (1754–93), second son of
the short-lived Dauphin Louis, succeeded his
grandfather Louis XV (see cat. nos. 40 and 86) in
1774. In 1770, he married Archduchess Marie-
Antoinette of Austria (1755–93), daughter of
Empress Maria Theresa (see cat. no. 90) by whom
he had four children. His political skills were limited
and he was beheaded during the French Revolution.
His wife and sister followed him to the guillotine
and the fate of his surviving son, declared King
Louis XVII, is unclear. For over twelve years after
his death, his two younger brothers became kings of
France as, successively, Louis XVIII and Charles X
(see cat. no. 97). Neuber's work has been

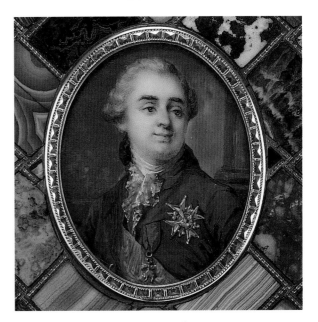

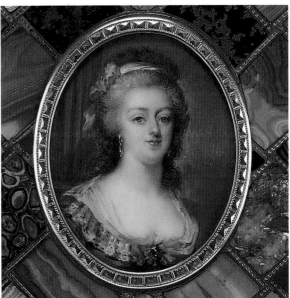

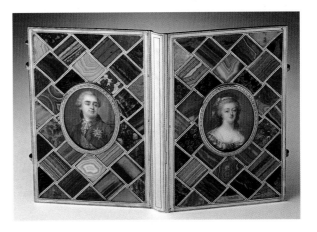

embellished with decorative miniatures in order to enhance its commercial value. Although the miniatures may possibly be of the same period as the notebook, they are of poor artistic quality. The attribution to Louis XVI's court miniaturist Louis Sicardi (1746–1825) put forward in the 1975 sale catalogue has to be disregarded because of major stylistic and technical discrepancies. The portrait of the King has probably been copied after a black and white print after Joseph Siffrein Duplessis's oil painting of 1775 (Constans, 1995, p. 286, no. 1592) which was engraved by Romanet in 1783, Le Mire, and Le Vachez fils in 1792. The cross sash has to be blue and not red in order to match the breast star of the Order of the Holy Ghost. The red sash would belong to the rather common French Military Order of Saint Louis and it is most improbable that the King would have been painted wearing it instead of the blue sash of the highest Royal French Order, the Holy Ghost.

FRENCH SCHOOL

88 *Madame de Maintenon in a Blue Dress*

France, second half of the nineteenth century
Watercolour and body colour on ivory, 4.4 × 3.7 cm (1³/₄ × 1⁷/₁₆ in), oval
Mounted on the lid of an oval Louis XVI enamelled gold snuffbox by Joseph-Etienne Blerzy, Paris, 1776–77.
1998.2 (GB200)

PROVENANCE: George IV of England; presented to Lord Glenlyon; Augustus Henry, 3rd Duke of Grafton; George, 4th Duke of Marlborough; Lady Churchill; Admiral the Hon. J.W.S. Spencer (until 1887); with S.J. Phillips (June 1995).

LITERATURE: Truman, 1999, pp. 18–9, no. 5.

EXHIBITION: Portland, 1995–97.

DESCRIPTION: The sitter is shown bust-length, facing right in a blue dress with a white lace border and red cloak, a jewelled pearl clasp at her right shoulder, wearing a pearl necklace, pearl earrings

and a pearl string in her curled dark hair.

COMMENTARY: Françoise d'Aubigné, Marquise de Rochechouart, Madame de Maintenon (1635–1719), married firstly the poet Paul Scarron in 1652. After his death, the '*Veuve Scarron*' was in charge of the education of the children of Louis XIV. The Sun King married her in 1683. Her religious fanaticism pushed the King into revoking the Edict of Nantes in 1685 which set off the persecution of French Protestants and their exodus from France. This portrait is derived from the painting by Pierre Mignard, representing the sitter at the age of forty, engraved

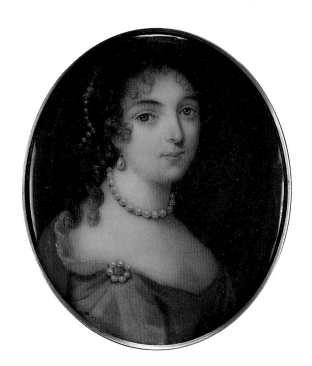

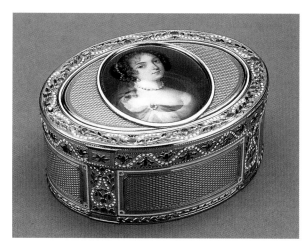

by Pierre Giffardin in 1687. It was also copied in enamel by Jean Petitot (illustrated in Schlumberger 1966, p. 89, no. 3), and the enamel later became part of the collection of Louis XVI. Seized during the French Revolution, the royal enamel collection was incorporated into the collections of the newly founded Louvre Museum. Petitot's enamel was produced during the reign of Emperor Napoleon III in 1864 (Ceroni, 1864, II, no. 1), and was from then onwards extensively copied. It was possibly during the second half of the nineteenth century that the present miniature was mounted on the Louis XVI box, perhaps in order to replace an unwanted, damaged or unattractive existing miniature. The poor artistic quality together with the subject's over-sweet expression confirms the date of the miniature as the second half of the nineteenth century.

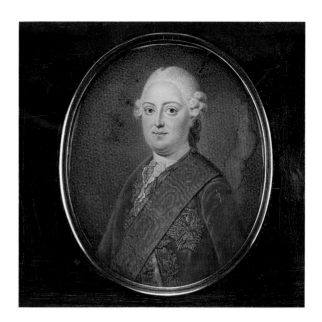

GERMAN SCHOOL

89 *Frederick Augustus III, Elector of Saxony, in a Red Coat*

Dresden, c. 1770/75
Watercolour and body colour on ivory, 4.4 × 3.6 cm (1³/₄ × 1⁷/₁₆ in), oval
Mounted on the inside of the cover of a rectangular gold and hardstone snuffbox by Johann Christian Neuber, Dresden, c. 1770/75
1996.487 (GB139)

PROVENANCE: Kugel, Paris (in 1989).

LITERATURE: Truman 1991, pp. 234–7, no. 80; *World of Interiors*, December 1996, p. 102.

EXHIBITIONS: Los Angeles/Memphis 1991–92.

DESCRIPTION: The sitter is shown waist-length, facing the spectator, in red velvet coat with embroidered border, white embroidered lace jabot, white curled wig, wearing the blue sash and breast star of the Royal Polish Order of the White Eagle.

COMMENTARY: Frederick Augustus III (1750–1827), son of Elector Frederick-Christian and his wife Maria Antonia Walpurgis (see cat. no. 91),

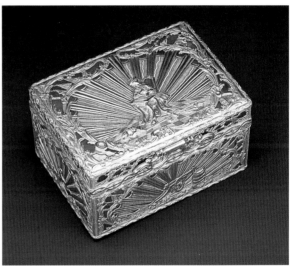

succeeded his short-lived father as Elector of Saxony in 1763, during the first five years under the regency of his uncle Prince Xaver of Saxony. Unlike his great-grandfather Augustus the Strong and his grandfather Augustus III, Frederick Augustus did not accept the crown of Poland offered to him in 1791 but tried to maintain the neutrality of Saxony. As a result of his good relations with Emperor Napoleon, he was, in 1806, made the first King of Saxony. Imprisoned after Napoleon's fall, he was released after the Congress of Vienna. He spent the last years of his reign in the reconstruction of his considerably reduced country and was given the epithet 'the Just'. The present miniature is inspired

by, although not taken after, the oil painting by
Anton Graff dated 1768 (Berckenhagen, 1967,
p. 122, no. 336), and shows the sitter with fuller
features and in a mauve coat. The miniature was
painted by a talented court miniaturist whose name
has not come through to us. It is quite exceptional
to find a miniature of a member of the House of
Saxony in the original presentation snuffbox by
Neuber who was appointed, in 1775, 'Hof-und
Kabinettsteinschneider' by the sitter depicted on
the present miniature. In many cases, the original
Saxon miniature was later replaced by a more
pleasant subject. The present box with its original
miniature is therefore an exceptionally important
item. An almost identical miniature of the same sitter, unidentified and catalogued as 'probably
Russian School c. 1750', is illustrated in Schaffers-
Bodenhausen/Tiethoff-Spliethoff, 1993, p. 441, no.
624.

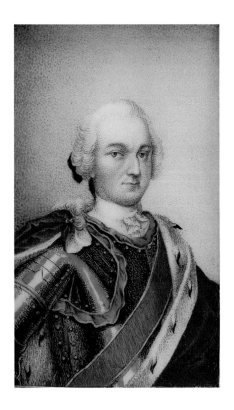

German School

90 *Elector Palatine Charles Theodore and Holy Roman Empress Maria Theresa*

Germany, possibly eighteenth or nineteenth century
Enamel on porcelain, each 6.5 × 3.7 cm (2⁹/₁₆ × 1⁷/₁₆
in), both rectangular
Painted on the interior of the two lids of a German
triple-opening porcelain snuffbox
1996.519 (GB170)

PROVENANCE: Christie's, Geneva (16 November
1992, lot 371); S.J. Phillips.

LITERATURE: Truman, 1999, pp. 49–50, no. 26.

EXHIBITION: Los Angeles/Memphis, 1991–2.

DESCRIPTION: The Elector Palatine is shown waist-
length, facing right in armour with blue borders,
ermine-lined purple cloak, decorated with the red
sash of the Bavarian Order of St Hubert, with white
short wig and black wig-bag; the Empress, waist-
length, facing left in low-cut lace-bordered yellow
dress with jewelled corsage, ermine-lined blue cloak,
a jewelled crown in her powdered long hair.

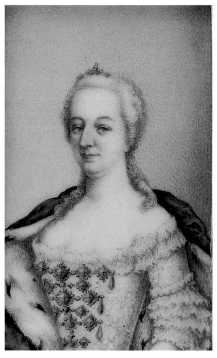

COMMENTARY: Charles Theodore (1724–99) became Elector Palatine in 1743 and Elector of Bavaria in 1777. He was married to Elisabeth Auguste of Sulzbach. He was a patron of the arts, a collector of antiques, a passionate musician and also corresponded with Voltaire. Maria Theresa (1717–80), Archduchess of Austria, Queen of Hungary and Bohemia, succeeded her father, Emperor Charles VI, in 1740, and was crowned as a Holy Roman Empress in 1745. She married Francis Stephen, Duke of Lorraine and their numerous children include Queen Marie-Antoinette of France (see cat. no. 87). Beaucamp-Markowsky (1985, pp. 138–9) illustrates an almost identical snuffbox, with minor differences in Maria Theresa's dress. She identifies the female sitter as Charles Theodore's wife Elisabeth Auguste but admits that there is a certain lack of resemblance, which she tries to explain, quite unconvincingly, by the position of the sitter's head slightly turned to the right. The portrait of the female sitter on her box is an inverse copy after Jean-Etienne Liotard's pastel portrait of Empress Maria Theresa (Loche/Roethlisberger,

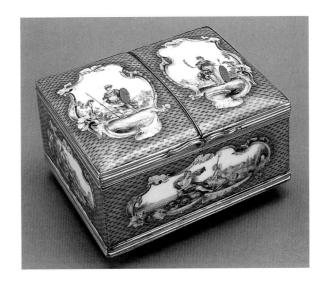

1978, p. 94, no. 64), and the only difference between Liotard's pastel and the miniature on the present box is the yellow dress with ruched sleeves. Beaucamp-Markowsky's tentative attribution of the miniatures to Johann Martin Heinrici cannot be substantiated owing to the poor artistic quality of the portraits.

CIRCLE OF JOHANN MARTIN HEINRICI (1713–86)

Johann Martin Heinrici was born in Lindau and arrived in Meissen in 1742. He was employed by the porcelain factory as a painter and, probably, as a gold box decorator. He was also an engraver, miniaturist and enameller, but not a single miniature or enamel can be attributed to him with certainty. Heinrici worked extensively for the Saxon court but left Meissen between 1757 and 1761.

91 *Maria Antonia Walpurgis, Electoral Princess of Saxony*

Circle of Johann Martin Heinrici (1713–86)
Meissen, c. 1750
Enamel on porcelain, 5.4 × 7.5 cm (2 1/8 in. × 2 15/16 in), rectangular
Painted on the inside of a rectangular gold-mounted

Meissen snuffbox
1996.518 (GB169)

PROVENANCE: Christie's, Geneva (16 November 1992, lot 365); with S.J. Phillips, London.

LITERATURE: Truman, 1999, p. 57, no. 33.

EXHIBITIONS: Los Angeles/Memphis, 1991–2.

DESCRIPTION: The sitter is shown bust-length, full face in pink-lined white satin dress with white lace underslip, ermine-lined blue velvet cloak fastened over her dress with jewelled clasps, decorated with the badge of the Order of the Starry Cross and the breast-star of the Imperial Russian Order of St Catherine, short powdered hair.

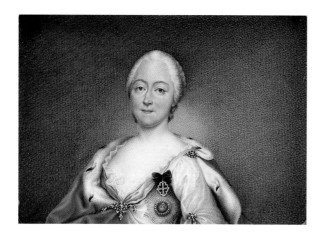

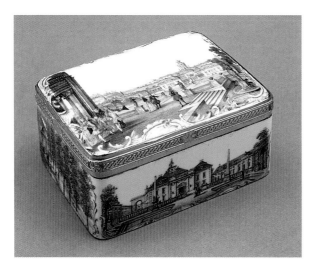

COMMENTARY: Maria Antonia Walpurgis (1724–80) was the daughter of Elector Charles Albrecht of Bavaria (Holy Roman Emperor under the name of Charles VII) and his wife Maria-Amalia of Habsburg. In 1747, she married the Saxon Hereditary Prince Frederick Christian who succeeded his father Frederick Augustus II in 1763 but died in December of the same year after a reign of only six weeks. Maria Antonia Walpurgis was an important patron of the arts and an accomplished composer, singer, poet and painter herself.

When the box was auctioned in 1992, the sitter was wrongly identified as Maria Josepha, wife of Elector Frederick Augustus II of Saxony. The large oil painting by Anton-Raphael Mengs of 1751, depicting the sitter with her regalia (illustrated inversed in Sponsel (1906, pl. 61, no. 148), now in the Gemäldegalerie, Dresden (inv. no. 2163), leaves no doubt about the identity of the sitter. Still closer to the present porcelain miniature is an oval water-colour on vellum miniature depicting Maria Antonia Walpurgis, sold at Christie's, Geneva (16 November 1993, lot 145).

Although the present miniature is of high quality, it is not possible to attribute it to the legendary Heinrici, whose works must have strongly resembled the present portrait.

For a miniature of the sitter's eldest son, see cat. no. 89.

GIOVANNI MARRAS

Giovanni Marras (Juan Maras) worked in New York in 1801 and 1802 and thereafter in Spain. When, in 1818, he applied for the appointment of professor at the Naples Academy, he was living in Spain and gave his titles as painter to the King of Spain and painter to the Grand Duke of Tuscany. About 1830 he was recorded as court painter to the Sultan of Turkey in Constantinople. Considering this late date, it is not clear if he is the same person as the miniaturist Marras born in Naples in 1765. His works, dated between 1803 and 1828, are rare. A miniature by him is in the Museum of Fine Arts, New Orleans.

92 *Mahmut II, Sultan of Turkey*

Attributed to Giovanni Marras
Constantinople, c. 1831
Watercolour and body colour on ivory, 2.8 × 2.4 cm
(1 1/8 × 15/16 in), oval
Mounted on the cover of a jewelled and enamelled
gold snuffbox attributed to Pierre-Etienne
Thérémin, St Petersburg, c. 1800, the base of the
box enamelled with a view of Rumeli Hisari on the
Bosphorus
1996.448 (GB98)

PROVENANCE: Prince Oskar of Prussia (in 1946);
Princess of Hohenzollern; S.J. Phillips, London.

LITERATURE: *Illustrated London News*, 2 February
1946, p. 128; *World of Interiors*, December 1996, pp.
104–105; Truman, 1991, pp. 380–2, no. 132.

EXHIBITIONS: Los Angeles/Richmond/New York
1986–87, no. 23; Los Angeles/Memphis 1991–92.

DESCRIPTION: The sitter is depicted bust-length,
facing left, in brown uniform with gold buttons
and red fez, the jewel of the Turkish Order of
Nishan-el-Iftikhar suspended from his neck.

COMMENTARY: The hitherto unpublished identification of the sitter could be established by comparison
with the oil painting of the Sultan by Henri-
Guillaume Schlesinger, presented by the sitter in
1839, the year of his death, to Louis-Philippe, King
of the French (Constans, 1995, II, p. 823, no. 4653).
Mahmut II (1785–1839), Ottoman Sultan of Turkey,
succeeded his brother Mustafa IV in 1808. His reign
saw the loss to Russia of Bessarabia, the autonomy
of Egypt under Muhammed Ali, and the independence of Serbia and Greece. It was during the Greek
struggle for independence against Mahmut's troops
that Lord Byron died in Greece in 1824. Despite
suffering numerous defeats on land and sea,
Mahmut tried to carry out a major reorganisation
of the state designed to strengthen the power
of the sultan and the central government. He
easserted control over the provincial administration,
previously in the hands of semi-independent local
rulers, and suppressed the corps of janissaries, often

the instrument of palace revolutions, replacing it
with a new regular army on the European model.
On the present miniature, Mahmut II is wearing the
jewel of the Order of Glory 'Nishan-el-Iftikhar',
founded by himself in 1831. This date and the presence of Marras as court painter in Constantinople
around 1830 confirm both the attribution of the
artist and the identification of the sitter. The
mediocre artistic quality of the miniature contrasts
with the splendour of the jewelled presentation box.
As pointed out by Truman (1991, p. 382), the box
may have initially contained an Imperial Russian
presentation miniature given by the Tsar to the
Sultan. It was probably replaced by an image of the
Sultan himself and presented to another ruler,
possibly to a member of the Royal Prussian family,
which may explain the princely provenance of the
piece. The Koran prohibits the representation
of human figures; the existence of the present
miniature depicting a Muslim ruler – even though
painted by a Christian – is a rare witness to the need
of political representation over religion.

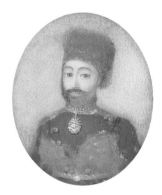

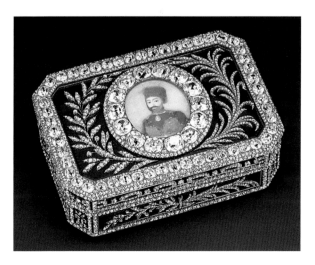

CIRCLE OF FRANCISCO ANTONIO MELÉNDEZ (1682–1752)

Francisco Antonio Meléndez, born in Orviedo, was the younger brother of Philip V's court painter Miguel Jacinto Meléndez. He was a soldier and worked as a painter and miniaturist in Italy between 1699 and 1717. In 1726, he encouraged the foundation of the Academy of San Fernando. He trained his son José Agustin Meléndez who became a miniaturist in Cadiz.

93 *Philip V of Spain in a Blue Coat*

Continental School
Madrid (or France), c. 1710/15
Watercolour and body colour on parchment, 4.2 × 5.7 cm (1⅝ × 2¼ in), cartouche-shaped rectangular
Mounted on the inside of the cover of a French gold and tortoiseshell snuffbox with marks for Paris, 1717–22, the cover with crowned mirrored monogram *FE* for Felipe and Elisabeth.
1996.497 (GB149)

PROVENANCE: Hôtel Drouot, Paris (16 March 1966, lot 53); Christie's, Geneva (10 November 1987, lot 390); with S.J. Phillips, London (1989).

LITERATURE: Truman, 1991, pp. 30–1, no. 1.

EXHIBITIONS: Los Angeles/Memphis 1991–92; San Francisco, 1996.

DESCRIPTION: The sitter is depicted three-quarters length, with steel breastplate over gold-figured blue velvet coat, gold-bordered red cloak, decorated with the jewel of the Order of the Golden Fleece and the blue sash of the Royal French Order of the Holy Ghost, his right hand on a baton next to the royal crown on a cushion, red canopy of estate and column background.

COMMENTARY: Philip (1683–1746), born and raised in France as Philippe, Duc d'Anjou, was a grandson of Louis XIV, the Sun King, who proclaimed him King of Spain in 1700 after the death of Philip's great-uncle, Charles II 'the Bewitched'. Philip ruled as Felipe V until 1724 when he abdicated in favour of his son Louis I. After the sudden death of his son in the same year, Felipe had to resume the throne and reigned until his death in 1746.

Truman (1991, p. 31) has pointed out that the love symbols on the base of the present box may refer to the marriage of the King to Elisabeth Farnese (1692–1766) of Parma in 1714. At this date, Philip was about thirty years old, and the features of the King correspond to those of someone of this age. This would also explain the initials 'F' for Felipe and 'E' for Elisabeth.

It has not been possible to find the source after which the present miniature was copied. It does not resemble any of the official portraits of the King painted by Hyacinthe Rigaud, Jean Ranc or Louis-

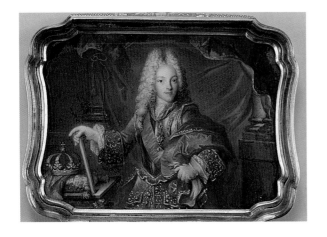

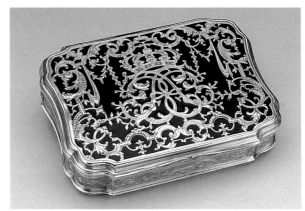

Michel van Loo (see Moran Turina, 1990, *passim*). Stylistically, it comes closest to the portraits by Miguel Jacinto Meléndez (1672–after 1726), who is said to have painted miniatures too. Several miniatures by his younger brother Francisco Antonio Meléndez are recorded and have a certain technical resemblance to the present portrait (see exhibition catalogue Madrid 1990–91). Nevertheless, the possibility that this well-painted miniature was executed in France in order to fit the box cannot be excluded.

ATTRIBUTED TO LOUIS-BERTIN PARANT (1768–1851)

Louis-Bertin Parant was a painter, miniaturist and porcelain painter. He exhibited at the Paris Salon from 1800 to 1834 and was awarded medals in 1806 and 1808. For many years he worked for the Sèvres porcelain factory. He specialised in profile portraits and scenes simulating cameos.

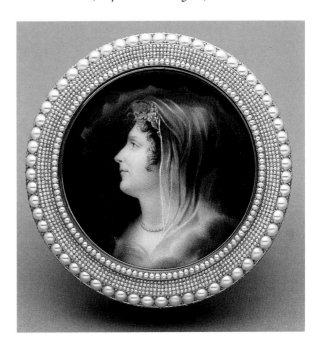

94 *Empress Joséphine in Profile*

Paris, c. 1805
Enamel on porcelain, 5.3 cm (2¹/₁₆ in) diameter, circular
Mounted on a circular gold bonbonnière covered with pearls.
1996.398 (GB35)

PROVENANCE: S.J. Phillips, London.

LITERATURE: Habsburg-Lothringen, 1983, p. 22, no. 3; Truman, 1991, pp. 350–1, no. 122; *Orient Express Magazine*, 1996, pp. 23.

EXHIBITIONS: Los Angeles/Richmond/New York, 1986–87; Los Angeles/Memphis, 1991–92.

DESCRIPTION: The sitter is shown bust-length in profile to the left, wearing a floral diadem with veil, pearl necklace, against a background simulating flecked tortoiseshell.

COMMENTARY: Marie Josèphe Rose Tascher de La Pagerie, called Joséphine (1763–1814), married Vicomte Alexandre de Beauharnais in 1779. They had two children, Eugène and Hortense. During the French Revolution, her husband was guillotined and Joséphine herself imprisoned. After she was freed, she led a frivolous life style which ended when she married General Napoléon Bonaparte in 1796. In 1809, Napoléon, now Emperor of France, became desperate for an heir and divorced her in order to marry Archduchess Marie-Louise of Austria in 1810. Joséphine was richly compensated and kept her title of Empress. Two ivory miniatures by Parant depicting Empress Joséphine in a similar way are in the Louvre (Grandjean, 1981, no. 292, and Jean-Richard, 1994, p. 270, no. 492). Truman (1991, p. 351) relates that the background of the miniature simulating flecked tortoiseshell corresponds to a technique used at the Sèvres porcelain factory for an imperial dinner service in 1802.

PORTUGUESE SCHOOL

95 *John VI of Portugal as Prince Regent, in Scarlet Coat*

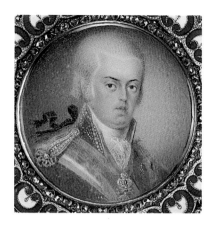

Portugal, c. 1802
Watercolour and body colour on ivory, 3.5 cm
(1³/₈ in) diameter, circular
Mounted on the cover of a circular Russian jewelled
and enamelled gold bonbonnière by David Rudolph
1998.32 (GB197)

PROVENANCE: Guilhou Collection, Paris, sold at
Hôtel Drouot, Paris (14–15 May 1906, lot 41);
Christie's, Geneva (8 May 1979, lot 120); Sotheby's,
New York (6 December 1994, through S.J. Phillips,
London).

LITERATURE: Solodkoff, 1981, pp. 172–3, no. 181;
Truman, 1999, pp. 85–6, no. 53.

EXHIBITION: Portland, 1995–97.

DESCRIPTION: The sitter is shown bust-length,
facing right in scarlet coat, decorated with the sash
and combined breast star (called the 'Sacred Heart
of Jesus') of the three Portuguese main orders of
the Christ, St Benedict of Aviz and St James of the
Sword, the blue sash of the Royal Portuguese Order
of the Tower and Sword, and the jewel of the Order
of the Golden Fleece suspended from a red ribbon
about his neck, short powdered hair and black
knotted ribbon.

COMMENTARY: John VI of Portugal (1767–1826),
son of Queen Maria I and Peter III of Portugal, held
the title of Prince of Brazil from 1788 onwards. He
was successively Regent (1792–1816) and King of
Portugal. When the Napoleonic troops invaded his
country in 1807, he fled to Brazil and returned to
Portugal as king in 1816. He recognised the independence of Brazil under his son, Emperor Pedro I
in 1825 but assumed the title of Emperor of Brazil
for life. In 1785, he married the Infanta Carlota
Joaquima of Spain. The date of c. 1802 is confirmed
by a very similar dated miniature of Prince Regent
John (with Galerie Kugel, Paris). Solodkoff (1981,
p. 173) relates that the box was originally a gift from

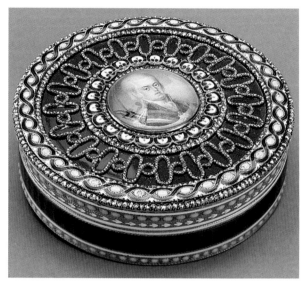

Tsarina Catharine the Great to Queen Mary of
Portugal and that the miniature had been added
later. Now fitted with the portrait of the Prince
Regent, it was – according to a later inscription on
the lid – presented by him to Admiral Sir John
Jervis, Earl St Vincent (1734–1823) who led a fleet
in a pre-emptive show of force to Lisbon in 1806.
For a similar case of a Russian presentation box con-
verted into a local presentation box, see cat. no. 91.

RUSSIAN SCHOOL

96 *Empress Elizabeth Petrovna of Russia*

St Petersburg, c. 1750
Watercolour and body colour on ivory, 5.8 × 4.5 cm
(2⁵/₁₆ × 1³/₄ in), oval
Mounted on the inside of a rectangular gold-
mounted amethystine-quartz snuffbox decorated
with the scrolling gold cypher of the sitter.
1998.35 (GB213)

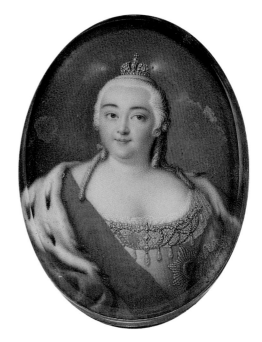

PROVENANCE: Empress Maria Feodorovna of Russia
(in 1904); Empress Alexandra Feodorovna of Russia
(by 1909); Ball & Graupe, Berlin (25 September
1930, lot 66); Sotheby's, Geneva (13 May 1996, lot
235); with S.J. Phillips, London.

LITERATURE: Prachoff, 1907, pp. 196–7, illustrations
86 and 87; *Les Arts* 1908, p. 13, pl. II; Truman, 1999,
pp. 35–6, no. 17.

EXHIBITIONS: St Petersburg, 1904; Portland,
1996–97.

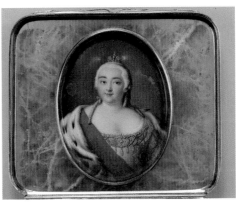

DESCRIPTION: The sitter is shown waist-length, full
face in low-cut jewel-encrusted grey satin dress,
ermine-lined saffron yellow cloak, decorated with
the blue sash and breast star of the Imperial Russian
Order of St Andrew, small jewelled crown in curled
powdered hair.

COMMENTARY: Elizabeth Petrovna (1709–62) was
the daughter of Tsar Peter the Great. She reigned
from 1741 until 1762 and was notorious for her cru-
elty. The present miniature is after the state portrait
by Louis Caravaque. Whereas the box is probably of
German origin, the miniature may just as well have
been painted in Russia. Nevertheless, it may have
been painted for the box-maker by a German
miniaturist after an engraving after Caravaque.

DANIEL SAINT (1778–1847)

Daniel Saint, born in Saint-Lô, was a pupil of Jean-
Baptiste Isabey, Regnault and Aubry. He became
one of the most important collaborators in Isabey's
studio, producing miniatures of Emperor Napoleon
I which were mounted on presentation snuffboxes.
He exhibited at the Paris Salon between 1804 and
1839 and was awarded a second-class medal in 1806
and a first-class medal in 1808. Under Kings
Charles X and Louis-Philippe, he was undoubtedly
the most fashionable miniaturist in Paris. Saint
produced numerous official miniatures of King
Charles X, whose court miniaturist he was, and of

his successor Louis-Philippe. He was a keen collector of portrait miniatures and paintings and his famous collection was auctioned in 1846. Miniatures by Saint are to be found in the Louvre, the Malmaison, the Musée Jacquemart-André, Paris, the Museum of Narbonne, the Musée des Arts Décoratifs, Bordeaux, the Museum of Saint-Lô, the Wallace Collection, the Musei Civici di Arte Antica, Bologna, the Museum Briner und Kern, Winterthur and in the Russian Museum, St Petersburg.

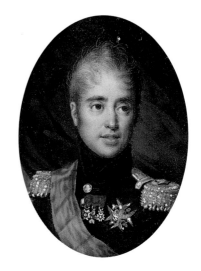

97 *The Count of Artois, future King Charles X of France, as 'Monsieur'*

Daniel Saint
Paris, c. 1820
Bearing false signature, lower right *J. Isabey*.
Watercolour and body colour on ivory, 4.7 × 3.2 cm (1⁷/8 × 1¹/₄ in), oval
Mounted on the lid of an oval enamelled gold snuff-box by Adrien-Jean-Maximilien Vachette, Paris, 1809–1819
1996.392 (GB28)

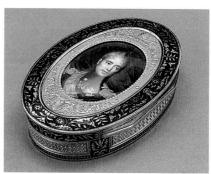

PROVENANCE: Sotheby's, Zurich (17 November 1976, lot 142); Sotheby's, Geneva (16 May 1995, lot 78, through S.J. Phillips).

LITERATURE: Truman, 1999, p. 27, no. 10.

EXHIBITION: Portland, 1995–97.

DESCRIPTION: The sitter is shown bust-length, facing right in dark uniform with a general's gold epaulettes, gold buttons and black stock, decorated with the blue sash and breast star of the Royal French Order of the Holy Ghost, the three badges of the Royal French Orders of Saint-Louis and the Legion of Honour surrounding the Golden Fleece, green curtain background.

COMMENTARY: Charles Philippe, Count of Artois (1757–1836), youngest brother of Kings Louis XVI and Louis XVIII, succeeded the latter in 1824 under the name of Charles X. His conservative politics caused a rebellion in 1830 and he abdicated in favour of his grandson, the Duke of Bordeaux. He fled first to Scotland, then to Prague and finally to Goeritz where he died. Daniel Saint was the King's court miniaturist and executed numerous portraits of his sovereign (see for example Le Corbeiller, 1966, no. 233). A very similar version, signed and dated 1824 and depicting the King slightly older than on the present portrait, is in the Louvre (illustrated in Lespinasse, 1929, pl. XLI, no. 145, and in Jean-Richard, 1994, pp. 312–13, no. 567). The present piece was probably painted in about 1820; a very similar signed large miniature by Saint was sold at Fontainebleau, Hôtel des Ventes (4 May 1986, lot 31). The splendid presentation frame was engraved with the inscription *Offert au Marquis de Rivière par Monsieur, Comte d'Artois (futur Charles X) le 25 Août 1819*. The Isabey signature on the present miniature is a later addition, possibly from the period when the miniature was mounted on the box. The miniature is a good example of Saint's official style adopted in Isabey's studio which made him so popular at court.

LEONARD TEMMINCK (1753–1813)

Leonard Temminck was born in the Hague and baptised on 7 September 1753. A pupil of Bolomey at the Academy 'Pictura' at the Hague, he was awarded a gold medal in 1783 and became a member of the guild in 1785. One year later he was appointed vice-director of the Academy and director in 1787. He died in 1813 in the Hague. For a detailed account on Temminck, see Staring, 1924, pp. 254–57.

Works by Temminck are to be found in the Gemeente-Museum, the Hague, the Rijksmuseum, and the Frans Hals Museum, Rotterdam.

98 *A Young Boy in a Green Coat*

Leonard Temminck
The Hague, c. 1788
Watercolour and body colour on ivory, 3.6 × 2.9 cm (1⁷/₁₆ × 1¹/₈ in), oval
Set on the lid of a circular enamelled gold bonbonnière with split-pearl borders by Pierre-Claude Pottier, Paris, 1787/1788; signed with monogram, mid-right *LT*; inscriptions 1998.36 GB217)

PROVENANCE: Hancocks, London (July 1996).

LITERATURE: Truman, 1999, p. 22, no. 7.

DESCRIPTION: The sitter is depicted bust-length, facing to the right in green coat with gilt buttons, white collar with frill border, long dark hair.

COMMENTARY: Although Temminck is not known to have worked in or travelled to Paris, the miniature appears to have belonged to the box from the

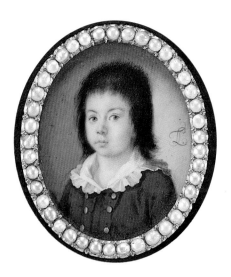

beginning. The date of the box coincides with the climax of Temminck's career and also corresponds with the period when the sitter's clothes were fashionable. It is possible that the box was commissioned in order to present the portrait of the client's son. Temminck's miniatures are characterised by a very fine brushstroke (producing long hatchings), yellowish colours and a slightly provincial style, as can be seen in the present portrait.

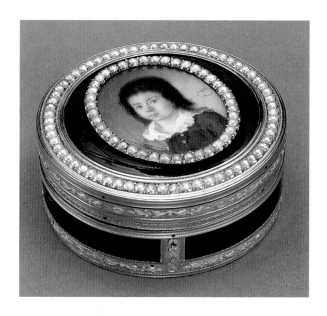

FRANCESCO TENDERINI (C. 1800–50)

Count Francesco Tenderini, born in about 1800 at
Fivizzano, was first a student of law before taking up
miniature painting. He was a member of the
Accademia di S. Luca in Rome. He died in Corsica
in 1850. Miniatures by his hand are extremely rare.

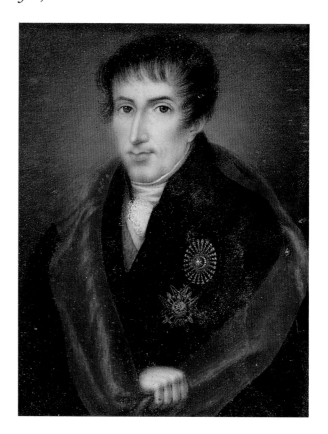

99 *Sir William Drummond in Fur-trimmed Coat*

Francesco Tenderini
Italy, c. 1828
Signed, lower right *Tenderini*
Watercolour and body colour on ivory, 8.2 × 6.4 cm
(3¹/₄ × 2¹/₂ in), rectangular
Mounted on the inside of the lid of a rectangular
gold and hardstone snuffbox, signed *Fratelli Mascelli
a Roma*
1996.392 (GB28)

PROVENANCE: Earl of Lonsdale, Lowther Castle sale
(22 April 1947, lot 1208); Sotheby's, Zurich (17
November 1976, lot 219); S.J. Phillips, London (in
1979).

LITERATURE: Habsburg-Lothringen, 1983, pp. 27–8,
no. 6; Truman, 1991, pp. 420–2, no. 147; Massinelli,
2000, p. 157.

EXHIBITIONS: Los Angeles/Richmond/New York
1986–87, no. 19; Los Angeles/Memphis 1991–92.

DESCRIPTION: The sitter is shown waist-length, in
dark fur-trimmed jacket and red-lined cloak,
decorated with the breast-stars of the Royal
Neapolitan Order of St Januarius, the Turkish
Order of the Crescent and the red sash of and order,
either of the Order of St Januarius or of the British
Order of the Bath.

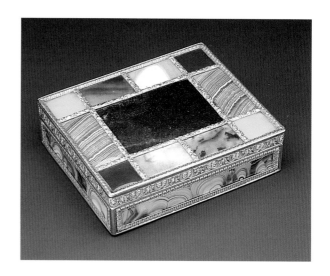

COMMENTARY: The identification of the sitter is
supplied by an engraved inscription below the
portrait, on the interior of the bezel of the box:
Right honourable Sir William Drummond 1828. Sir
William Drummond, KCB (?1770–1828), scholar,
writer, diplomat and MP, was Envoy Extraordinary

and Plenipotentiary to the Court of Naples in 1801 and 1806. Between 1803 and 1806, he acted as Ambassador to the Ottoman Porte at Constantinople. He died in Rome in 1828.

A slightly larger version of this miniature, 9.5 × 8 cm (3³/₄ × 3¹/₈ in) was sold at the Hôtel Drouot, Paris (21 November 1994, lot 28, sitter and artist unidentified despite apparent signature).

Tenderini's slightly naïve and coarse style corresponds with that of most of the Italian miniaturists of his time.

ADOLF THEER (1811–68)

Adolf Theer was born in Johannisberg in Austrian Silesia. He and his two brothers, the famous miniature painters Albert and Robert Theer, were brought to Vienna in 1820 by their father and became pupils at the Vienna Academy. Adolf exhibited at the Academy from 1832 to 1847 and in 1852 at the Österreichischer Kunstverein. Although he was mainly known for his ivory miniatures, he also painted watercolours on paper and printed lithographs. L. Schidlof (1964, II, p. 827) considered him a good miniaturist, although inferior to his brothers Robert and Albert. His clientele included the Austrian court, aristocracy and bourgeoisie. Miniatures by his hand are to be found in the Albertina, Vienna, and in the Hermitage, St Petersburg.

100 *Ferdinand Charles of Habsburg, Archduke of Austria-Este, in Uniform*

Adolf Theer
Austria, probably Vienna, c. 1840
Signed on front, lower left *Adolf Theer*
Watercolour and body colour on ivory, 17.2 × 14.1 cm (6³/₄ × 5⁹/₁₆ in), oval
Gilt-metal mount within later gilt-wood frame; label on reverse '*Arciduca Maxmiliano* [sic] *d'Austria L (?) Theer*'.
1996.824 (MIN55)

PROVENANCE: Charles III (1823–54), Duke of Parma, husband of Princess Maria Theresa of Bourbon and nephew of the sitter; their eldest daughter Margareta (1847–1909), wife of Don Carlos VII of Spain, Infante of Spain, Duke of Madrid; their only son, Don Jaime, Infante of Spain, Duke of Madrid (1870–1931); his sister, Infanta Beatrix (b. 1874), Princess Fabrizio Massimo; thence by direct descent until 1994; Christie's, Geneva (15 November 1994, lot 123, through S.J. Phillips).

EXHIBITION: Portland, 1994–95.

DESCRIPTION: The sitter is shown with curling greying hair and moustache, three quarters left, wearing a scarlet Hussar's uniform with gold frogging and aiguillettes, a gold-braided white dolman bordered with brown fur draped over his left shoulder, wearing the Order of the Golden Fleece at his neck, the badge of the Imperial Austrian Order of Maria Theresa, the breast stars of the Royal Prussian Order of the Black Eagle, the Royal Hungarian Order of St Stephen, and the Guelphic Order of Hanover.

COMMENTARY: Archduke Ferdinand Charles of Austria-Este (1781–1850) was the second son of Archduke Ferdinand of Austria-Este and his wife Maria-Beatrice of Este-Modena. At the age of twelve, he owned the 3rd Hussar regiment and entered the military academy of Wiener Neustadt in 1796, joining the army in 1799. His military success earned him the award of the Cross of the Military Order of Maria Theresa as early as 1800. He struggled against the French troops until 1815 and resigned from the army in 1846. He was the brother of Empress Maria Ludovika of Austria.

This exceptionally well-painted and expressive miniature may be considered as one of Adolf Theer's masterworks. Its quality is in no way inferior to the portraits by the hand of his two better-known brothers.

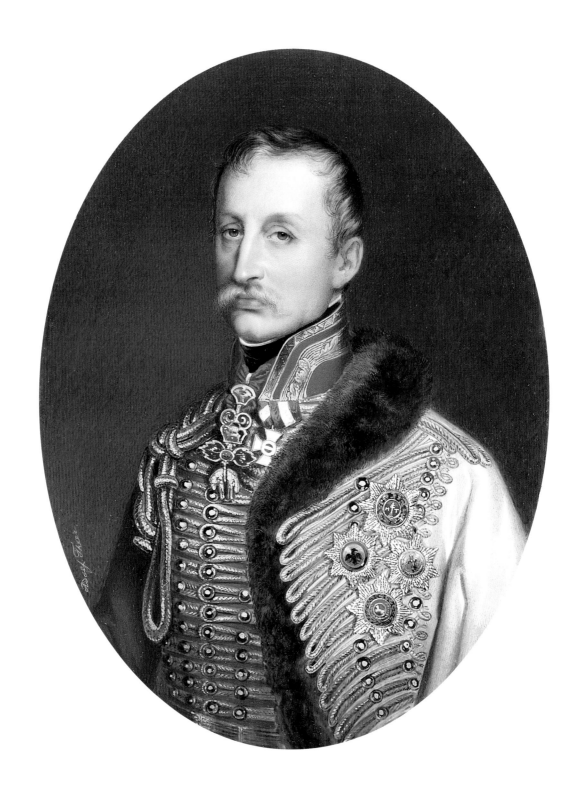

AUGUSTUS TOUSSAINT (C. 1750–1800)

Born in London, the miniaturist Augustus Toussaint was also a jeweller and the son of a jeweller. That he was a competent miniaturist is reinforced by the fact that he exhibited at the Royal Academy in 1775–88. The entry for 1775 shows him at No. 5, Denmark Street, Soho, where he exhibited three miniatures (nos. 310–12). In 1785, no. 290 was listed as 'Portrait of a Lady in enamel'. Although most of his miniatures were not listed as enamels, it is possible that some were, as enamelling was not always indicated in the catalogue.

Foskett states 'he is reputed to have been friendly with J. Smart, and to have devoted much of his time to designing elaborate frames for miniatures, including some for Smart and, in particular, the one which contained the miniature of Smart's son John who died in infancy' (1987, p. 664). She repeats Long's statement (1929, p. 440) that Toussaint inherited property from his father and retired to Lymington, where he died between 1790 and 1800 and was buried in the churchyard. Assuming he created this frame in 1799 or 1800, he must have died no earlier than 1800.

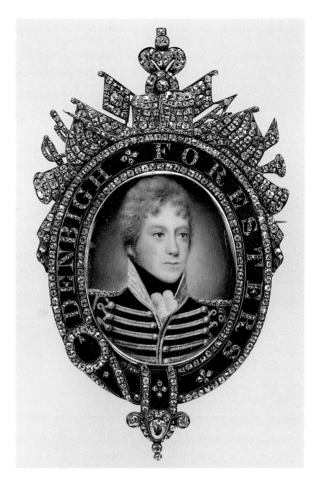

101 *An Officer, probably Captain Richard Lloyd*

Attributed to Augustus Toussaint
England, c. 1800
Unsigned on front
Watercolour on ivory, with card fill to borders,
4.4 × 3.5 cm (1¾ × 1⅜ in), oval
Frame with *Denbigh Foresters* and topped with military trophies, and oval gold-backed frame within original blue enamel diamond frame; included is a blue leather DSL case
1998.28 (MIN63)

PROVENANCE: Robert H. Rockliff, Esq; sold at Sotheby's, London (11 Nov 1947, lot 131); purchased by F. Partridge; D.S. Lavender, London (July 1996).

DESCRIPTION: The officer is shown bust length facing slightly right, with short fair hair, wearing his uniform.

COMMENTARY: It seems likely that Toussaint made both the frame and painted the miniature. The use of the fill at the borders appears to have originally been to widen the oval of a narrow piece of ivory, rather than as an later adaptation to marry it with the frame. A miniature sold at Sotheby's, New York Arcade (22 January, 1997, lot 331 by Toussaint, signed with the initials 'A.T', and of similar style, also had an enamel frame, albeit less elaborate. In 1777, he exhibited as no. 316 'a frame [referring to an exhibition frame] with five orders belonging to the Lodge of the Nine Muses, in enamel from designs by Mr. Cipriani'. In other years, various miniatures are listed including, in 1784 no. 272 'Portrait of a Gentleman (Lieutenant Stone)'. When this miniature was sold from the Rockliff Collection, it was described as a 'Superb Diamond and Enamel Miniature Frame probably by Toussaint', with a miniature of an officer 'perhaps by John Smart, jun.' The footnote said 'the "Denbigh Foresters" was the unofficial name for the Denbigh Yeomanry Cavalry, a troop raised in 1799, and a body of Infantry known as the Denbigh Legion under the command of Lieutenant Colonel Viscount Kirkwall, which were combined in 1800.' According to Mr David Bownes of Amgueddfa, the Royal Welsh Fusiliers Regimental Museum, Captain R. Lloyd was in command of the Denbigh Yeomanry Cavalry when it was raised in July 1799.[1] Thus the identification of Lloyd as the subject

seems reasonable. The troop was raised as part of preparations against a potential French invasion. The troop became known as the Denbigh Legion (also the Denbigh Foresters) when it was attached to the local volunteer infantry, in 1800, called the Denbighshire Yeomanry Cavalry. It was disbanded in 1808.

[1] Letter to Heather Trust, 6 Oct 1999.

IVAN WINBERG (FL. FIRST HALF NINETEENTH CENTURY)

Ivan Winberg was probably of Swedish origin and became an *agrée* at the St Petersburg Academy in 1830, and a full member in 1846. He was Imperial court miniaturist and he together with Alois Gustav Rockstuhl were certainly the most important miniaturists active during the reign of Tsar Nicholas I. His short-lived son Ivan Ivanovich Winberg (1834–52) was also a miniaturist. Miniatures by Ivan Winberg are to be found in most major Russian museums and in the Museum Briner and Kern, Winterthur.

102 *Tsar Nicolas I of Russia in a Dark Green Uniform*

Ivan Winberg
Russia, probably St Petersburg, c. 1850
Signed, mid-right *Winberg*
Watercolour and body colour on ivory, 16.7 × 12.6 cm (6⁹/₁₆ × 4¹⁵/₁₆ in), oval
Carved polygonal oval wood frame in Russian folk style with easel stand, the reverse with old paper labels with *HVvW / GvR / Privat. Eigentum / No 1035* and *PEvW / Privat Eigentum / No [. . .]*
1996.814 (MIN48)

PROVENANCE: Grand Duchess Olga Nicholaievna of Russia (1822–92), later Queen of Württemberg, daughter of the sitter; Grand Duchess Vera

Constantinovna of Russia (1854–1912), later Duchess of Württemberg, niece of the latter; thence by family descent; a German Princess, Bavaria; Christie's, Geneva (18 May 1994, lot 301, through S.J. Phillips).

EXHIBITION: Portland, 1994–95.

DESCRIPTION: The sitter is shown turned three-quarter left, with receding dark hair, moustache and side-whiskers, in dark green uniform with gold-embroidered red collar and gold epaulettes, decorated with the blue *moiré* sash and breast star of the Imperial Russian Order of St Andrew the First Called, the star of the Imperial Russian Order of St Vladimir combined with the English Order of the Garter, the Imperial badge for thirty years of Distinguished Military Services, the badge of the Imperial Russian Order of St George and the Imperial Russian Medal for the Turkish Campaign 1828–29 and the badge of the Royal Order of the Crown of Württemberg.

COMMENTARY: Nicholas I (1796–1855) was the third son of Tsar Paul I of Russia. In 1816, he married Princess Charlotte Louise, daughter of Frederick William III, King of Prussia. When his eldest brother Tsar Alexander I died in 1825, Nicholas, who was unpopular with the army, insisted upon the formal abdication of his elder brother Constantine before assuming the crown. In 1826, this led to the uprising of the Decembrists. The subsequent harsh punishments that they suffered, including death sentences and exile, plus the creation of a secret police, added to his unpopularity. Schidlof (1964, II, p. 884) cites three miniatures of Tsar Nicholas I by Winberg, and numerous variants of the present miniature are known. The present piece is nevertheless a particularly large and impressive portrait, which was certainly conceived as a more personal present to the sitter's daughter, Grand Duchess Olga.

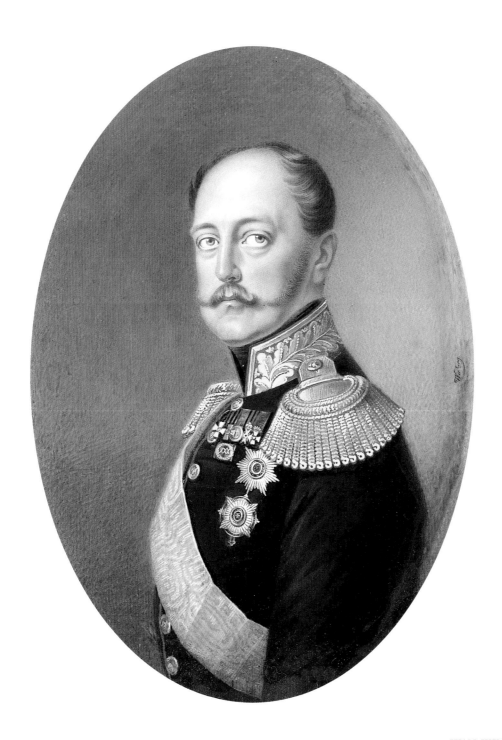

Bibliography

BAYNE-POWELL 1985:
Bayne-Powell, Robert, *Catalogue of Portrait Miniatures in the Fitzwilliam Museum, Cambridge*, Cambridge, 1985.

BEAUCAMP-MARKOWSKY 1985:
Beaucamp-Markowsky, Barbara, *Porzellandosen des 18. Jahrhunderts*, Fribourg/Munich, 1985.

BEAUCAMP-MARKOWSKY 1988:
Beaucamp-Markowsky, Barbara, *Collection of 18th Century Porcelain Boxes on loan to the Rijksmuseum Amsterdam*, Amsterdam, 1988.

BÉNÉZIT 1999:
Bénézit, Emmanuel, *Dictionnaire critique et documentaire des peintres, sculpteurs, dessinateurs et graveurs de tous les temps et de tous les pays*, Paris, 1999.

BENJAMIN 1983:
Benjamin, Susan, *Enamels*, Washington, 1983.

BENTON 1970:
Benton, Eric, 'The Bilston Enamellers', *English Ceramic Circle Transactions*, 7, part 3, 1970.

BERCKENHAGEN 1967:
Berckenhagen, Ekhart, *Anton Graff*, Berlin, 1967.

BIERMANN/BRINCKMANN 1917:
Biermann, Georg/Brinckmann, *Die Miniaturen-Sammlung seiner Königlichen Hoheit des Grossherzogs Ernst Ludwig von Hessen und bei Rhein*, Berlin/Leipzig, 1917.

BLONDEL 1907:
Blondel, Auguste, 'Nicolas Soret-Duval, peintre sur émail', *Nos anciens et leurs œuvres*, VII, 1907, pp. 25–30.

BOECKH 1982:
Boeckh, Hans, *Emailmalerei auf Genfer Taschenuhren vom 17. bis zum beginnenden 19. Jahrhundert*, Freiburg im Breisgau, 1982.

BOECKH 1989:
Boeckh, Hans, 'Remarques sur l'origine et la place de la peinture en émail dans l'œuvre de Liotard', *Genava*, XXXVII, 1989, pp. 117–130.

BOECKH 1994:
Boeckh, Hans, 'En fläkt av Whitehall', in Olausson, Magnus (ed.), *Europeiskt Miniatyrmåleri*, Stockholm, 1994, pp. 26–45.

BOECKH 1996:
Boeckh, Hans, 'Les arts du feu à Augsbourg et a Genève, ou comment différencier les deux écoles entre 1680 et 1710.', *Genava*, XLIV, 1996, pp. 81–94.

BOECKH 1999:
Boeckh, Hans, 'La miniature sur émail au XIXe siècle à Genève', in Genoud, Jean-Claude (ed.), *100 ans de miniatures suisses 1780–1880*, Geneva, 1999, pp. 129–138.

BONE:
Bone, Henry, *Bone Drawings*, Three Volumes of squared and numbered drawings by Henry Bone in the National Portrait Gallery (some unpublished, others see Walker 1999), London.

BOUCHOT 1910:
Bouchot, Henri, *La miniature française 1750–1825*, Paris, 1910.

BREJON DE LAVERGNÉE/ THIÉBAUT 1981:
Brejon de Lavergnée, Arnauld/Thiébaut, Dominique, *Catalogue sommaire illustré des peintures du musée du Louvre*, Paris, 1981.

BRUN 1917:
Brun, Carl, *Schweizerisches Künstler-Lexikon*, Frauenfeld, 1905– 1917.

BUCHHEIT 1911:
Buchheit, Hans, *Katalog der Miniaturbilder im Bayerischen Nationalmuseum*, Munich, 1911.

BURCHFIELD 1951:
Burchfield, Louise H./Milliken, William M. et al., *Portrait Miniatures, The Edward B. Greene Collection.* The Cleveland Museum of Art, Cleveland, 1951.

BURY 1982:
Bury, Shirley, Jewellery Gallery. *Summary Catalogue.Victoria and Albert Museum*, London, 1982.

CAVALLI-BJÖRKMAN 1981:
Cavalli-Björkman, Görel, *Svenskt Miniatyrmåleri*, Stockholm, 1981.

CERONI 1862:
Ceroni, L., *Les émaux de Petitot du musée Impérial du Louvre*, Paris, 1862–1864.

CLASEN 1993:
Clasen, Carl-Wilhelm, *Peter Boy*, Cologne, 1993.

CLOUZOT 1919:
Clouzot, Henri, '*L'école genevoise de peinture sur émail*', La renaissance de l'art français et des industries de luxe, March 1919, pp. 107–110.

CLOUZOT 1923:
Clouzot, Henri, 'Les maîtres de la miniature sur émail au musée Galliéra', *Gazette de Beaux-Arts*, VIII, 5e période, July–August 1923, pp. 53–62.

CLOUZOT 1924:
Clouzot, Henri, *Dictionnaire des miniaturistes sur émail*, Paris, 1924.

CLOUZOT 1925:
Clouzot, Henri, *La miniature sur émail en France*, Paris, n. d. [about 1925].

COLDING 1991:
Colding, Torben Holck, *Miniature-og Emaillemåleri i Danmark 1606– 1850*, Aalborg, 1991.

COLDING 1994:
Colding, Torben Holck, 'Danska miniatyrer i Stockholm', in Olausson, Magnus (ed.), *Europeiskt Miniatyrmåleri*, Stockholm, 1994, pp. 78–99.

CONSTANS 1995:
Constans, Claire, *Musée national du château de Versailles. Les Peintures*, Paris, 1995.

COOMBS 1998:
Coombs, Katherine, *The Portrait Miniature in England*, London, 1998.

DEMÔLE 1917:
Demôle, J.-Henri, 'Les émaux et les miniatures à l'exposition du Centenaire', *Nos anciens et leurs œuvres*, 1917, 2e série, VII, pp. 63–85.

DEONNA 1947:
Deonna, Waldemar, 'Anciens émaux de Genève', *Pro Arte*, 63/64, July–August 1947, pp. 313–333.

DORIVAL 1976:
Dorival, Bernard, *Philippe de Champaigne 1602–1674*, Paris, 1976.

DUSSIEUX 1841:
Dussieux, L., *Recherches sur l'histoire de la peinture sur émail*, Paris, 1841.

EDWARDS 1997:
Edwards, Sebastien/Bryant, Julius/Reynolds, Graham/Dejardin, Ian/Ribeiro, Aileen. *Miniatures at Kenwood, The Draper Gift*, London, 1997.

ELWARD 1905:
Elward, Robert, *On Collecting Miniatures, Enamels and Jewellery*, London, 1905.

FARINGTON:
Farington, Joseph, *The Diary of Joseph Farington*, Garlick, Kenneth/McIntyre, Angus (ed), New Haven/London, 1978–84.

FITZROY 1979:
FitzRoy, Virginia, 'The London Art Market, Miniatures', *The Connoisseur*, October 1979, pp. 38–40.

FLEMING 1959:
Fleming, John, 'Giuseppe MacPherson: A
Florentine Miniaturist', *The Connoisseur*, November
1959, pp. 160–167.

FOSKETT 1972:
Foskett, Daphne, *A Dictionary of British Miniature
Painters*, London, 1972.

FOSKETT 1979:
Foskett, Daphne, *Collecting Miniatures*, Woodbridge,
1979.

FOSKETT 1987:
Foskett, Daphne, *Miniatures: Dictionary and Guide*,
Woodbridge, 1987.

FRIESEN 2000:
Friesen, Margareta, *Französische Bildnisminiaturen
von 1770 bis 1880*, Darmstadt, 2000.

FURCY-RAYNAUD 1912:
Furcy-Raynaud, Marc, 'Les tableaux et objets d'art
saisis chez les émigrés et condamnés et envoyés au
Muséum central', *Archives de l'Art français*, nouvelle
période, 1912, VI, pp. 245–343.

GAUTHEY 1975:
Gauthey, Marcel, *Emaux peints de Genève*, XVIIe et
XVIIIe siècles, Geneva, 1975.

GEISMEIER/BUROCK 1986:
Geismeier, Irene/Burock, Bernd, *Staatliche Museen
zu Berlin. Gemäldegalerie Berlin. Miniaturen. 16.–19.
Jahrhundert*, Berlin, 1986.

GILLET/JEANNERAT/CLOUZOT 1957:
Gillet, Louis/Jeannerat, Carlo/Clouzot, Henri,
*Miniatures and enamels from the D. David-Weill
Collection*, Paris, 1957.

GONZÁLEZ-PALACIOS 1977:
González-Palacios, Alvar, *The Art of Mosaics: Selection
from the Gilbert Collection*, Los Angeles, 1977.

GONZÁLEZ-PALACIOS/ROETTGEN 1982:
González-Palacios, Alvar/Roettgen, Steffi, *The Art
of Mosaics: Selection from the Gilbert Collection* (revised
edition), Los Angeles, 1982.

GOULDING 1916:
Goulding, Richard, *The Welbeck Abbey Miniatures: a
Catalogue Raisonné*, Oxford, 1916.

GRANDJEAN 1981:
Grandjean, Serge, *Les tabatières du musée du Louvre*,
Paris, 1981.

GRAVES 1905:
Graves, Algernon, *The Royal Academy of Arts
Exhibitions 1769–1904*, London, 1905.

GUIFFREY 1880–1881:
Guiffrey, Jules-Marie-Joseph, 'Objets d'art acquis
pour l'impératrice de Russie par le Baron de
Grimm', *Nouvelles archives de l'art français*, 2e série,
II, 1880–1881, pp. 329–331.

HABSBURG-LOTHRINGEN 1983:
Habsburg-Lothringen, Géza von, *Gold Boxes from
the Collection of Rosalinde and Arthur Gilbert*, London,
1983.

HALES-TOOKE 1957:
Hales-Tooke, John, 'A Century of Wonder', *The
Connoisseur Yearbook*, 1957, pp. 64–71.

HENNINGER-TAVCAR 1995:
Henninger-Tavcar, Karin, *Miniaturporträts*,
Pforzheim, 1995.

HOFSTETTER 1994:
Hofstetter, Bodo, 'Franska 1700–talsminiatyrer i
Nationalmuseum', in Olausson, Magnus (ed.),
Europeiskt Miniatyrmåleri, Stockholm, 1994, pp.
54–77.

HOFSTETTER 1999:
Hofstetter, Bodo, 'La miniature sur émail suisse à la
fin du XVIIIe siècle', in Genoud, Jean-Claude (ed.),
100 ans de miniatures suisses 1780–1880, Geneva,
1999, pp. 47–73.

HOLZHAUSEN 1935:
Holzhausen, Walter, *Johann Christian Neuber*,
Dresden, 1935.

HUMBERT/REVILLIOD/TILANUS 1897
Humbert, Ed./Revilliod, Alphonse/Tilanus, J. W.
R., *La vie et les œuvres de Jean Etienne Liotard*,
Amsterdam, 1897.

JEAN-RICHARD 1994:
Jean-Richard, Pierrette, *Miniatures sur ivoire. Musée
du Louvre. Musée d'Orsay*, Paris, 1994.

KALIAZINA 1987:
Kaliazina, Ninel et al., *Russkaia emal' XII–nachala
XX veka iz sobraniia gosudarstvennogo Ermitazha* [in
cyrillic] (*Russian Enamels of the Twelfth to the Early-
Twentieth Century from the Collection of the
Hermitage*), Leningrad, 1987.

KAREV 1989:
Karev, Andrej Aleksandrovich, *Miniatyrn'ij Portret i
Rossii XVIII veka* [in cyrillic], Moscow, 1989.

KEIL 1999:
Keil, Robert, *Die Porträtminiaturen des Hauses
Habsburg*, Vienna, 1999.

KENNEDY 1917:
Kennedy, Hannah A., *Early English Portrait
Miniatures in the Collection of the Duke of Buccleuch*,
London, 1917.

KERSLAKE 1977:
Kerslake, John, National Portrait Gallery. *Early
Georgian Portraits*, London, 1977.

KOMELOVA 1995:
Komelova, Galina N., *Russkaia miniatjura na emali*
[in cyrillic] (*Russian Enamel Miniatures*), St
Petersburg, 1995.

KOMELOVA/PRINTSEVA 1986:
Komelova, Galina N./Printseva, Galina A., *Portrait
Miniature in Russia. XVIII-early XX century from the
Collection of The Hermitage*, Leningrad, 1986.

LANGEDIJK 1981:
Langedijk, Karla, T*he Portraits of the Medici*,
Florence, 1981.

LAPAIRE 1990:
Lapaire, Claude et al., *Musée de l'horlogerie Genève*,
Geneva, 1990.

LE CORBEILLER 1966:
Le Corbeiller, Clare, *European and American Snuff
Boxes 1730–1830*, New York, 1966.

LES ARTS 1908:
'Une exposition rétrospective à Saint-Pétersbourg',
Les Arts, December 1908.

LESPINASSE 1929:
Lespinasse, Pierre, *La miniature en France au XVIIIe
siècle*, Paris/Brussels, 1929.

LIGHTBOWN 1968:
Lightbown, Ronald W., 'Jean Petitot and Jacques
Bordier at the English court', *The Connoisseur*, June
1968, pp. 82–91.

LLOYD/REMINGTON 1996:
Lloyd, Christopher/Remington, Vanessa,
*Masterpieces in little. Portrait Miniatures from the
Collection of Her Majesty Queen Elizabeth II*, London,
1996.

LOCHE/ROETHLISBERGER 1978:
Loche, Renée/Roethlisberger, Marcel, *L'opera completa di Liotard*, Milan, 1978.

LONG 1923:
Long, Basil S., Victoria and Albert Museum.
*Catalogue of the Jones Collection. Part III – Paintings
and Miniatures*, London, 1923.

LONG 1929:
Long, Basil S., *British Miniaturists*, London, 1929
(reprint 1966).

LONG 1929 'Crosse':
Long, Basil S., 'Richard Crosse, Miniaturist and
Portrait Painter', *The Walpole Society*, XVII, 1929.

LONG 1930:
Long, Basil S., *Handlist of Miniature Portraits and
Silhouettes in the Victoria and Albert Museum*,
London, 1930.

LUNDBERG 1987:
Lundberg, Gunnar W., *Charles Boit 1662–1727 émailleur-miniaturiste suédois*, Paris, 1987.

MASSINELLI 2000:
Massinelli, Anna Maria, *The Gilbert Collection. Hardstones*, London, 2000.

MAZE-SENCIER 1885:
Maze-Sencier, Alphonse, *Le livre des collectionneurs*, Paris, 1885.

MIKHAILOVA/SMIRNOV 1974:
Mikhailova, Kira Vladimirovna/Smirnov, Georgii Victorovich, *Miniatures from the Collection of the Russian Museum*, Leningrad, 1974.

MILLAR 1963:
Millar, Oliver, *The Tudor, Stuart an Early Georgian Pictures in the Collection of Her Majesty the Queen*, London, 1963.

MILLAR 1972:
Millar, Oliver, *The Age of Charles I, Painting in England, 1620–1649*, London, 1972.

MILLAR 1974:
Millar, Oliver, 'Samuel Cooper at the National Portrait Gallery', *Burlington Magazine*, CXVI, June 1974, pp. 346–349.

MORAN TURINA 1990:
Moran Turina, Miguel, *La imagen del rey Felipe V y el arte*, Madrid, 1990.

MURDOCH 1981:
Murdoch, John/Murrell, Jim/Noon, Patrick J./Strong, Roy, *The English Miniature*, New Haven/London, 1981.

MURDOCH 1997:
Murdoch, John, *Seventeenth-Century English Miniatures in the Collection of the Victoria & Albert Museum*, London, 1997.

NAVILLE 1974:
Naville, René, 'Souvenirs de Nicolas Soret, peintre ordinaire de Catherine II de Russie', *Genava*, XXII, 1974, pp. 347–363.

NICHOLAS MIKHAILOVICH 1906:
Nicholas Mikhailovich, Grand Duke, *Portraits Russes des XVIIIe et XIXe siècles*, St Petersburg, 1906–1909.

NORTON/NORTON 1938:
Norton, Richard/Norton, Martin, *A History of Gold Snuff Boxes*, London, 1938.

ODOM 1996:
Odom, Anne, *Russian Enamels*, London, 1996.

OLAUSSON 1994:
Olausson, Magnus (ed.), *Europeiskt Miniatyrmåleri*, Stockholm, 1994.

PEPPER 1988:
Pepper, Stephen, *Guido Reni. L'opera completa*, Novara, 1988.

PIPER 1958:
Piper, David, 'The Contemporary Portraits of Oliver Cromwell', *The Walpole Society 1952–1954*, XXXIV, 1958.

POLOVTSOFF 1939:
Polovtsoff, Alexandre, *Les favoris de Catherine la Grande*, Paris, 1939.

PRACHOFF 1907:
Prachoff, Adrien, *Album de l'exposition rétrospective d'objets d'art de 1904 à St Pétersbourg*, St Petersburg, 1907.

REYNOLDS 1980:
Reynolds, Graham, *Wallace Collection. Catalogue of Miniatures*, London, 1980.

REYNOLDS 1999:
Reynolds, Graham, *The Sixteenth and Seventeenth-Century Miniatures in the Collection of Her Majesty The Queen*, London, 1999.

RIGAUD 1876:
Rigaud, J.-J., *Renseignements sur les Beaux-Arts à Genève*, Geneva, 1876.

ROGERS 1875:
Rogers, J. Jope, *Notice of Henry Bone, RA and his works Together with those of his son, Henry Pierce Bone and other members of the Family*, Turo, [1875?].

ROWORTH 1992:
Roworth, Wendy Wassyng, Angelica Kauffman: *A Continental Artist in Georgian England*, Stockbridge, 1992 (reprint 1993).

SCHAFFERS-BODENHAUSEN/ TIETHOFF-SPLIETHOFF 1993:
Schaffers-Bodenhausen, Karen/Tiethoff-Spliethoff, Marieke, *The Portrait Miniatures in the Collections of The House of Orange-Nassau*, Zwolle, 1993.

SCHIDLOF 1911:
Schidlof, Leo R., *Die Bildnisminiatur in Frankreich im XVII., XVIII. und XIX. Jahrhundert*, Vienna/Leipzig, 1911.

SCHIDLOF 1964:
Schidlof, Leo R., *The miniature in Europe*, Graz, 1964.

SCHLUMBERGER 1966:
Schlumberger, Eveline, 'La vie méritoire de Petitot, le miniaturiste le plus reputé du XVIIe siècle', *Connaissance des arts*, 170, April 1966, pp. 88–91.

SCHNEEBERGER 1958:
Schneeberger, Pierre-Francis, 'Les peintres sur émail genevois au XVIIe et au XVIIIe siècle', *Genava*, VI, fasc. 2–3, July 1958, pp. 77–216.

SCHNETZLER 1981:
Schnetzler, Barbara, 'Johann Heinrich Hurter', in *Schaffhauser Biographien*, IV, Thayngen, 1981, pp. 97–100.

SEELER 1983:
Seeler, Margarete, *The Art of Enamelling*, New York, 1983.

SOLODKOFF 1981:
Solodkoff, Alexander von, *Russische Goldschmiedekunst 17.–19. Jahrhundert*, Fribourg, 1981.

SPEEL 1988:
Speel, Erika, 'Enamel Portrait Miniatures', *The Antique Collector*, December 1988, pp. 54–57.

SPEEL 1998:
Speel, Erika, *Dictionary of Enamelling*, London, 1998.

SPENCER 1831:
Spencer, Earl, *Catalogue of the Pictures at Althorpe House in the County of Northampton*, London, 1831.

SPONSEL 1906:
Sponsel, Jean Louis, *Fürsten-Bildnisse aus dem Hause Wettin*, Dresden, 1906.

STARING 1924:
Staring, Adolphe, 'Leonard Temminck. Een Haagsch portretminiaturist', *Jaarboek 'Die Haghe'*, 1924, pp. 254–257.

STRŒHLIN 1905:
Strœhlin, Ernest, *Jean Petitot et Jaques Bordier*, Geneva, 1905.

STURM 1975:
Sturm, Fabienne-Xavière, *Emaux peints de Genève, XVIIIe et XIXe siècles*, Geneva, 1975.

STURM 1997:
Sturm, Fabienne-Xavière, 'The painted enamels of Geneva Switzerland', *The Magazine Antiques*, CLII, no. 3, September 1997, pp. 346–353.

STURZENEGGER-STIFTUNG 1992:
Sturzenegger-Stiftung Schaffhausen im Museum zu Allerheiligen Schaffhausen, Katalog der Erwerbungen 1987– 1991, Schaffhouse, 1992.

THIEME/BECKER 1909–1951:
Thieme, Ulrich/Becker, Felix, *Allgemeines Lexikon der bildenden Künstler von der Antike bis zur Gegenwart*, Leipzig, 1909–1951.

TOMÁS 1953:
Tomás, Mariano, *La miniatura retrato en España*, n. l. [Spain], 1953.

TRUMAN 1991:
Truman, Charles, *The Gilbert Collection of Gold Boxes*, Los Angeles, 1991.

TRUMAN 1999:
Truman, Charles, *The Gilbert Collection of Gold Boxes – Volume Two*, London, 1999.

VERTUE 1930–1955:
Vertue, George, 'Notebooks', I–VI (ed. Earl of Ilchester), *The Walpole Society*, XVIII (1930), XX (1932), XXII (1934), XXIV (1936), XXVI (1938), XXIX (1947), XXXIV (1955).

WALKER 1992:
Walker, Richard, *Miniatures in the Collection of Her Majesty the Queen. The Eighteenth and Early Nineteenth Centuries*, Cambridge, 1992.

WALKER 1997:
Walker, Richard, *Miniatures. A selection of miniatures in the Ashmolean Museum*, Oxford, 1997.

WALKER 1998:
Walker, Richard, *Miniatures. 300 Years of the English Miniature Illustrated from the Collections of the National Portrait Gallery*, London, 1998.

WALKER 1999:
Walker, Richard, 'Henry Bone's Pencil Drawings in the National Portrait Gallery', *The Walpole Society*, LXI, 1999, pp. 305–367.

WATERFIELD 1971:
Waterfield, Hermione, 'Miniature Portraits in Enamel', *A Thousand Years of Enamel*, London, 1971.

WATNEY/CHARLESTON 1966:
Watney, Bernard/Charleston, R. J., 'Petitions for Patents concerning Porcelain, Glass and Enamels [...]'/'The Great Toyshop of Europe', *English Ceramic Circle Transactions*, VI, part 2, 1966.

WEBSTER 1972:
Webster, Mary, 'The Work of Giuseppe MacPherson', *Country Life*, 8 June 1972, pp. 1445–1446.

WILLIAMSON 1897:
Williamson, George C., *Richard Cosway*, London, 1897.

WILLIAMSON 1904:
Williamson, George C., *The History of Portrait Miniatures*, London, 1904.

WILLIAMSON 1926:
Williamson, George C., *Signed Enamel Miniatures of the XVIIth, XVIIIth & XIXth Centuries*, London, n. d. [1926]

YAKOVLEVA 1997:
Yakovleva, Larissa, *Artistic Enamels from the Hermitage Collection. Swiss Watches and Snuff-Boxes, 17th–20th Centuries*, St Petersburg, 1997.

YUNG 1981:
Yung, K. K., *National Portrait Gallery. Complete Illustrated Catalogue 1856–1979*, London, 1981.

Exhibition History

Berlin 1991:
Kaiserlicher Kunstbesitz, Berlin, Charlottenburg Castle, 1991.

Brussels 1912:
Exposition de la miniature, Brussels, Hôtel Goffinet, 1912.

Cleveland 1951:
The Edward B. Green Collection, Cleveland Art Museum, 1951.

Douvres-La Délivrande 1960:
Grandes collections particulières du Calvados, Douvres-La Délivrande, Baronnie, 1960.

Edinburgh 1965:
British Portrait Miniatures, Edinburgh, The Arts Council Gallery, 1965.

Edinburgh 1996–1997:
Portrait Miniatures from the Collection of the Duke of Buccleuch, Edinburgh, Scottish National Portrait Gallery, 1996–1997.

Ghent 1979:
Meesterwerken uit Genève, Ghent, Bijlokemuseum, 1979.

Geneva 1953:
Les deux grands siècles de Versailles, Geneva, musée d'art et d'histoire, 1953.

Geneva 1956:
Chefs-d'œuvre de la miniature et de la gouache, Geneva, musée d'art et d'histoire, 1956.

Geneva/Paris 1992:
Dessins de Liotard, Geneva, musée d'art et d'histoire/Paris, Musée du Louvre, 1992.

The Hague 1991:
Portretten in miniatuur, The Hague, Mauritshuis, 1991.

Lausanne 1999–2000:
100 ans de miniatures suisses 1780–1880, Lausanne, Musée historique, 1999–2000.

London 1861:
Antiquities and Works of Art, exhibited at Ironmongers' Hall, London, London, Ironmongers' Hall, 1861 (catalogue London, 1869).

London 1862:
Special Exhibition of Works of Art [...] on loan at the South Kensington Museum, London, South Kensington Museum (Victoria & Albert Museum), 1862.

London 1865:
Special Exhibition of Portrait Miniatures on loan at the South Kensington Museum, London, South Kensington Museum (Victoria & Albert Museum), 1865.

London 1887:
Art Exhibition at Spencer House, London, Spencer House, 1887.

London 1889:
Exhibition of Portrait Miniatures, London, Burlington Fine Arts Club, 1889.

London 1932:
British Antique Dealers' Association Art Treasures Exhibition, London, 1932.

London 1961:
An exhibition of important 18th century & 19th century miniatures and enamels at Garrard, London, Garrard's, 1961.

London 1968:
British Antique Dealers' Association Golden Jubilee Exhibition, London, Victoria & Albert Museum, 1968.

London 1972:
The Age of Charles I, Painting in England 1620–1649, The Tate Gallery, London, 1972.

London 1975:
British Antique Dealers' Association Exhibition, London, Grosvenor House Hotel, 1975.

London/Los Angeles/Atlanta/San Antonio/Richmond/Seattle 1975–1979:
The Art of Mosaics and Monumental Silver, London, Victoria & Albert Museum/Los Angeles, Los Angeles County Museum of Art/Atlanta, High Museum of Art/San Antonio, Witte Museum/Richmond, Virginia Museum of Fine Art/Seattle, Seattle Art Museum, 1975–1979.

London 1979:
British Antique Dealers' Association Art Treasures Exhibition, London, Somerset House, 1979.

London 1993:
The Monarchy in Portrait Miniatures from Elizabeth I to Queen Victoria, London, D. S. Lavender (Antiques) Ltd., 1993.

London 1994:
Anatole Demidoff Prince of San Donato (1812–70), London, The Wallace Collection, 1994.

London 1999:
The Kings' Head. Charles I: King and Martyr, London, The Queen's Gallery, Buckingham Palace, 1999.

Los Angeles/Richmond/New York 1986–1987:
Gold Boxes from the Gilbert Collection, Los Angeles, Los Angeles County Museum of Art/Richmond, Virginia Museum of Fine Art/New York, A la Vielle Russie, 1986–1987.

Madrid 1990–1991:
Miguel Jacinto Meléndez, Madrid, Museo Municipal del Ayuntamiento, 1990–1991.

Milan 1978–1879:
Neoclassico e Troubadour nelle miniature di Giambattista Gigola, Milan, Museo Poldi Pezzoli, 1978–1979.

New Haven 1979–1980:
English Portrait Drawings & Miniatures, New Haven (CT), Yale Center for British Art, 1979–1980.

New York/San Marino/Richmond/London 1996–1997:
Portrait Miniatures from the Collection of Her Majesty Queen Elizabeth II, New York, The Metropolitan Museum of Art/San Marino, The Huntington Library/Richmond, Virginia Museum/of Fine Arts/ London, The Queen's Gallery, 1996–1997.

Paris 1923:
Exposition de la Verrerie et de l'Emaillerie modernes. Section rétrospective, Paris, musée Galliéra, 1923.

Paris 1956–1957:
Donation de D. David-Weill au musée du Louvre. Miniatures et émaux, Paris, Musée du Louvre, Cabinet des Dessins, 1956–1957.

Paris 1998:
Chaumet Paris, deux siècles de création, Paris, Musée Carnavalet, 1998.

Philadelphia 1990:
The Intellectual World of Benjamin Franklin, Philadelphia, Arthur Ross Gallery and the Van Pelt Library, 1990.

Schaffhousen 1983:
Schaffhauser Kunst und Kultur im 18. Jahrhundert, Schaffhouse, Museum zu Allerheiligen, 1983.

St Petersburg 1904:
Exposition rétrospective d'Objets d'Art, St Petersburg, Empress Alexander III Russian Museum, 1904.

Index

Numbers in bold refer to catalogue numbers. A question mark in brackets indicates that there is some uncertainty as to where the work originates.